Women in American History
Since 1880

Uncovering the Past: Documentary Readers in American History
Series Editors: Steven Lawson and Nancy Hewitt

The books in this series introduce students in American history courses to two important dimensions of historical analysis. They enable students to engage actively in historical interpretation, and they further students' understanding of the interplay between social and political forces in historical developments.

Consisting of primary sources and an introductory essay, these readers are aimed at the major courses in the American history curriculum, as outlined further below. Each book in the series will be approximately 225–50 pages, including a 25–30 page introduction addressing key issues and questions about the subject under consideration, a discussion of sources and methodology, and a bibliography of suggested secondary readings.

Published

Paul G. E. Clemens
The Colonial Era: A Documentary Reader

Sean Patrick Adams
The Early American Republic: A Documentary Reader

Stanley Harrold
The Civil War and Reconstruction: A Documentary Reader

Robert P. Ingalls and David K. Johnson
The United States Since 1945: A Documentary Reader

Brian Ward
The 1960s: A Documentary Reader

Steven Mintz
African American Voices: A Documentary Reader, 1619–1877

Camilla Townsend
American Indian History: A Documentary Reader

Steven Mintz
Mexican American Voices: A Documentary Reader

Nancy Rosenbloom
Women in American History Since 1880: A Documentary Reader

In preparation

Jeremi Suri
American Foreign Relations Since 1898: A Documentary Reader

Women in American History Since 1880

A Documentary Reader

Nancy J. Rosenbloom

WILEY-BLACKWELL

A John Wiley & Sons, Ltd., Publication

Blackwell Publishing was acquired by John Wiley & Sons in February 2007. Blackwell's publishing program has been merged with Wiley's global Scientific, Technical, and Medical business to form Wiley-Blackwell.

Registered Office
John Wiley & Sons Ltd, The Atrium, Southern Gate, Chichester, West Sussex, PO19 8SQ, United Kingdom

Editorial Offices
350 Main Street, Malden, MA 02148-5020, USA
9600 Garsington Road, Oxford, OX4 2DQ, UK
The Atrium, Southern Gate, Chichester, West Sussex, PO19 8SQ, UK

For details of our global editorial offices, for customer services, and for information about how to apply for permission to reuse the copyright material in this book please see our website at www.wiley.com/wiley-blackwell.

The right of Nancy J. Rosenbloom to be identified as the author of the editorial material in this work has been asserted in accordance with the UK Copyright, Designs and Patents Act 1988.

Wiley also publishes its books in a variety of electronic formats. Some content that appears in print may not be available in electronic books.

Designations used by companies to distinguish their products are often claimed as trademarks. All brand names and product names used in this book are trade names, service marks, trademarks or registered trademarks of their respective owners. The publisher is not associated with any product or vendor mentioned in this book. This publication is designed to provide accurate and authoritative information in regard to the subject matter covered. It is sold on the understanding that the publisher is not engaged in rendering professional services. If professional advice or other expert assistance is required, the services of a competent professional should be sought.

Library of Congress Cataloging-in-Publication Data

A catalogue record for this book is available.

ISBN 978-1-4051-9050-3 (hardback)
      978-1-4051-9049-7 (paperback)

Set in 10/12.5pt Sabon by SPi Publisher Services, Pondicherry, India
Printed in Singapore by Markono Print Media Pte Ltd

01 2010

To Harvey and Ethel Rosenbloom

Contents

Series Editors' Preface   xii

Acknowledgments   xv

Introduction   1

**Chapter 1: The Boundaries of Convention in the Gilded Age,
1880–1900**   12

WORK   12
  1 Atlanta Washing Society, 1881   12
  2 Lynn Shoe Stitchers, 1886 and 1888   15

CITIZENSHIP   17
  3 Frances Willard, Women and Organization, 1891   17
  4 Elizabeth Cady Stanton, The Solitude of Self, 1892   20
  5 Ida B. Wells, Lynch Law, 1892   23

REPRESENTATIONS   28
  6 Kate Chopin, Regret, 1897   28
  7 Zitkala-Ša (Gertrude Bonnin), The Beadwork, 1900   31

DOMESTIC LIVES   34
  8 Woman's Christian Temperance Union, Rules and
  regulations for the Hope and Help Rooms, 1887   34
  9 Dr. Clelia Duel Mosher, The Mosher Survey, 1892 to 1913   36
  10 Leong Shee's Testimony, 1893 and 1929   39

Chapter 2: Reform and Revolt in the Modern Era, 1900–20   47

WORK   47

1   Maimie Pinzer, Letters to Fanny Howe, 1911   47
2   A Negro Nurse, More Slavery at the South, 1912   52

CITIZENSHIP   58

3   Elizabeth Gurley Flynn, Women in Industry Should
    Organize, 1911   58
4   Louis D. Brandeis and Josephine Goldmark,
    The Brandeis Brief, 1908   63
5   Nannie Helen Burroughs, Black Women and Reform, 1915   74
6   Sonya Levien, The Struggles of Immigrant Women, 1918   75
7   Crystal Eastman, Our War Record: A Plea for Tolerance, 1918   79

REPRESENTATIONS   80

8   Virginia Arnold Holding a Kaiser Wilson Banner, 1918   80
9   Women Rivet Heaters and Passers On, 1919   82

DOMESTIC LIVES   83

10 Elinore Pruitt Stewart, The Homesteader's Marriage and
    A Little Funeral, 1912   83
11 Lutiant, Letter to a Friend, 1918   86

Chapter 3: Sex and Politics in an Age of Conservatism, 1920–33   89

WORK   89

1   Caroline Manning, The Immigrant Woman and Her Job, 1930   89
2   Christine Galliher Describes her Participation in a
    Walkout Strike, 1929   92

CITIZENSHIP   96

3   National Consumer's League, Why It Should Not Pass:
    The Blanket Equality Bill Proposed by the National
    Woman's Party, 1922   96
4   Carrie Chapman Catt, Poison Propaganda, 1924   101
5   Eleanor Roosevelt, Women Must Learn to Play the Game
    as Men Do, 1928   107

REPRESENTATIONS   114

6   Betty Boop's Bamboo Isle, 1932   114
7   Ethel Waters, No Man's Mamma Now, 1925   115

DOMESTIC LIVES   116

8   Margaret Sanger, Address of Welcome, 1925   116
9   Alice Hamilton, Poverty and Birth Control, 1925   118

Chapter 4: Work and Family in Times of Crisis, 1933–48   122

WORK   122
1   Jennie Matyas and the ILGWU, 1937   122
2   Emma Tenayuca, Pecan Shellers Strike, 1938   127
3   Anna Mae Dickson, It's Something Inside You, 1930s   130

CITIZENSHIP   133
4   *New York Times,* Women Will Form a Ferry
    Command, 1942   133
5   Sue Kunitomi Embrey Describes her Experience as an
    Internee at Manzanar, 1940s   135

REPRESENTATIONS   142
6   Rosie the Riveter, 1942   142
7   Still Image of Joan Crawford from *Mildred Pierce*, 1945   143

DOMESTIC LIVES   144
8   Tennessee Valley Authority, Office Memorandum Re:
    Mattie and Jim Randolph, 1936   144
9   Eudora Welty, To Play Dolls, 1936   149
10 Letters from Polly to William Crow, 1944 to 1945   150

Chapter 5: The Second Sex in America, 1948–68   156

WORK   156
1   Michael Wilson, *Salt of the Earth*, 1954   156
2   *Los Angeles Times,* Classified Advertisements, 1960   161
3   Betty Friedan, The Sexual Sell, 1963   162

CITIZENSHIP   169
4   Dorothy Kenyon and Phyllis J. Shampanier,
    Hoyt v. Florida, 1961   169
5   Casey Hayden and Mary King, A Kind of Memo, 1965   173
6   Fannie Lou Hamer, Testimony Before the Credentials
    Committee at the Democratic National Convention, 1964   176

REPRESENTATIONS   179
7   Esmeralda Santiago, A *Nena Puertorriquena Decente,* 1960s   179
8   *Life Magazine,* How Nice to be a Pretty Girl and Work in
    Washington, 1962   181

DOMESTIC LIVES   182
9   Del Martin, President's Message to the Daughters of
    Bilitis, 1956   182
10 Susan Tracy, We Know What You've Done, 1968   183

**Chapter 6: Race, Class, Gender, and the Redefinition
of America, 1968–88**   188

WORK   188
1   *Ms. Magazine,* To Love, Honor and ... Share: A Marriage
    Contract for the Seventies, 1973   188
2   Barbara Kingsolver, Ask Any Miner, 1983   191
3   Seth Mydans, Children of Chinatown Get a Day-Care
    Center, 1984   196

CITIZENSHIP   197
4   Angela Davis, Free Angela Davis, 1972   197
5   Letter from Esther Peterson to Martha Griffiths, 1971   202
6   Phyllis Schlafly, Women Should Not Serve in Combat, 1979   203
7   Sister Theresa Kane, Welcome to Pope John Paul II,
    October 7, 1979   207

REPRESENTATIONS   208
8   Bil Keane, When I Grow Up, 1973   208
9   Gloria Anzaldúa, To Live in the Borderlands means
    you, 1999   209

DOMESTIC LIVES   211
10 Barbara Susan Kaminsky, An Abortion Testimonial, n.d.   211
11 Senator George McGovern, The Pill and Informed
    Consent, 1970   212
12 New Jersey Lesbian Caucus, How Do You Define
    "Lesbianism?" 1976   215

**Chapter 7: Globalization, Glass Ceilings, and the Good
Life? 1988–2008**   219

WORK   219
1   Felice N. Schwartz, Management Women
    and the New Facts of Life, 1989   219
2   *New York Times,* More and More, Women Risk
    All to Enter U.S., 2006   223

CITIZENSHIP   227
3   Anita Hill, Statement to the U.S. Senate Judiciary
    Committee for the Hearings on Clarence Thomas, 1991   227
4   Rebecca Walker, Becoming the Third Wave, 1992   232
5   Carolyn Maloney, The Spirit of Stonewall, 1999   235

REPRESENTATIONS   236
  6   Guerilla Girls, Do Women Have to Be Naked to
      Get into the Met. Museum? 1989   236
  7   Susan Power, Museum Indians, 2002   237

DOMESTIC LIVES   240
  8   National Center for Health Statistics, Death Rates for
      Selected Causes of Death for White and Black Women, 1970
      and 1993   240
  9   Barbara Seaman, The Doctors' Case Against the Pill 1969,
      1995   241
 10   Antonia I. Castañeda, History and the Politics
      of Violence Against Women, 1995   248

Bibliography   255
Index   260

Series Editors' Preface

Primary sources have become an essential component in the teaching of history to undergraduates. They engage students in the process of historical interpretation and analysis and help them understand that facts do not speak for themselves. Rather, students see how historians construct narratives that recreate the past. Most students assume that the pursuit of knowledge is a solitary endeavor; yet historians constantly interact with their peers, building upon previous research and arguing among themselves over the interpretation of documents and their larger meaning. The documentary readers in this series highlight the value of this collaborative creative process and encourage students to participate in it.

Each book in the series introduces students in American history courses to two important dimensions of historical analysis. They enable students to engage actively in historical interpretation, and they further students' understanding of the interplay among social, cultural, economic, and political forces in historical developments In pursuit of these goals, the documents in each text embrace a broad range of sources, including such items as illustrations of material artifacts, letters and diaries, sermons, maps, photographs, song lyrics, selections from fiction and memoirs, legal statutes, court decisions, presidential orders, speeches, and political cartoons.

Each volume in the series is edited by a specialist in the field who is concerned with undergraduate teaching. The goal is not to offer a comprehensive selection of material but to provide items that reflect major themes and debates; that illustrate significant social, cultural, political, and economic dimensions of an era or subject; and that inform, intrigue, and inspire undergraduate students. The editor of each volume has written an introduction that discusses the central questions that have occupied historians in this field and the ways historians have used primary sources to answer them.

In addition, each introductory essay contains an explanation of the kinds of materials available to investigate a particular subject, the methods by which scholars analyze them, and the considerations that go into interpreting them. Each source selection is introduced by a short head note that gives students the necessary information and a context for understanding the document. Also, each section of the volume includes questions to guide student reading and stimulate classroom discussion.

Nancy Rosenbloom's *Women in American History Since 1880* uses a wide array of documents to trace the diverse experiences of women in the United States from the late nineteenth to the early twenty-first century. Divided into seven chronological sections, Rosenbloom encourages students to explore women's work, citizenship, representations, and domestic lives while recognizing differences rooted in race, class, ethnicity, and education. These readings document working-class struggles alongside advances in women's education and occupations, social activism alongside changes in housework and domestic technology, political and scientific advances alongside the upheavals of war and economic depression, challenges to dominant representations of women alongside continued cultural stereotyping, feminist mobilizations alongside systemic economic and legal discrimination. The volume covers all regions of the United States, highlighting the impact of western expansion, industrialization, urbanization, immigration, technological innovation, economic depression, war and globalization on women. At the same time, it chronicles women's efforts both to shape and challenge national agendas, institutions and ideals through unions, reform movements, political campaigns, and grassroots activism as well as through literature, music, and film. Beginning with the lives of washerwomen, shoe stitchers, temperance advocates, anti-lynching campaigners, and American Indian and southern writers in the late 1800s, Rosenbloom carries us through the rapid economic, political, and cultural changes of the early twentieth century and the economic and military crises of the 1930s and 1940s. She then tracks the early efforts of Mexican American, African American and native-born white women to challenge the racial, class, and gender hierarchies that defined post-World War II America while recognizing the continued power of older ideas about women's proper place. In the final two sections, Rosenbloom introduces us to the critical battles of the 1960s and beyond for social justice and women's liberation as well as the backlash against such movements and the persistence of racial, economic, and gender inequality. To trace the lives of ordinary women and the contributions of individuals who gained a public stage through their writing, art, political leadership, or organizing ability requires a range of sources. This volume offers a wide array of documents including newspaper and magazine articles, speeches, court decisions, investigative reports, letters, photographs, posters, surveys, Congressional testimony, memoirs and mani-festos, movie stills and advertisements, want ads and cartoons, poetry and oral histories. Taken together, they inspire students to explore the represen-tations and experiences of women across the vast landscape of modern American history. *Women in American History Since 1880* captures the multi-faceted character of women's lives and the ways they were repre-sented by themselves and others. It provides students with the sources to understand women's history in all of its complexities and provides a valu-able bibliography to guide students in pursuing their own research projects.

Steven F. Lawson and Nancy A. Hewitt, Series Editors

Acknowledgments

It is a pleasure to acknowledge the help of many people on this project. I want to thank my students who have inspired and challenged me in 30 years of college teaching. I am particularly thankful to Mariel Volk for proofreading the manuscript and for her suggestions.

The dedicated library staff at Canisius College and especially Jessica Blum and Ami Lake helped me locate a number of texts included in this manuscript. I would also like to thank Paula McNutt, Dean of Arts and Sciences, and Julie Gibert, Chair of the History Department, for their support. Dorinda Hartmann at the Wisconsin Center for Film and Theater Research at the Wisconsin Historical Society helped me locate an intriguing still from *Mildred Pierce*.

The resources available online from the Library of Congress, National Archives, and Alexander Street Press greatly enriched the possibilities for this project. I am indebted to the Manuscript Division at the Huntington Library for access to the Sonya Levien materials. Nancy C. Unger at Santa Clara University directed me to her essay "Teaching 'Straight' Gay and Lesbian History" which appeared in the *Journal of American History* in 2007.

This manuscript has benefitted from the expertise and keen insight of its anonymous readers. Galen Smith and Peter Coveney at Wiley-Blackwell have been extraordinarily helpful in this process from beginning to end. The series editors, Nancy Hewitt and Steven Lawson, have been truly wonderful and offered kind and wise advice at every stage of this book. Nancy is a long-time friend and a very gracious and generous colleague.

Larry Eugene Jones, my colleague and husband, has encouraged me in all things big and small, and our sons Matthew and Daniel keep me focused on connecting the past to the future.

Finally, this book reflects many conversations with my mother Ethel L. Rosenbloom, who was born in 1920, and whose experiences were shaped by so many of the trials and tribulations examined in the pages that follow. Like the voices of the women included in this text, her life and its meaning are so much more than the sum of its parts.

Introduction

Zora Neale Hurston begins *Their Eyes Were Watching God* with an elegant contrast between the power of memory in the lives of men and women. She writes "Now, women forget all those things they don't want to remember, and remember everything they don't want to forget. The dream is the truth. Then they act and do things accordingly." Hurston's training as an anthropologist in the 1920s led her to the folklore of African American life and inspired her to write the novels for which she is best known. Historians might dispute her road to the truth but they nevertheless have much to learn from her insight. For as historians use artifacts – both visual and literary – to explore how women shape and are shaped by the economic, political and familial events of the past, Hurston's appeal sensitizes us to the potential of these texts to reveal the trials and tribulations of the individual and collective lives of America's women. At the same time, she reminds us of the important role that memory plays in how women organize their experiences and how they come to tell those stories that so greatly enrich the present. The documents in *Women in American History Since 1880* address the myriad ways in which American women – in all their diversity – have defined and continue to define themselves in the context of modern life.

Goals

This *Reader* provides primary sources that deepen student understanding of and promote critical thinking about women's historical experiences. To that end, this collection strives to meet five specific goals each intended to enhance students' ability to analyze relationships both within historical periods and across the twentieth century.

First, it develops students' critical-thinking skills by encouraging them to evaluate how race, class, ethnicity, sexual orientation, and life cycle affected women's work, politics, and domestic life. Second, it encourages students to analyze the relationships among political, social, and economic institutions and their impact on women's lives in specific historical periods. Third, it facilitates the study of the connections between the public and private lives of women, frequently studied in opposition to one another. Fourth, it clarifies how women's search for self, both individually and collectively, has been informed by the historical intersections of class, race, and ethnicity. And finally, it reinforces the fact that women shaped their own lives, often self-consciously voicing their needs, their desires, and their hopes, through actions and words.

Some of the selections are representative of common experiences that women have shared, while others document a specific individual or distinct perspective. Together, the documents represent a broad spectrum of voices, valuing equally the marginalized and the elite, the common and the uncommon.

Chronology

Women in American History Since 1880 is divided into seven units and moves forward in time generally by increments of 15 to 20 years. The rationale for these units is twofold, one theoretical and the other practical. First, major historical events including urbanization and industrial growth, war, economic crisis, civil rights, and the rise of the New Right, have shaped and been shaped by women's active membership in the world around them. Women's participation in the public arena and the dynamic relationship between American political culture and the personal and domestic lives of women challenge students to reconsider their understanding of politics and power and the ties that link self and society. Second, this chronological approach, organized with reference to clearly defined periods in the development of our nation state, provides a sense of historical narrative and context.

Women confronted the boundaries of social convention everywhere at the end of the nineteenth century. Pushing the limits of respectability meant challenging the status quo in print and in public, through labor and political organizations, singly and collectively. For women of color, in particular, such challenges involved great personal risk. Most women, regardless of race and ethnicity, did not enjoy much leisure. They worked long hours at home, in factories, on the land, in offices and schools, experiencing a reality often at odds with the images of a more leisured domesticity that appeared in household manuals and popular media. Throughout the period the expectation of motherhood remained a core component of the female experience. Thus women's activism in political and economic life challenged the imaginary boundary between public and private life in the Gilded Age.

Historians estimate that in 1900 one-third of all single, urban women worked for wages outside the home. Among female wage earners, over half were foreign born or nonwhite and the average woman worker earned half what the average male worker earned. Some women worked in offices, others in professional fields including law, medicine, and social work, and still others as industrial, domestic, and farm labor. By 1920, over one fifth of the labor force was female. Throughout the period, women challenged a social order that despite its rhetoric remained especially harsh for many women and children. Perceived as a key reform, support for a federal suffrage amendment guaranteeing voting rights to women gained momentum after 1910. Women and men from diverse backgrounds effectively organized to support the amendment. Their efforts, some more militant than others, helped convince President Wilson to endorse the amendment in 1918. The combined and orchestrated work of many pro-suffrage women in "the winning plan" culminated in ratification of the Nineteenth Amendment in August 1920. Nevertheless, profound differences among women who struggled to be heard within American political, social, and economic life suggest the tensions that remained a powerful part of everyday life in America even after women achieved federal sanction for voting rights.

Developments in the 1920s illuminate these differences and the tensions they reveal. The metaphor of the flapper in the jazz age often evokes the freedoms experienced by many women during the 1920s. For some women this era did bring new opportunities in professional work like medicine, law, social work, and academe, but the majority of working women in cities and on farms labored in factories and fields, homes and offices. Frustration and anger grew among women workers in this period when their expectations for advancement, or at least a decent living, remained unfulfilled. Some female workers, such as those in southern textile factories, went on strike. In Elizabethon, Tennessee, and Gastonia, North Carolina, they were supported by labor reformers at the Bryn Mawr Summer School and together they sought to challenge inequities in the workplace. Still debate raged among women activists over how to promote freedom and equality for women: should it be through an equal rights amendment, labor legislation to protect women and children, strikes and other forms of direct protest, government support for mother's pensions, or other means? And what about women of color during this period when the Ku Klux Klan and those in favor of restricting immigration used incendiary language to keep America white and its women pure?

The Great Depression and World War II posed new challenges for women as they struggled to support themselves and their families during this extended period of crisis. As the federal government developed programs to provide relief and to facilitate recovery in the economic sector, American women, particularly among the working poor and the disenfranchised stood up for themselves and the needs of their families even if it meant confronting powerful economic and political institutions. When war came in 1941, women served the national good in various ways. The media, directed by the Office of War Information, projected new images of women that encouraged their entry into jobs previously done by men. At the end of World War II, many working women returned to traditionally female sectors of the economy where they were once again paid lower wages.

This return to traditional jobs reflected the dominant rules of life in the 1950s, which emphasized conformity in politics, social life, race relations, and leisure. For women, particularly those coming of age in Cold War America, opportunities to define their own lives appeared to be more limited and social norms more restrictive. The standard of white middle-class respectability defined ideal womanhood as wives, daughters, and professionals. Yet under this façade, women did challenge male authority, sometimes in the name of holding their family together, sometimes in pursuit of independence. The inroads made by labor and African Americans in the 1930s and 1940s served as a foundation as women sought ways to redress social, political, and economic inequalities most visibly in the growth of the civil rights movement in the late 1950s and early 1960s. And, for all the attention paid to conformity, the 1953 publication in English of *The Second Sex*, by French philosopher Simone de Beauvoir, energized American women. Here was a modern philosophical justification for self-determination that spoke to women seeking emancipation from traditional strictures at the core of female identity.

The 20 years from 1968 to 1988 formed a period of dramatic and fundamental change for American women. The tumultuous and divisive events of the 1960s often polarized American women: the rise of the New Right and the New Left, feminism and its backlash, and the debate over abortion rights. This period of intense questioning by women across the spectrum of race, class, ethnicity, and sexual orientation was accompanied by real changes in the workplace as increasing numbers of women claimed their rights and responsibilities as citizens with equal protection under the law. Still, the ties of some women to family and traditional cultural norms created tensions as they sought ways to integrate their work, family, and domestic lives.

Since 1988 hitherto private issues have become more public and more political. The Supreme Court's curtailment of some abortion rights in the

Webster decision (1989) is emblematic of what has been called a "backlash against women" that includes violence against those seeking and providing abortions as well as changes in affirmative action legislation. The enduring problems of sexual harassment in the workplace and violence in the home afflict women regardless of class, color, and ethnicity. Sexual orientation, too, is openly addressed in the public arena both by private citizens and public figures. At the same time, women's activism in contemporary politics builds on decades of past experience. Child labor, immigration, and human trafficking are among the international problems that have pushed women into the political world for the past century. And for many women, their public lives continue to be built around the needs of family. The recognition that some women have gained more of the good life in part because other women provide badly needed domestic services challenges any notion that sisterhood has been achieved.

Themes

The documents are organized around four major themes to facilitate discussion within each chronological unit and to show change or stasis over time. These themes are chosen to reflect four decades of work by historians of women: women and work, women and citizenship, representations of women, and domestic lives. Each of these themes connects to the overarching questions at the heart of this *Reader*, namely how, when, and why have American women participated in the nation's political, social, and economic life; how have women forged relationships and defined social networks among themselves that empowered them collectively and as individuals; and how have literary/visual artifacts reflected modern conceptions of culture, identity, and self-representation.

- The first theme examines how women have participated in economic life as producers and consumers, as well as advocates and critics of capitalism. Under this broad umbrella are topics as diverse as urbanization, wage labor, unionization, the feminization of poverty, and household management.
- The second theme highlights questions that pertain to women and citizenship. Under this rubric fall topics such as suffrage, participation in political parties and office holding, voting, and other forms of civic engagement such as lobbying and volunteerism, civil rights, and military service.
- The third theme considers representations of women in the arts such as literature, film, and other graphic arts and their influence on a variety of audiences who engaged these representations.

- The fourth theme explores the domestic lives of women and centers on life-cycle events as well as questions pertaining to women's health and sexuality.

Women Historians and American Women's History

In the 75 years since Mary Ritter Beard first wrote about women as "a force in history," historians have sought to collect, archive, and analyze sources that document the range of activities, public and private, that have defined the lives of American women. A handful of historians produced monographs in the 1950s and early 1960s that highlighted the major achievements of extraordinary women, such as those discussed in Eleanor Flexner's *The Century of Struggle*, a history of the battle for women's suffrage. By the late 1960s and 1970s, the enthusiasm for women's history as an academic discipline intensified partly in response to the feminist movement. Since that time, women's historians have joined other scholars in seeking to understand more clearly the dynamic interactions among social institutions such as work, family, religion, education, and law and their impact on the individual and collective experiences of American women. The documents in this *Reader* have been chosen and organized in an effort to understand more fully the diverse, sometimes contradictory, experiences of American women specifically with regard to work, citizenship, and domesticity, as well as the ways that women have been represented in visual and literary culture since 1880.

The diversity of women's experiences has provided an organizational motif in American women's history for the past 25 years. Among the first in a generation of scholars and activists who insisted on writing a narrative that included women of color and specifically African American women, Gerda Lerner had a tremendous impact on the discipline. Having suffered as a young Jewish woman in Nazi Europe, Lerner was especially sensitive to the complex ways that people used categories like race, gender, and ethnicity to determine people's political and civil rights. In the heightened awareness born of the civil rights revolution and grassroots activism against political, social, and economic injustice, women's historians continue to celebrate the diversity in how American women have worked, played, and organized their lives over the past century. In addition to race and ethnicity, historians use the category of social class to explain what appears to be a stark contrast in how women lived. In this context, the landmark article by Gerda Lerner, "The Lady and the Mill Girl," argues that industrialization in the nineteenth century displaced women's productive labor from home to factory and in so doing altered expectations for middle-class women and created new strata of women wage earners. Subsequent research has expanded our understanding of how work, paid and unpaid, plays a central role in the experiences of American women and how women have shaped and been shaped by attempts to assert control of their labor.

At the same time that women's historians explored the diversity of women's experiences, they also sought to integrate women's lives into a more inclusive narrative of American history. Beginning in the 1970s, scholars like Elizabeth Fox-Genovese attempted to show how, when, and where women's experiences fit into the most significant themes of our nation's past, not as tokens but as full-fledged participants. Fox-Genovese focused initially on the nineteenth-century South, reminding historians that the household – where black and white women and men lived in close proximity – was central to the plantation system. To understand that system and the various axes of race, class, and sexual power that defined it, scholars needed to examine the plantation household and all its complex relations. By the 1980s, questions of identity and culture demanded attention as historians sorted through the myriad ways that women defined themselves or were defined by others. In this context, Fox-Genovese turned from explorations of southern women's lives in the nineteenth century to representations of them in the twentieth century. In her interdisciplinary study, "Scarlett O'Hara: The Southern Lady as New Woman," Fox-Genovese examined depictions of southern belles in the mass media including film and popular literature. Her psychoanalytic approach offered a unique perspective for understanding the dynamic between women's past lives and the ways they are depicted in later periods.

Efforts to integrate women's experiences into the main historical narrative and to rewrite the contours of that narrative have found a complement in a woman-centered history. Carroll Smith-Rosenberg wrote extensively on domestic life and women's empowerment through a distinctly female world built around and made meaningful by shared experiences. This perspective has focused on the private lives of women and on issues of domesticity, maternity, intimacy, and sexuality. Beginning in the mid-1970s, Smith-Rosenberg urged historians to listen carefully to women's words, to study women as actors in their own lives by finding them in places where they exerted authority, and even power. Explorations of women's colleges, family relationships, child rearing, birth control, abortion, and sexuality enhanced critical thinking about women's multifaceted experiences in the private sphere and how they shaped women's agency. Recent studies of reproductive rights extend this important work by focusing on the interrelationship between the private and public lives of women and by gaining critical perspective on the role that race and ethnicity play in women's decision making about the most intimate aspects of their lives.

In this regard, histories of sexuality engage a range of complex issues that expose the multiple perspectives that women bring to emotionally charged arenas like reproductive rights. In the 1960s, radical feminists argued in support of a woman's right to control her own body. They challenged legislatures and courts to repeal laws criminalizing abortion, a movement that resulted in 1973 in the historic *Roe v. Wade* Supreme Court decision that granted women and their physicians the right to make decisions about abortion in private, at least for the first trimester of a pregnancy. Yet for many women of color, *Roe v. Wade* was only a partial victory. For them, reproductive rights required choices beyond abortion. Such rights included not only family planning and legalized abortion, but also economic guarantees that made it possible to give birth to and raise healthy children. Moreover, exposing deeply racist practices such as the forced sterilization of poor women – a practice that had occurred at least since the 1930s – and the experimental trials of the birth control pill in Puerto Rico in the 1950s brings attention to the dynamic interplay of freedom and control, of rights and abuse.

Sexuality and reproductive rights is also a key arena for understanding the interplay between family dynamics and state policy. Historians have moved towards a more nuanced understanding of the role that government – not always a disinterested partner – has played and continues to play in influencing women's most private and personal decisions. In doing so, they have recast the relationship between public and private boundaries that dominated much of the post-1960s' scholarship in women's history. As students continue to debate how women achieved suffrage and what happened in the aftermath of the Nineteenth Amendment, scholars explore the ways that reproductive rights and gay rights tie together the most personal and most public aspects of women's individual and collective lives. This work clarifies the important roles that class, ethnicity, race, and gender play in any historical understanding of the relationships between American women and the nation state.

Whether exploring the most intimate aspects of women's lives or integrating them into the main historical narrative, scholars who sought to shed light on the experiences of women of color faced unique challenges. Historians of African American women, for instance, had to excavate long-lost documents, read traditional sources against the grain, and employ newer methods like oral history in order to bring the voices of black women into the historical narrative. They discovered strong women everywhere, in the North as well as the South, in cities and on farms, in churches, schools, and hospitals, as organizers and club members, as entrepreneurs and secretaries, in government and in political clubs. Their understanding of the richness of African American women's lives complicated the dual identity or "double consciousness" of Black America so poignantly described a century ago by

W.E.B. DuBois. Yet even as history revealed multiple ways that black women organized on behalf of themselves and played leadership roles in challenging racial stereotypes, achieving suffrage, and securing civil rights, so too did it show how difficult it is to generalize about their experiences. As Deborah Gray White demonstrates in *Too Heavy a Load*, black women struggled over the course of the twentieth century to secure their civil and political rights, but they did not always do so as a unified force. Differences of class, color, political ideology, region, and sexuality affected black women's lives as they did the lives of other women. Similarly, historians of Latinas and Chicanas, American Indian women, Asian American women, and women from other racial and ethnic communities have discovered unsung heroines, traced women's leadership in local and national movements for change, and revealed differences of class, ideology, and other characteristics within each group.

Nature of Sources

The primary sources available to students exploring American women's history today are breathtaking by virtue of both abundance and quality. Among the sources available are personal narratives, letters, diaries, fiction and speeches before Congressional committees, on the campaign trail, or published in newspapers, magazines, and manifestos. Demographic and census materials provide context for women's voices and are significant in studying family and community history. Finally, cultural artifacts produced for and by women including film, television, cookbooks, and fashion have the potential to stimulate critical and imaginative historical analysis. The documents chosen for this volume offer a sampling of the range of sources available. Oral interviews appear throughout this *Reader* and affirm the popularity of oral history among women's historians. These interviews provide a wealth of information about individual lives and events. Like memoirs and other forms of personal narratives, interviews are authentic but not always accurate representations of the past. Like all documents, they require careful reading, corroboration from other sources, and above all critical evaluation.

Using the Sources

How do historians use documents? Historians are trained to examine documents and texts in relationship to time and place, in connection to other documents produced at the same time, and with the perspective of change or continuity over time. In women's history the dynamic tension between contemporary affairs and historical understanding is especially close, tempting the historian to evaluate documents through the subjective lens of the present. While it is often impossible to attain perfect objectivity, historians nevertheless strive to balance their craft by using multiple sources to build a logical and coherent interpretation of the past. While careful selection and evaluation of documents is essential, good historical writing often begins with curiosity and empathy. Who, what, when, where, how, and ultimately why, are questions frequently raised in historical inquiry.

Generally historians approach each document with a series of questions. First it is important to know who wrote or produced the document and to whom it was addressed. Most often writers have a particular audience in mind which informs the content and style of the document. The historian should evaluate who is writing, when, and whether she intended others to read the document. For example, when the Negro Nurse described her work day for a 1912 issue of the magazine *The Independent*, she did so knowing that it would be read largely by a white middle-class audience. In contrast, Eudora Welty took a candid photograph of two young girls playing with dolls on a Saturday afternoon in Jackson, Mississippi in 1933. Almost 50 years later, after she became a prize-winning author, she selected this picture for public exhibition about her home state of Mississippi at a particular historical moment. Why Welty snapped this particular photo, what she wanted to capture about this moment in 1933, when she was an unknown field agent working for the WPA, and why she chose to make it public in 1970 in the aftermath of school desegregation suggest the complexity and the fun of analyzing documents.

A second set of questions historians raise when analyzing documents involves the relationship between text and historical context. External events help locate the document in time and place. Although historians often attempt to sort through documents by categorizing them as political, social, or economic, for example, most documents are not written in a vacuum. When the Women's Bureau, a government agency created in 1922 to gather information about working women, published its case studies in 1930, it did so in the wake of the October 1929 crash. Today we know that the Great Depression went on for nearly a decade, with slowdowns in factory production that affected thousands of working women. But in 1930, the federal government had better hindsight than foresight and the work of the Women's Bureau agents was informed by the violence of strikes by women textile workers at Elizabethon, Tennessee, and in mills at Gastonia, North Carolina. It is important for the historian to examine the document and also to look outside the document to understand its context.

A third approach that historians employ when analyzing documents is to compare and contrast documents from the same time period. Sometimes texts will corroborate each other but sometimes historians will find radically different positions. By allowing the documents to work together historians are able to interpret the past from a critical perspective. This is particularly important in women's history where the intersection of race, class, ethnicity, sexual orientation, and other characteristics have a significant impact. It is easy to see that women, even women of the same social class and economic position, have never voted as a bloc or shared one common ideology.

The documents in this *Reader* are a beginning. Two students looking at the same document will arrive at different interpretations in part because each brings a different lens through which to look and in part because each starts with a different question he or she wants to answer. The documents leave a paper trail; the historian creates his or her own journey through them.

Chapter 1

The Boundaries of Convention in the Gilded Age, 1880–1900

WORK

1 Atlanta Washing Society, 1881

In July 1881, the Atlanta Washing Society, a group of 20 women and men, established a uniform rate of one dollar per 12 pounds of wash. Several weeks later they organized a strike to secure a higher rate and involved washerwomen all over the city in the action, including a few white women. They met head on the threat of displacement by Chinese commercial laundries and an "industrial steam laundry" that employed "smart Yankee girls." Despite pressure from police and the city council in the form of arrests, fines, and taxes, the washerwomen persevered. These so-called "Washing Amazons" defiantly challenged their exploitation as domestic household laborers in a most public and political way.

THE DOUGHTY WASHWOMEN

Holding out for an Advance in Wages

The washerwomen's strike is assuming vast proportions and despite the apparent independence of the white people, is causing quite an inconvenience among our citizens.

In one instance the demand for one dollar per dozen was acceded to. Those who decline to give this price are still wanting washers. Several families who decline to pay the price demanded, have determined to send their clothing to

Marietta where they have secured laundry service. The strikers hold daily meetings and are exhorted by the leaders, who are confident that the demands will be granted. The committees still visit the women and induce them to join the strike and when a refusal is met with threats of personal violence are freely indulged in to such an extent as to cause a compromise with their demands. There are some families in Atlanta who have been unable to have any washing done for more than two weeks.

Not only the washerwomen, but the cooks, house servants and nurses are asking an increase. The combinations are being managed by the laundry ladies.

THE WET CLOTHES

The Washerwomen Bring Home

The Story of the Organization Fully Told by Captain Starnes, Who Says a White Man and $300 Back the Strikers – The Way the Ranks are Increased.

Police court was well attended yesterday morning, and Recorder Glenn added $166 to the city treasury by fines imposed.

Among other cases disposed of were those against Mattida Orawford, Sallie Bell, Carrie Jones, Dora Jones, Ophetia Turner and Sarah A. Coilier. This sixtette of ebony hued damsels was charged with disorderly conduct and quarreling, and in each case, except the last, a fine of five dollars was imposed, and subsequently paid. In the case of Sarah A. Collier, twenty dollars was assessed, and the money not being paid, the defendant's name was transcribed to the chain-gang book, where it will remain for forty days.

Each of these cases resulted from the washerwomen's strike. As members of that organization they have visited women who are taking no part in the strike and have threatened personal violence unless their demands were acceded to and their example followed. During their rounds they met with persons who opposed the strike and who declined to submit to their proposition to become members. This opposition caused an excessive use of abusive and threatening language and the charge of disorderly conduct and quarreling was the result.

Soon after court a CONSTITUTION representative heard Captain Starnes remark, "Well, Glenn's a good one; he put the fine on the strikers and tomorrow we will have additional subjects for his consideration." This remark caused the reporter to ask Starnes if he knew what he was talking about.

"Of course I do," was the reply. "Bagby and I have been working on this matter ever since the strike began, and if anybody in town knows anything about, I guess we do."

"Well, tell us what you know."

"Well, you see this society was first organized about one year ago. The first meeting was held in the church on Summer Hill, but only a few women attended. They tried hard to get up a strike but could not succeed and the thing soon broke because no one would join This year however, they have been successful and to-day nearly 3,000 negro women are asking their white friends who supported them during the cold, hard winter to pay them a dollar a dozen for washing."

"You say they organized a year ago?"

"Yes, but that organization went to pieces. The society that now exists is about two weeks old. Next Saturday night three weeks ago twenty negro women and a few negro men met in Summer Hill church and discussed the matter. The next night the negro preachers in all the churches announced a mass meeting of the washerwomen for the following night at Summer Hill church. The meeting was a big one and the result was an organization. Officers were elected, committees appointed and time and places for meeting read out. Since then there has been meetings every night or two, and now there is a club or society in every ward in the city and the strikers have increased from twenty to about 8,000 in less than three weeks."

"What do they do at these meetings?"

"Make speeches and pray. They swear they never will wash another piece for less than one dollar a dozen, but they will never get it and will soon give in. In fact, they would have caved before this but for the white man who is backing the strike."

"Do you know that there is a white man behind these strikers, or is it a rumor?"

"I know it, and I'll tell you who it is if you want to know,"

"No, never mind his name. Tell me how you know,"

"I have heard it from several responsible parties. There is Dora Watts, who lives at Mr. Wolfe's, 144 Jones street, who swears that a white man addressed a meeting last week. She also says that he will speak to them next Monday night. This man tells them that he will see them through all right. They have a fund of $300 and feel confident of getting what they ask."

"They are trying to prevent those who are not members from washing, are they not?"

"Yes. The committee first goes to those who have no connection with the organization and try to persuade them to join. Failing in this they notify them that they must not take any more washing at less than one dollar a dozen, and then threaten them with cowhides, fire and death if they disobey. Out on Walker street there lives a white lady, a Mrs. Richardson, who has had but one washerwoman for eight years. Her name is Sarah Gardner. Her husband joined the strikers and would not let his wife take the washing

Mrs. Richardson hired another woman who took her clothes away Monday but brought them back in the afternoon saying that the "committee wouldn't let her wash for less than a dollar a dozen." Mrs. Richardson then induced a girl she had in the house to undertake the washing but yesterday evening while she was at work on Mrs. Richardson's place, a committee composed of Dora Shorter, Annie King and Sam Gardner came up and threatened to kill her if she didn't stop, and when the lady, Mrs. Richardson, came out and ordered them away, they refused to go, and began to abuse her. I heard of it and now all three are in here, and Spyers has the key. He is fond of locking, but hates to unlock a door. I guess Recorder Glenn will catch 'em for $20 each."

"So they are on their muscle?"

"Well, I should say so. The men are as bad as the women. When a woman refuses to join the society, their men threaten to 'whip 'em,' and the result is that the ranks are daily swelling, why, last night there was a big meeting at New Hope church, on Green's Ferry street, and fifty additions were made to the list. They passed resolutions informing all women not members of the society to quit work, or stand the consequences. I tell you, this strike is a big thing, but if Glenn will only stand to Bagby and myself we will break it up. I am going to arrest every one who threatens any woman, and I am going to try to get the chain gang full, then they will stop. Why, let me tell you, out here on Spring street is an old white woman who lives over her wash tub. The infernal scoundrels went to her house yesterday and threatened to burn the place down and to kill her if she took another rag. Emma Palmer, Jane Webb and Sarah Collier, with two white women, are doing the work, but I think Spyers will get a chance to lock 'em up before dark."

Source: *Atlanta Constitution*, July 21, 29, 1881. © AJC Reprints.

2 Lynn Shoe Stitchers, 1886 and 1888

Descriptions of the lady shoe stitchers in Lynn, Massachusetts, appeared in both the Lynn Bee *and the* Boston Herald *in the mid-1880s. Census records from 1880 suggest that 51 percent of the total female labor force in Lynn were wives and daughters in male-headed families, while the rest of the wage-earning women were either self-supporting boarders or heads of families. Whereas the majority of these Lynn workers came from New England and included American-born daughters of Irish and French Canadian immigrants, still a significant number were foreign born. Lynn boasted an active labor movement, but The Lady Stitchers' Assembly of the Knights of Labor included only those women employed in boot and shoe making.*

The female operatives in the shoe manufactories of Lynn differ materially from the [present day] factory operatives of Lowell, Lawrence and Fall River. In the latter cities the foreign element predominates – almost entirely prevails at the present day. In Lynn comparatively few are employed who are not strictly American, by birth and blood. Once this could have been said of the factory operatives of those cities. A generation ago their factories were largely filled with ambitious and self respecting daughters of New England, who flocked to them for employment that could not be obtained nearer home....

The Lynn female operative occupies an important social position in the community. In the intervals of her employment she sometimes does valuable service in charitable work, and every Sabbath finds her attired in the very latest styles and the most costly fabrics, a constant and devout attendant at church and Sabbath school.... There she meets her employer and other employers on a perfect equality, and even sometimes become the leading spirit in movements in which she often exercises authority over their less enthusiastic temperaments.

Most of the shop girls employed in Lynn are permanent residents here, living with their parents.... Many, however, are compelled to live in the excellent boarding houses, for which Lynn is noted, and the lively times enjoyed after the day's work is done is [sic] the natural consequence of a gathering of youthful spirits released from all care. There is another class of provident female operatives who club together, and hiring a suite of rooms either cook for themselves, taking an occasional meal out, or go regularly to meals at some restaurant....

The comparatively strict discipline common in the factories of Lowell and Fall River is unknown in Lynn.... but it has been partially maintained by the self reliant and independent spirit of the operatives themselves, who never hesitate to chaff and torment any self-important overseer who may start out upon the idea of requiring implicit obedience to any code of rules and regulations.... The Yankee girl is proverbially a girl of mischievous spirit, and she never hesitates to assert herself... whatever be her comparative station in life....

    ... if these thirteen ladies were representatives of their class of Lynn shoe girls, they certainly bore out the description already given in the *Herald* of them, for they were well and tastefully dressed, ladylike in bearing and demeanor, and their conversation evinced an intelligence and refinement that would do credit to the best of their sex.

    ... They showed their intelligent appreciation of the subject by pointing out the embarrassment which might occur in the event of large numbers of young women being attracted to Lynn with the expectation of earning high wages, when in reality they could only hope for the barest subsistence, and at that would be taking the work from the hands of those who already had too little to do for their own comfort and hope of independence.

... There are now said to be 180 manufacturing rooms and 300 stitching rooms [shops] in Lynn, each employing 150 to 200 girls.

["] ... A great deal of my time [said one stitcher] has been spent among the poor girls of Lynn connected with the shoe industry, and I know that their lot is not to be envied. Often, after getting a few weeks' pay, they are thrown out on to the world, and all the winter and spring there is any amount of poverty among them. Many at these times have to live on bread and water in order to get along. There is a large class in Lynn of these homeless girls, who, for a great part of the time, undergo such hardships as I have described.... Some of them drift off to Boston, which is already overstocked with the unemployed of their class. I say I have had to do with these girls, and I have had them come to me a dozen times in the week for help or advice, telling me they had no money to pay for their room or to pay for food or for a nurse or for medicine.... I should say that one third of the girls of Lynn are homeless and subject to these changes of fortune.... ["]

Source: *Lynn Bee*, February 16, 1886, and *Boston Herald*, July 29, 1888, in *We Will Rise in Our Might: Working-women's Voices from Nineteenth-Century New England*, ed. Mary H. Blewett (Ithaca, NY: Cornell University Press, 1991), pp. 161–2, 171. Copyright © 1991 by Cornell University used by permission of the publisher, Cornell University Press.

CITIZENSHIP

3 Frances Willard, Women and Organization, 1891

The Woman's Christian Temperance Union (WCTU) was the largest temperance organization and included women of various racial and class backgrounds although it appealed largely to white middle-class women. It organized its members in productive ways to "Do Everything" for "Home Protection." The WCTU shared some goals with the more overtly populist National Farmer's Alliance, including a reform agenda that empowered women at the grassroots level. Frances Willard (1839–98), president of the WCTU from 1879 until her death, championed suffrage as a means to purify the home of alcohol. In her 1891 address to the Woman's National Council, Willard sought to find common ground with Elizabeth Cady Stanton and the National American Woman Suffrage Association (NAWSA) created in 1890 through the merger of the National Woman Suffrage Association and the American Woman Suffrage Association.

Beloved Friends and Comrades in a Sacred Cause:
"A difference of opinion on one question must not prevent us from working unitedly in those on which we can agree."

These words from the opening address before the International Council convened in this auditorium three years ago were the key-note of a most tuneful chorus. The name of her who uttered words so harmonious is Elizabeth Cady Stanton, and it shall live forever in the annals of woman's heroic struggle up from sexhood into humanhood.

Our friends have said that, as President of the National American Woman Suffrage Association, Mrs. Stanton leads the largest army of women outside, and I the largest one inside, the realm of a conservative theology. However this may be, I rejoice to see the day when, with distinctly avowed loyalty to my Methodist faith, and as distinctly avowed respect for the sincerity with which she holds to views quite different, I can clasp hands in loyal comradeship with one whose dauntless voice rang out over the Nation for "woman's rights" when I was but a romping girl upon a prairie farm. . . .

"Something solid, and superior to any existing society, is what we want." This is the commentary of women with whom I have talked, and the foregoing outline is offered as a possible help toward meeting this very natural and reasonable requirement. Such a National society would, indeed, incalculably increase the world's sum total of womanly courage, efficiency, and *esprit de corps;* widening our horizon, correcting the tendency to an exaggerated impression of one's own work as compared with that of others, and putting the wisdom and expertness of each at the service of all. Nor would it require a vast amount of effort to bring such a great movement into being, for the work of organizing is already done, and the correlating of societies now formed could be divided among our leaders, each one taking a state or a number of chief towns and cities.

Being organized in the interest of no specific propaganda, this great Association would unite in cordial sympathy all existing societies of women, that with a mighty aggregate of power we might move in directions upon which we could agree.

Moreover, the tendency would be vastly to increase the interest of individual women in associated work and the desire of local societies to be federated nationally, individual women and isolated societies of women being ineligible to membership in the councils, whether local, State, or National.

But the greatest single advantage will perhaps be this, that while each society devoted to a specific end will continue to pursue these by its own methods, every organization will have the moral support of all others and will be in a position to add its influence to that of all others, for such outside movements of beneficence as it may approve. For instance, without a dissenting voice, the International Council of 1888 put itself on record to the following effect:

> It is the unanimous voice of the Council that all institutions of learning and of professional instruction, including schools of theology, law, and medicine, should, in the interests of humanity, be as freely opened to women as to men; that opportunities for industrial training should be as generally and as liberally provided for one sex as for the other, and the representatives of organized womanhood in this Council will steadily demand that in all avocations in which both men and women engage equal wages shall be paid for equal work; and, finally, that an enlightened society should demand, as the only adequate expression of the high civilization which it is its office to establish and maintain, an identical standard of personal purity and morality for men and women.

Probably there is not an intelligent woman in America who would not subscribe to this declaration. The only point of possible difference would be the opening of theological schools to women; and since Oberlin and Hartford, Boston and Evanston theological seminaries have done this and it does not necessarily involve the ordination of women, that difference would not be likely to arise.

Were there such a council of women in town and city, State and Nation, we should have our representatives constantly at the State and National capitals, and should ask unitedly for advantages that have heretofore been asked for only by separate societies. Laws for the better protection of women, married and single; laws protecting the property rights of married women and giving them equal power with their husbands over their children; laws making the kindergarten a part of the public school system; requiring lessons in physical culture and gymnastics to be given in all grades of the public school with special reference to health and purity of personal habitudes; National and State appropriations for common school and industrial education, and appropriations for institutions helpful to women – surely we might together strive for all of these.

Locally a woman's council should, in the interest of that "mothering" which is the central idea of our new movement, seek to secure for women admission to all school committees, library associations, hospital and other institutional boards intrusted with the care of the defective, dependent, and delinquent classes; also to boards of trustees in school and college and all professional and business associations; also to all college and professional schools that have not yet set before us an open door; and each local council should have the power to call in the united influence of its own State council, or, in special instances, of the National Council, if its own influence did not suffice.

I am confident that the development of this movement will impart to women such a sense of strength and courage, and their corporate self-respect will so increase, that such theatrical bills as we now see displayed will not be permitted for an hour, without our potent protest; and the exhibitions of women's forms and faces in the saloons and cigar stores, which women's self-respect will never let them enter, and the disgraceful literature now for sale on so many public news-stands, will not be tolerated by the womanhood of any town or city. An "Anatomical Museum" that I often pass on a Chicago street bears the words: "Gentlemen only admitted." Why do women passively accept these flaunting assumptions that men are expected to derive pleasure from objects that they would not for a moment permit their wives to see? Some day women will not accept them passively, and then these base exhibitions will cease, for women will purify every place they enter, and they will enter every place. Catholic and Protestant women would come to a better understanding of each other through working thus for mutual interests; Jew and Gentile would rejoice in the manifold aims of a practical Christianity; women who work because they must; women, true-souled enough to work because they ought, or, best of all, great-souled enough to work because they love humanity, will all meet on one broad platform large enough and strong enough to furnish standing room for all. Later on, who knows but that by means of this same Council we women might free ourselves from that stupendous bondage which is the basis of all others – the unhealthfulness of fashionable dress! "Courage is as contagious as cowardice," and the courage of a council of women may yet lead us into the liberty of a costume tasteful as it is reasonable, and healthful as it is chaste.

Source: *Address of Frances E. Willard, President of the Woman's National Council of the United States . . . at its First Triennial Meeting, Albaugh's Opera House, Washington, D.C., February 22–25, 1891* (Washington, DC, 1891), pp. 1–2, 6–8. Library of Congress, American Memory Collection.

4 Elizabeth Cady Stanton, The Solitude of Self, 1892

Elizabeth Cady Stanton (1815–1902) wrote and then delivered The Solitude of Self *in a rare appearance of a female before the judiciary committee of the United States Congress in 1892. Twenty-five years after having stomped through Kansas with Susan B. Anthony in pursuit of women's suffrage, she remained a leader of the woman's rights movement.* The Solitude of Self *reflected a profound commitment to the tenets of natural rights philosophy and of the rights of the individual, female as well as male, at the center of emancipation. Three years later she authored* The Woman's Bible *where she argued defiantly in support of a feminist reinterpretation of scripture.*

The point I wish plainly to bring before you on this occasion is the individuality of each human soul; our Protestant idea, the right of individual conscience and judgment; our republican idea, individual citizenship. In discussing the rights of woman, we are to consider, first, what belongs to her as an individual, in a world of her own, the arbiter of her own destiny, an imaginary Robinson Crusoe, with her woman, Friday, on a solitary island. . . .

The strongest reason for giving woman all the opportunities for higher education, for the full development of her faculties, her forces of mind and body; for giving her the most enlarged freedom of thought and action; a complete emancipation from all forms of bondage, of custom, dependence, superstition; from all the crippling influences of fear – is the solitude and personal responsibility of her own individual life. The strongest reason why we ask for woman a voice in the government under which she lives; in the religion she is asked to believe; equality in social life, where she is the chief factor; a place in the trades and professions, where she may earn her bread, is because of her birthright to self-sovereignty; because, as an individual, she must rely on herself. No matter how much women prefer to lean, to be protected and supported, nor how much men desire to have them do so, they must make the voyage of life alone, and for safety in an emergency, they must know something of the laws of navigation. To guide our own craft, we must be captain, pilot, engineer; with chart and compass to stand at the wheel; to watch the winds and waves, and know when to take in the sail, and to read the signs in the firmament over all. It matters not whether the solitary voyager is man or woman; nature, having endowed them equally, leaves them to their own skill and judgment in the hour of danger, and, if not equal to the occasion, alike they perish.

To appreciate the importance of fitting every human soul for independent action, think for a moment of the immeasurable solitude of self. We come into the world alone, unlike all who have gone before us, we leave it alone, under circumstances peculiar to ourselves. No mortal ever has been, no mortal ever will be like the soul just launched on the sea of life. There can never again be just such a combination of prenatal influences; never again just such environments as make up the infancy, youth and manhood of this one. Nature never repeats herself, and the possibilities of one human soul will never be found in another. No one has ever found two blades of ribbon grass alike, and no one will ever find two human beings alike. Seeing, then, what must be the infinite diversity in human character, we can in a measure appreciate the loss to a nation when any class of the people is uneducated and unrepresented in the government. . . .

The young wife and mother, at the head of some establishment, with a kind husband to shield her from the adverse winds of life, with wealth, fortune and position, has a certain harbor of safety, secure against the ordinary ills of life. But to manage a household, have a desirable influence in society, keep her friends and the affections of her husband, train her children and servants well, she must have rare common sense, wisdom, diplomacy, and a knowledge of human nature. . . .

In age, when the pleasures of youth are passed, children grown up, married and gone, the hurry and bustle of life in a measure over, when the hands are weary of active service, when the old arm chair and the fireside are the chosen resorts, then men and women alike must fall back on their own resources. If they cannot find companionship in books, if they have no interest in the vital questions of the hour, no interest in watching the consummation of reforms with which they might have been identified, they soon pass into their dotage. The more fully the faculties of the mind are developed and kept in use, the longer the period of vigor and active interest in all around us continues. If, from a life-long participation in public affairs, a woman feels responsible for the laws regulating our system of education, the discipline of our jails and prisons, the sanitary condition of our private homes, public buildings and thoroughfares, an interest in commerce, finance, our foreign relations, in any or all these questions, her solitude will at least be respectable, and she will not be driven to gossip or scandal for entertainment. . . .

Nothing strengthens the judgment and quickens the conscience like individual responsibility. Nothing adds such dignity to character as the recognition of one's self-sovereignty; the right to an equal place, everywhere conceded – a place earned by personal merit, not an artificial attainment by inheritance, wealth, family and position. Conceding, then, that the responsibilities of life rest equally on man and woman, that their destiny is the same, they need the same preparation for time and eternity. . . .

But when all artificial trammels are removed, and women are recognized as individuals, responsible for their own environments, thoroughly educated for all positions in life they may be called to fill; with all the resources in themselves that liberal thought and broad culture can give; guided by their own conscience and judgment, trained to self-protection, by a healthy development of the muscular system, and skill in the use of weapons and defence; and stimulated to self-support by a knowledge of the business world and the pleasure that pecuniary independence must ever give; when women are trained in this way, they will in a measure be fitted for those hours of solitude that come alike to all, whether prepared or otherwise. As in our extremity we must depend on ourselves, the dictates of wisdom point to complete individual development.

In talking of education, how shallow the argument that each class must be educated for the special work it proposes to do, and that all those faculties not needed in this special work must lie dormant and utterly wither for want of use, when, perhaps, these will be the very faculties needed in life's greatest emergencies! Some say, "Where is the use of drilling girls in the languages, the sciences, in law, medicine, theology. As wives, mothers, housekeepers, cooks, they need a different curriculum from boys who are to fill all positions. The chief cooks in our great hotels and ocean steamers are men. In our large cities, men run the bakeries; they make our bread, cake and pies. They manage the laundries; they are now considered our best milliners and dressmakers. Because some men fill these departments of usefulness, shall we regulate the curriculum in Harvard and Yale to their present necessities? If not, why this talk in our best colleges of a curriculum for girls who are crowding into the trades and professions, teachers in all our public schools, rapidly filling many lucrative and honorable positions in life?" . . .

And yet, there is a solitude which each and every one of us has always carried with him, more inaccessible than the ice-cold mountains, more profound than the midnight sea; the solitude of self. Our inner being which we call ourself, no eye nor touch of man or angel has ever pierced. It is more hidden than the caves of the gnome; the sacred adytum of the oracle; the hidden chamber of Eleusinian mystery, for to it only omniscience is permitted to enter.

Such is individual life. Who, I ask you, can take, dare take on himself the rights, the duties, the responsibilities of another human soul?

Source: Elizabeth Cady Stanton, *The Solitude of Self. Address before the U.S. Senate Committee on Woman Suffrage, February 20, 1892*, in *The Woman's Column*, January 1892, pp. 2–3.

5 Ida B. Wells, Lynch Law, 1892

Ida B. Wells (1862–1931) lived with danger and opportunity in Memphis, Tennessee, between 1880 and her forced exile in 1892. She worked for a decade as a teacher and might have assumed roles as wife, mother, and member of the rising black middle class. But Ida B. Wells sued the Chesapeake, Ohio, and Southwestern Railroad after having been forced to leave the "Ladies Car," which was reserved exclusively for white women. Subsequently she became a social and political activist, writer, editor, and part owner of the Memphis Free Speech and Headlight. *In 1892 she wrote an editorial in the* Free Speech *"Eight Men Lynched." When threats against her own life forced her to remain in the North, she challenged others to join in a campaign against "Southern Horrors." Within this context, she exposed a fundamental ideological difference with Frances Willard and the WCTU (Woman's Christian Temperance Union).*

LYNCHING AND RECONSTRUCTION

May 21, 1892
Eight Negroes lynched since last issue of the *Free Speech* one at Little Rock, Ark., last Saturday morning where the citizens broke (?) into the penitentiary and got their man; three near Anniston, Ala., one near New Orleans; and three at Clarksville, Ga., the last three for killing a white man, and five on the same old racket – the new alarm about raping white women. The same programme of hanging, then shooting bullets into the lifeless bodies was carried out to the letter. Nobody in this section believes the old threadbare lie that Negro men assault white women. If Southern white men are not careful, they will over-reach themselves and public sentiment will have a reaction; a conclusion will then be reached which will be very damaging to the moral reputation of their women.

PREFACE

The greater part of what is contained in these pages was published in the *New York Age* June 25, 1892, in explanation of the editorial which the Memphis whites considered sufficiently infamous to justify the destruction of my paper, *The Free Speech*.

Since the appearance of that statement, requests have come from all parts of the country that "Exiled," (the name under which it then appeared) be issued in pamphlet form. Some donations were made, but not enough for that purpose. The noble effort of the ladies of New York and Brooklyn Oct 5 have enabled me to comply with this request and give the world a true, unvarnished account of the causes of lynch law in the South.

This statement is not a shield for the despoiler of virtue, nor altogether a defense for the poor blind Afro-American Sampsons who suffer themselves to be betrayed by white Delilahs. It is a contribution to truth, an array of facts, the perusal of which it is hoped will stimulate this great American Republic to demand that justice be done though the heavens fall.

It is with no pleasure I have dipped my hands in the corruption here exposed. Somebody must show that the Afro-American race is more sinned against than sinning, and it seems to have fallen upon me to do so. The awful death-roll that Judge Lynch is calling every week is appalling, not only because of the lives it takes, the rank cruelty and outrage to the victims, but because of the prejudice it fosters and the stain it places against the good name of a weak race.

The Afro-American is not a bestial race. If this work can contribute in any way toward proving this, and at the same time arouse the conscience of the

American people to a demand for justice to every citizen, and punishment by law for the lawless, I shall feel I have done my race a service. Other considerations are of minor importance.

MISS WILLARD'S ATTITUDE

No class of American citizens stands in greater need of the humane and thoughtful consideration of all sections of our country than do the colored people, nor does any class exceed us in the measure of grateful regard for acts of kindly interest in our behalf. It is, therefore, to us, a matter of keen regret that a Christian organization so large and influential as the Woman's Christian Temperance Union, should refuse to give its sympathy and support to our oppressed people who ask no further favor than the promotion of public sentiment which shall guarantee to every person accused of crime the safeguard of a fair and impartial trial, and protection from butchery by brutal mobs. Accustomed as we are to the indifference and apathy of Christian people, we would bear this instance of ill fortune in silence, had not Miss Willard gone out of her way to antagonize the cause so dear to our hearts by including in her Annual Address to the WCTU Convention at Cleveland, November 5, 1894, a studied, unjust and wholly unwarranted attack upon our work.

In her address Miss Willard said:

The zeal for her race of Miss Ida B. Wells, a bright young colored woman, has, it seems to me, clouded her perception as to who were her friends and well-wishers in all high-minded and legitimate efforts to banish the abomination of lynching and torture from the land of the free and the home of the brave. It is my firm belief that in the statements made by Miss Wells concerning white women having taken the initiative in nameless acts between the races she has put an imputation upon half the white race in this country that is unjust, and, save in the rarest exceptional instances, wholly without foundation. This is the unanimous opinion of the most disinterested and observant leaders of opinion whom I have consulted on the subject, and I do not fear to say that the laudable efforts she is making are greatly handicapped by statements of this kind, nor to urge her as a friend and well-wisher to banish from her vocabulary all such allusions as a source of weakness to the cause she has at heart.

This paragraph, brief as it is, contains two statements which have not the slightest foundation in fact. At no time, nor in any place, have I made statements "concerning white women having taken the initiative in nameless acts between the races." Further, at no time, or place nor under any circumstance, have I directly or inferentially "put an imputation upon half the white race in this country" and I challenge this "friend and well-wisher" to give proof of the truth of her charge....

What I have said and what I now repeat – in answer to her first charge – is, that colored men have been lynched for assault upon women, when the facts were plain that the relationship between the victim lynched and the alleged victim of his assault was voluntary, clandestine and illicit. For that very reason we maintain, that, in every section of our land, the accused should have a fair, impartial trial, so that a man who is colored shall not be hanged for an offense, which, if he were white, would not be adjudged a crime. Facts cited in another chapter – "History of Some Cases of Rape" – amply maintain this position. The publication of these facts in defense of the good name of the race casts no "imputation upon half the white race in this country" and no such imputation can be inferred except by persons deliberately determined to be unjust....

Then the question was asked what the great moral reformers like Miss Frances Willard and Mr. Moody[1] had done to suppress Lynch Law and again I answered – nothing. That Mr. Moody had never said a word against lynching in any of his trips to the South, or in the North either, so far as was known, and that Miss Willard's only public utterance on the situation had condoned lynching and other unjust practices of the South against the Negro. When proof of these statements was demanded, I sent a letter containing a copy of the New York Voice, Oct. 23, 1890, in which appeared Miss Willard's own words of wholesale slander against the colored race and condonation of Southern white people's outrages against us. My letter in part reads as follows:

But Miss Willard, the great temperance leader, went even further in putting the seal of her approval upon the southerners' method of dealing with the Negro. In October, 1890, the Woman's Christian Temperance Union held its national meeting at Atlanta, Georgia. It was the first time in the history of the organization that it had gone south for a national meeting, and met the southerners in their own homes. They were welcomed with open arms. The governor of the state and the legislature gave special audiences in the halls of state legislation to the temperance workers. They set out to capture the northerners to their way of seeing things and without troubling to hear the Negro side of the question...

Said Miss Willard: "Now, as to the 'race problem' in its minified, current meaning, I am a true lover of the southern people – have spoken and worked in, perhaps, 200 of their towns and cities; have been taken into their love and

---

[1]   Rev. Dwight L. Moody, an internationally recognized evangelist from Northfield, Massachusetts, is perhaps best known as the founder of the Chicago Bible Institute (now the Moody Bible Institute).

confidence at scores of hospitable firesides; have heard them pour out their hearts in the splendid frankness of their impetuous natures. And I have said to them at such times: 'When I go North there will be wafted to you no word from pen or voice that is not loyal to what we are saying here and now.' Going South, a woman, a temperance woman, and a Northern temperance woman – three great barriers to their good will yonder – I was received by them with a confidence that was one of the most delightful surprises of my life. I think we have wronged the South, though we did not mean to do so. The reason was, in part, that we had irreparably wronged ourselves by putting no safeguards on the ballot box at the North that would sift out alien illiterates. They rule our cities today; the saloon is their palace, and the toddy stick their sceptre. It is not fair that they should vote, nor is it fair that a plantation Negro, who can neither read nor write, whose ideas are bounded by the fence of his own field and the price of his own mule, should be entrusted with the ballot. We ought to have put an educational test upon that ballot from the first. The Anglo-Saxon race will never submit to be dominated by the Negro so long as his altitude reaches no higher than the personal liberty of the saloon, and the power of appreciating the amount of liquor that a dollar will buy. New England would no more submit to this than South Carolina. 'Better whisky and more of it' has been the rallying cry of great dark-faced mobs in the Southern localities where local option was snowed under by the colored vote. Temperance has no enemy like that, for it is unreasoning and unreasonable. Tonight it promises in a great congregation to vote for temperance at the polls tomorrow; but tomorrow twenty-five cents changes that vote in favor of the liquor-seller.

"I pity the southerners, and I believe the great mass of them are as conscientious and kindly-intentioned toward the colored man as an equal number of white church-members of the North. Would-be demagogues lead the colored people to destruction. Half-drunken white roughs murder them at the polls, or intimidate them so that they do not vote. But the better class of people must not be blamed for this, and a more thoroughly American population than the Christian people of the South does not exist. . . .

"The fact is that illiterate colored men will not vote at the South until the white population chooses to have them do so; and under similar conditions they would not at the North." Here we have Miss Willard's words in full, condoning fraud, violence, murder, at the ballot box; rapine, shooting, hanging and burning; for all these things are done and being done now by the Southern white people. She does not stop there, but goes a step further to aid them in blackening the good name of an entire race, as shown by the sentences quoted in the paragraph above. These utterances, for which the colored people have never forgiven Miss Willard, and which Frederick Douglass has denounced as false, are to be found in full in the Voice of October 23, 1890, a temperance organ published at New York city.

Source: *A Red Record* in *Southern Horrors and Other Writings: The Anti-Lynching Campaign of Ida B. Wells, 1892–1900*, ed. Jacqueline Jones Royster (Bedford, 1997), pp. 1, 50, 140–3.

REPRESENTATIONS

6 Kate Chopin, Regret, 1897

Educated by nuns at the St. Louis Academy of the Sacred Heart, Kate Chopin (1851–1904) married into a prominent Creole family and spent 14 years in Louisiana. She returned to St. Louis with her six children after her husband died and began to write stories that reflected the rich heritage of the Louisiana Bayou. In 1899 she published The Awakening, *her first and only novel. In this novel, Chopin offended the tastes of polite society by creating a heroine, Edna Pontellier, who did not act as a proper wife or mother. Her earlier story "Regret" explores the emotional conflicts of an economically self-sufficient, middle-aged Creole woman confronted unexpectedly and briefly with the demands of others. It appeared in* A Night in Acadie *(1897), the second of two well-received collections of her stories.*

REGRET

Mamzelle Aurélie possessed a good strong figure, ruddy cheeks, hair that was changing from brown to gray, and a determined eye. She wore a man's hat about the farm, and an old blue army overcoat when it was cold, and sometimes topboots.

Mamzelle Aurélie had never thought of marrying. She had never been in love. At the age of twenty she had received a proposal, which she had promptly declined, and at the age of fifty she had not yet lived to regret it.

So she was quite alone in the world, except for her dog Ponto, and the negroes who lived in her cabins and worked her crops, and the fowls, a few cows, a couple of mules, her gun (with which she shot chicken-hawks), and her religion.

One morning Mamzelle Aurélie stood upon her gallery, contemplating, with arms akimbo, a small band of very small children who, to all intents and purposes, might have fallen from the clouds, so unexpected and bewildering was their coming, and so unwelcome. They were the children of her nearest neighbor, Odile, who was not such a near neighbor, after all.

The young woman had appeared but five minutes before, accompanied by these four children. In her arms she carried little Elodie; she dragged Ti

Nomme by an unwilling hand; while Marcéline and Marcélette followed with irresolute steps.

Her face was red and disfigured from tears and excitement. She had been summoned to a neighboring parish by the dangerous illness of her mother; her husband was away in Texas – it seemed to her a million miles away; and Valsin was waiting with the mule-cart to drive her to the station.

"It's no question, Mamzelle Aurélie; you jus' got to keep those youngsters fo' me tell I come back. Dieu sait, I would n' botha you with 'em if it was any otha way to do! Make 'em mine you, Mamzelle Aurélie; don' spare 'em. Me, there, I'm half crazy between the chil'ren, an' Léon not home, an' maybe not even to fine po' maman alive encore!" – a harrowing possibility which drove Odile to take a final hasty and convulsive leave of her disconsolate family.

She left them crowded into the narrow strip of shade on the porch of the long, low house; the white sunlight was beating in on the white old boards; some chickens were scratching in the grass at the foot of the steps, and one had boldly mounted, and was stepping heavily, solemnly, and aimlessly across the gallery. There was a pleasant odor of pinks in the air, and the sound of negroes' laughter was coming across the flowering cotton-field.

Mamzelle Aurélie stood contemplating the children. She looked with a critical eye upon Marcéline, who had been left staggering beneath the weight of the chubby Elodie. She surveyed with the same calculating air Marcélette mingling her silent tears with the audible grief and rebellion of Ti Nomme. During those few contemplative moments she was collecting herself, determining upon a line of action which should be identical with a line of duty. She began by feeding them.

If Mamzelle Aurélie's responsibilities might have begun and ended there, they could easily have been dismissed; for her larder was amply provided against an emergency of this nature. But little children are not little pigs; they require and demand attentions which were wholly unexpected by Mamzelle Aurélie, and which she was ill prepared to give.

She was, indeed, very inapt in her management of Odile's children during the first few days. How could she know that Marcélette always wept when spoken to in a loud and commanding tone of voice? It was a peculiarity of Marcélette's. She became acquainted with Ti Nomme's passion for flowers only when he had plucked all the choicest gardenias and pinks for the apparent purpose of critically studying their botanical construction.

"'Tain't enough to tell 'im, Mamzelle Aurélie," Marcéline instructed her; "you got to tie 'im in a chair. It's w'at maman all time do w'en he's bad: she tie 'im in a chair." The chair in which Mamzelle Aurélie tied Ti Nomme was roomy and comfortable, and he seized the opportunity to take a nap in it, the afternoon being warm.

At night, when she ordered them one and all to bed as she would have shooed the chickens into the hen-house, they stayed uncomprehending before her. What about the little white nightgowns that had to be taken from the pillow-slip in which they were brought over, and shaken by some strong hand till they snapped like ox-whips? What about the tub of water which had to be brought and set in the middle of the floor, in which the little tired, dusty, sunbrowned feet had every one to be washed sweet and clean? And it made Marcéline and Marcélette laugh merrily – the idea that Mamzelle Aurélie should for a moment have believed that Ti Nomme could fall asleep without being told the story of *Croque-mitaine* or *Loup-garou*, or both; or that Elodie could fall asleep at all without being rocked and sung to.

"I tell you, Aunt Ruby," Mamzelle Aurélie informed her cook in confidence; "me, I'd rather manage a dozen plantation' than fo' chil'ren. It's terrassent! Bonté! Don't talk to me about chil'ren!"

"'Tain' ispected sich as you would know airy thing 'bout'em, Mamzelle Aurélie. I see dat plainly yistiddy w'en I spy dat li'le chile playin' wid yo' baskit o' keys. You don' know dat makes chillun grow up hard-headed, to play wid keys? Des like it make 'em teeth hard to look in a lookin'-glass. Them's the things you got to know in the raisin' an' manigement o' chillun."

Mamzelle Aurélie certainly did not pretend or aspire to such subtle and far-reaching knowledge on the subject as Aunt Ruby possessed, who had "raised five an' bared (buried) six" in her day. She was glad enough to learn a few little mother-tricks to serve the moment's need.

Ti Nomme's sticky fingers compelled her to unearth white aprons that she had not worn for years, and she had to accustom herself to his moist kisses – the expressions of an affectionate and exuberant nature. She got down her sewing-basket, which she seldom used, from the top shelf of the armoire, and placed it within the ready and easy reach which torn slips and buttonless waists demanded. It took her some days to become accustomed to the laughing, the crying, the chattering that echoed through the house and around it all day long. And it was not the first or the second night that she could sleep comfortably with little Elodie's hot, plump body pressed close against her, and the little one's warm breath beating her cheek like the fanning of a bird's wing.

But at the end of two weeks Mamzelle Aurélie had grown quite used to these things, and she no longer complained.

It was also at the end of two weeks that Mamzelle Aurélie, one evening, looking away toward the crib where the cattle were being fed, saw Valsin's blue cart turning the bend of the road. Odile sat beside the mulatto, upright and alert. As they drew near, the young woman's beaming face indicated that her home-coming was a happy one.

But this coming, unannounced and unexpected threw Mamzelle Aurélie into a flutter that was almost agitation. The children had to be gathered.

Where was Ti Nomme? Yonder in the shed, putting an edge on his knife at the grindstone. And Marcéline and Marcélette? Cutting and fashioning doll-rags in the corner of the gallery. As for Elodie, she was safe enough in Mamzelle Aurélie's arms; and she had screamed with delight at sight of the familiar blue cart which was bringing her mother back to her.

The excitement was all over, and they were gone. How still it was when they were gone! Mamzelle Aurélie stood upon the gallery, looking and listening. She could no longer see the cart; the red sunset and the blue-gray twilight had together flung a purple mist across the fields and road that hid it from her view. She could no longer hear the wheezing and creaking of its wheels. But she could still faintly hear the shrill, glad voices of the children.

She turned into the house. There was much work awaiting her, for the children had left a sad disorder behind them; but she did not at once set about the task of righting it. Mamzelle Aurélie seated herself beside the table. She gave one slow glance through the room, into which the evening shadows were creeping and deepening around her solitary figure. She let her head fall down upon her bended arm, and began to cry. Oh, but she cried! Not softly, as women often do. She cried like a man, with sobs that seemed to tear her very soul. She did not notice Ponto licking her hand.

Source: Kate Chopin, *The Awakening and Selected Stories* (New York: Random House, 1981), pp. 96–101.

7 Zitkala-Ša (Gertrude Bonnin), The Beadwork, 1900

Zitkala-Ša (1876–1938) used the power of her writing for political purposes. Born Gertrude Simmons, she began to write under her Dakota name Zitkala-Ša in the late 1890s. "The Beadwork," part of "Impressions of an Indian Childhood" written for Atlantic Monthly *in 1900, is a finely crafted memory of her childhood and her mother. After her marriage to Richard Bonnin, who was part Dakota and part French-American, Zitkala-Ša sometimes used her married name. In 1916 she published "The Indian's Awakening" in the opening issue of* The American Indian Magazine, *in conjunction with the work of the Society of American Indians. After passage of the Nineteenth Amendment, she appealed to her suffrage friends in the General Federation of Women's Clubs and the League of American Pen Women, to support Indian citizenship and the legal rights it entailed.*

Soon after breakfast mother sometimes began her beadwork. On a bright, clear day, she pulled out the wooden pegs that pinned the skirt of our wigwam to the ground, and rolled the canvas part way up on its frame of slender poles. Then the cool morning breezes swept freely through our dwelling, now and then wafting the perfume of sweet grasses from newly burnt prairie.

Untying the long tasseled strings that bound a small brown buckskin bag, my mother spread upon a mat beside her bunches of colored beads, just as an artist arranges the paints upon his palette. On a lapboard she smoothed out a double sheet of soft white buckskin; and drawing from a beaded case that hung on the left of her wide belt a long, narrow blade, she trimmed the buckskin into shape. Often she worked upon small moccasins for her small daughter. Then I became intensely interested in her designing. With a proud, beaming face, I watched her work. In imagination, I saw myself walking in a new pair of snugly fitting moccasins. I felt the envious eyes of my playmates upon the pretty red beads decorating my feet.

Close beside my mother I sat on a rug, with a scrap of buckskin in one hand and an awl in the other. This was the beginning of my practical observation lessons in the art of beadwork. From a skein of finely twisted threads of silvery sinews my mother pulled out a single one. With an awl she pierced the buckskin, and skillfully threaded it with the white sinew. Picking up the tiny beads one by one, she strung them with the point of her thread, always twisting it carefully after every stitch.

It took many trials before I learned how to knot my sinew thread on the point of my finger, as I saw her do. Then the next difficulty was in keeping my thread stiffly twisted, so that I could easily string my beads upon it. My mother required of me original designs for my lessons in beading. At first I frequently ensnared many a sunny hour into working a long design. Soon I learned from self-inflicted punishment to refrain from drawing complex patterns, for I had to finish whatever I began.

After some experience I usually drew easy and simple crosses and squares. These were some of the set forms. My original designs were not always symmetrical nor sufficiently characteristic, two faults with which my mother had little patience. The quietness of her oversight made me feel strongly responsible and dependent upon my own judgment. She treated me as a dignified little individual as long as I was on my good behavior; and how humiliated I was when some boldness of mine drew forth a rebuke from her!

In the choice of colors she left me to my own taste. I was pleased with an outline of yellow upon a background of dark blue, or a combination of red and myrtle-green. There was another of red with a bluish-gray that was more conventionally used. When I became a little familiar with designing and the various pleasing combinations of color, a harder lesson was given me. It was the sewing on, instead of beads, some tinted porcupine quills, moistened and flattened between the nails of the thumb and forefinger.

My mother cut off the prickly ends and burned them at once in the centre fire. These sharp points were poisonous, and worked into the flesh wherever they lodged. For this reason, my mother said, I should not do much alone in quills until I was as tall as my cousin Warca-Ziwin.

Always after these confining lessons I was wild with surplus spirits, and found joyous relief in running loose in the open again. Many a summer afternoon a party of four or five of my playmates roamed over the hills with me....

We delighted in impersonating our own mothers. We talked of things we had heard them say in their conversations. We imitated their various manners, even to the inflection of their voices. In the lap of the prairie we seated ourselves upon our feet, and leaning our painted cheeks in the palms of our hands, we rested our elbows on our knees, and bent forward as old women were most accustomed to do.

While one was telling of some heroic deed recently done by a near relative, the rest of us listened attentively, and exclaimed in undertones, "Han! han!" (yes! yes!) whenever the speaker paused for breath, or sometimes for our sympathy. As the discourse became more thrilling, according to our ideas, we raised our voices in these interjections. In these impersonations our parents were led to say only those things that were in common favor.

No matter how exciting a tale we might be rehearsing, the mere shifting of a cloud shadow in the landscape near by was sufficient to change our impulses; and soon we were all chasing the great shadows that played among the hills. We shouted and whooped in the chase; laughing and calling to one another, we were like little sportive nymphs on that Dakota sea of rolling green.

On one occasion I forgot the cloud shadow in a strange notion to catch up with my own shadow. Standing straight and still, I began to glide after it, putting out one foot cautiously. When, with the greatest care, I set my foot in advance of myself, my shadow crept onward too. Then again I tried it; this time with the other foot. Still again my shadow escaped me. I began to run; and away flew my shadow, always just a step beyond me. Faster and faster I ran, setting my teeth and clenching my fists, determined to overtake my own fleet shadow. But ever swifter it glided before me, while I was growing breathless and hot. Slackening my speed, I was greatly vexed that my shadow should check its pace also. Daring it to the utmost, as I thought, I sat down upon a rock imbedded in the hillside.

So! my shadow had the impudence to sit down beside me!

Now my comrades caught up with me, and began to ask why I was running away so fast.

"Oh, I was chasing my shadow! Didn't you ever do that?" I inquired, surprised that they should not understand.

They planted their moccasined feet firmly upon my shadow to stay it, and I arose. Again my shadow slipped away, and moved as often as I did. Then we gave up trying to catch my shadow.

Before this peculiar experience I have no distinct memory of having recognized any vital bond between myself and my own shadow. I never gave it an afterthought.

Returning our borrowed belts and trinkets, we rambled homeward. That evening, as on other evenings, I went to sleep over my legends.

Source: "Impressions of an Indian Childhood," *Atlantic Monthly* (1900), reprinted first in Zitkala-Ša, *American Indian Stories* (Washington: Hayworth Publishing House, 1921), and more recently in Zitkala-Ša, *American Indian Stories,* with an introduction by Susan Rose Dominguez (Lincoln, NE: University of Nebraska Press, 2003), pp. 18–24.

DOMESTIC LIVES

8 Woman's Christian Temperance Union, Rules and regulations for the Hope and Help Rooms, 1887

Members of the Woman's Christian Temperance Union (WCTU) campaigned against prostitution in the late nineteenth and early twentieth centuries. Some anti-vice and purity crusaders targeted prostitutes as social deviants in need of reform. Others saw young women, especially innocent newcomers to urban life, as unwitting victims who were forced into prostitution or what was commonly called white slavery. Such reformers worked towards the passage in 1910 of the Mann Act aimed at stopping human trafficking. This poster from the WCTU outlines appropriate conduct for the young women whose behavior they hoped to change.

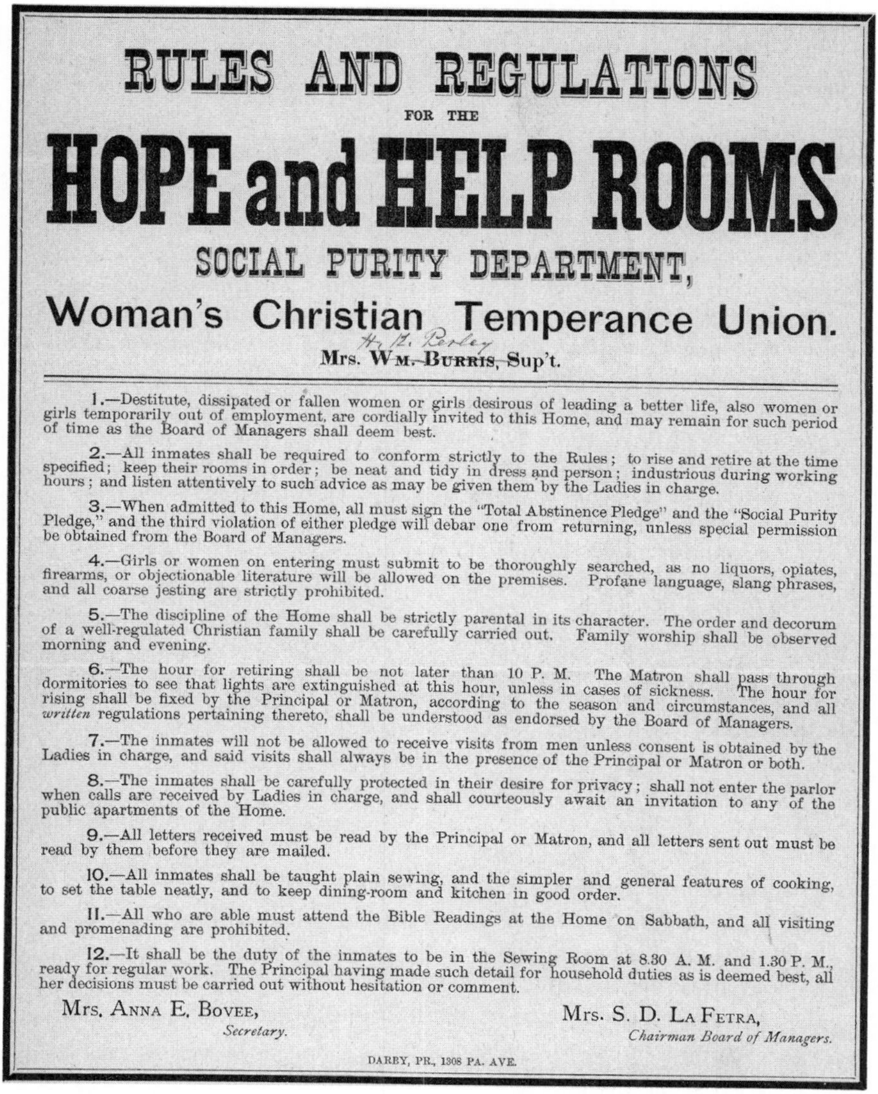

RULES AND REGULATIONS
FOR THE
HOPE and HELP ROOMS
SOCIAL PURITY DEPARTMENT,
Woman's Christian Temperance Union.
Mrs. Wm. Burris, Sup't.

1.—Destitute, dissipated or fallen women or girls desirous of leading a better life, also women or girls temporarily out of employment, are cordially invited to this Home, and may remain for such period of time as the Board of Managers shall deem best.

2.—All inmates shall be required to conform strictly to the Rules; to rise and retire at the time specified; keep their rooms in order; be neat and tidy in dress and person; industrious during working hours; and listen attentively to such advice as may be given them by the Ladies in charge.

3.—When admitted to this Home, all must sign the "Total Abstinence Pledge" and the "Social Purity Pledge," and the third violation of either pledge will debar one from returning, unless special permission be obtained from the Board of Managers.

4.—Girls or women on entering must submit to be thoroughly searched, as no liquors, opiates, firearms, or objectionable literature will be allowed on the premises. Profane language, slang phrases, and all coarse jesting are strictly prohibited.

5.—The discipline of the Home shall be strictly parental in its character. The order and decorum of a well-regulated Christian family shall be carefully carried out. Family worship shall be observed morning and evening.

6.—The hour for retiring shall be not later than 10 P. M. The Matron shall pass through dormitories to see that lights are extinguished at this hour, unless in cases of sickness. The hour for rising shall be fixed by the Principal or Matron, according to the season and circumstances, and all *written* regulations pertaining thereto, shall be understood as endorsed by the Board of Managers.

7.—The inmates will not be allowed to receive visits from men unless consent is obtained by the Ladies in charge, and said visits shall always be in the presence of the Principal or Matron or both.

8.—The inmates shall be carefully protected in their desire for privacy; shall not enter the parlor when calls are received by Ladies in charge, and shall courteously await an invitation to any of the public apartments of the Home.

9.—All letters received must be read by the Principal or Matron, and all letters sent out must be read by them before they are mailed.

10.—All inmates shall be taught plain sewing, and the simpler and general features of cooking, to set the table neatly, and to keep dining-room and kitchen in good order.

11.—All who are able must attend the Bible Readings at the Home on Sabbath, and all visiting and promenading are prohibited.

12.—It shall be the duty of the inmates to be in the Sewing Room at 8.30 A. M. and 1.30 P. M., ready for regular work. The Principal having made such detail for household duties as is deemed best, all her decisions must be carried out without hesitation or comment.

Mrs. Anna E. Bovee,
Secretary.

Mrs. S. D. La Fetra,
Chairman Board of Managers.

DARBY, PR., 1308 PA. AVE.

Figure 1.1

Source: *Rules and regulations for the Hope and Help Rooms, Social Purity Department, Woman's Christian Temperance Union* (Washington, DC: Darby Press, n.d. [1887]), Courtesy of Library of Congress.

9 Dr. Clelia Duel Mosher, The Mosher Survey, 1892 to 1913

Dr. Clelia Duel Mosher (1863–1940) gathered information regarding the "marital relation" for what she called the Study of the Physiology and Hygiene of Marriage with Some Consideration of the Birth Rate. *Never published, the research consisted of 45 questionnaires gathered over a period of 28 years. Reportedly, many of the women that completed her questionnaire were faculty wives whom she met during her time as a student at the University of Wisconsin, Stanford University, and Johns Hopkins Medical School. They were more highly educated, had fewer children, and were more comfortable with discussing sexual matters in a clinical way than many middle-class housewives. The questionnaires included each woman's case history and explored in a scientific manner menstruation, coitus, child birth, and sexual pleasure. These representative interviews from her study contrast two women each assigned a number in the survey. Number 15 was born in 1860 and graduated from Cornell University, worked as a librarian and has two children; number 22 was born in 1867, graduated from Radcliffe College, taught for five years and has one child.*

Blank No. 15

18.   Did conception occur by choice or accident?
      Choice.

22.   Is intercourse agreeable to you or not?
      It is agreeable when I wish it – would be unbearable if I did not.
      Do you always have a venereal orgasm?
      No. I have had but one during my whole married life, that one not complete and occasioned by my husband's being very near to me but not by intercourse.
      1. – When you do,
         (a)   Effect immediately afterwards?
         (b)   Effect next day?
      2. – When you do not,
         (a)   Effect immediately afterwards?
               Ten minutes to half an hour afterward I feel as usual, physically.
         (b)   Effect next day?
               None whatever.

23. What do you believe to be the true purpose of intercourse?
  (a) Necessity to man? to woman?
       It is my belief and my experience that intercourse is not to the
       comparatively normal man and woman necessary in the way in
       which food & drink are necessary. Whatever "necessity" there is
       is the same for man and woman alike and is a spiritual not a
       physical impulsion.
  (b) Pleasure
  (c) Reproduction?
       Both [pleasure and reproduction].
  (d) What other reasons beside reproduction are sufficient to warrant
       intercourse?
       The desire of both husband and wife for this expression of
       their union seems to me the first and highest reason for inter-
       course. The desire for offspring is a secondary, inci-
       dental, although entirely worthy motive but could never to me
       make intercourse right unless the mutual desire were also
       present.

24. Have you ever used any means to prevent conception? b) if so, what?
     Only the means of refraining from intercourse at the times when
     conception is most liable to take place.
  (b) Effect on your health?
       Refraining from all intercourse for as long as a year has not
       apparently affected my health one way or the other.

25. What, to you, would be an ideal habit?
     In general terms the ideal habit would be that which should most
     perfectly and completely serve as the physical expression of the
     spiritual union of husband and wife. My husband and I have not
     found yet what to us is an ideal habit. We believe in intercourse for
     its own sake – we wish it for ourselves and spiritually miss it, rather
     than physically, when it does not occur, because it is the highest,
     most sacred expression of our oneness. On the other hand there are
     sometimes long periods when we are not willing to incur even a slight
     risk of pregnancy, and then we deny ourselves the intercourse, feeling
     all the time that we are losing that which keeps us closest to each
     other.
     I wish to say that this need is absolutely spiritual so far as we can
     judge, possibly reacting somewhat upon the physical organization. We
     do not find health impaired in any way by the self denial.

Blank No. 22

18. Did conception occur by choice or accident?
We believe that it dated from a time chosen by my husband as one that would probably result in pregnancy though I did not know his thought at the time.

22. Is intercourse agreeable to you or not?
After it has begun, yes. If too long continued it wearies me.
Do you always have a venereal orgasm?
Never but once or twice.

    1. – When you do,
        (a) Effect immediately afterwards?
        Do not notice any.
        [Mosher's Note:] When she cares physically for it, [she has a] general sense of well being and relaxation & inclination to sleep. If she does not care physically for it, [she] is much more high strung & nervous. If intercourse is too much prolonged, she ceases to care for it, & becomes more & more nervous.
        (b) Effect next day?
        Do not notice any. Effects if any are always nervous.

    2. – When you do not,
        (a) Effect immediately afterwards?
        During the first six months of our intercourse I usually felt wearied & "distasteful" afterward; even when the act itself had been very pleasant; those last two weeks when I really enjoyed it, I felt contented & physically at rest afterwards.
        (b) Effect next day?
        Do not notice any.

23. What do you believe to be the true purpose of intercourse?
    (a) Necessity to man? to woman?
    From my own thinking I have always believed that there was no more *necessity* for it in a healthy, pure-minded, actively-employed man than for a woman of the same description as far as mere exercise of physical function goes.
    (b) Pleasure?
    In its right place and a minor purpose.
    (c) Reproduction?
    Yes, main reason.
    (d) What other reasons beside reproduction are sufficient to warrant intercourse?
    In the married condition my ideas as to the reasons for it have changed materially from what they were before marriage. I then

thought reproduction was the only object & that once brought about [i.e., after conception], intercourse should cease. But in my experience the habitual bodily expression of love has a deep psychological effect in making possible complete mental sympathy & perfecting the spiritual union that must be the lasting "marriage" after the passion of love has passed away with the years.

24. Have you ever used any means to prevent conception? a) if so, what? No.
(b) Effect on your health?

25. What, to you, would be an ideal habit?
To have it take place not more than from four to six times a month & then at the period that conception is least likely to take place (and ideally I should never have it take place then). Aside from that I should have intercourse entered upon for the purpose of reproduction with deliberate design on both sides in time and circumstances most favorable physically and spiritually for the accomplishment of an immensely important act. It amounts to separating times and objects of intercourse into (a) that of expression of love between man & woman (that act is frequently simply the extreme of causes of love's passion, which it would be a pity to limit it to once in two or three years) and (b) that of carrying on our share in the perpetuation of the race, which should be done carefully & prayerfully.

Source: Clelia Duel Mosher, *The Mosher Survey: Sexual Attitudes of Forty-Five Victorian Women*, ed. James MaHood and Kristin Wenburg (New York: Arno Press, 1980), pp. 175–6, 253–4.

10 Leong Shee's Testimony, 1893 and 1929

Leong Shee first arrived in San Francisco in 1893 in the shadow of federal laws restricting Chinese immigration. She was permitted entry on the basis of her husband Chin Lung's reported status as a merchant. She returned to China in 1904 with her five American-born children and remained there until 1921, when she rejoined her husband. Significantly, her daughters lost their American rights when they married foreigners. She was interviewed twice by immigration officers in San Francisco, first when she arrived in 1893 and once again when she departed for the last time in 1929. There are inconsistencies in these testimonies that reveal some of her fears, typical of Chinese-born women and indicative of the preconceived ideas others held of the Chinese.

Leong Shee's Testimony, April 18, 1893

San Francisco, April 18th, 1893.
Kind of Certificate, or Paper, Certificate of Identification *Ticket No.* 388.
Name of Passenger, Leong Yee & Ah Kum, child. *Sex*, Female.
Where born? China.
Here in U.S.? Yes. *Place of former residence in U.S.* San Francisco.
Date of departure from U.S.? Oct. 17/89.
Name of Vessel departed on, Belgic . . .
Do you speak English? No. *Destination*, San Francisco
Place of stopping in City, #808 Sacramento St.
Who bought your ticket to China? My brother-in-law.
With whom connected, Gurm Wo Jan – Jackson St., don't know number.
When did you first arrive in U.S.? 1879.

I was married in San Francisco on Dec. 15, 1885 to Chong [Chin] Lung of the firm of Sang Kee wholesale dealers in tea & rice #808 Sac. St. San Francisco. When I first came to this country I came with my father Leong Hoong Wum and my mother Lee Shee and lived at #613 Dupont St. My father was formerly connected with the firm of Sang Kee #808 Sac. St. My father died in this city Nov. 25, 1887. My mother died in this city 1883 so long ago I have forgotten the date. I went home to China with my brother-in-law Chun Gwun Dai and my daughter Ah Kum who was 4 years of age the time of departure. After I was married I lived on the 2nd floor over the store of Sang Kee #808 Sac. St where my daughter Ah Kum was born on the 28 day of December 1886. My daughter is 8 years old now. My brother-in-law Chun Gwun Dai returned to S.F. in the later part of year 1891. Lee Moon's wife went home in the same steamer with me. I do not know her name. There was also a woman named Sam Moy and a child Ah Yuck on board. I do not speak English and do not know the city excepting the names of a few streets as I have small feet and never went out.

H.S. Huff,
Interpreter
Leong X (her mark) Yee

Leong Shee's Testimony, July 24, 1929

U.S. Immigration Service
Port of San Francisco

12017/37232	Angel Island Station
Leong Shee	July 24, 1929
Laborer Departing	Exam. Inspector, H.F. Hewitt
	Interpreter, Yong Kay

Applicant, sworn and admonished that if at any time she does not understand the interpreter to at once so state. Also advised of the crime of perjury and the penalty therefor. Speaks the Heung Shan dialect.

Q: What are all your names?
A: Leong Shee; Leong Yee was my maiden name.
Q: How old are you?
A: 61.
Q: Where were you born?
A: Kay Boo village, H.S.D.,[2] China.
Q: When did you first come to the U.S.?
A: K.S. 19/3 (1893, April) ss "China."
Q: Were you accompanied when you came to the U.S. in K.S. 19 (1893)?
A: By my daughter, Chin Kum, and a clansman, Leong Wai Kun, a clansman of mine.
Q: Under what status were you admitted to the U.S. at that time, K.S. 19 (1893)?
A: I do not know; I came here to join my husband, Chin Lung, who was a merchant of Sing Kee Co., San Francisco.
Q: Who is this (showing photo attached to affidavit of Chin Lung,[3] contained in file 20437/2–6, Leong Shee, Wife of Mer., "Shinyo Maru," 7/14/29 – affidavit referred to attached to landing record April 18, 1893, Leong Yee & child, Ah Kum, ss "China")?
A: That is my photo.
Q: Who is represented in the photo of the child next attached to the photo which you claim is of yourself?
A: My daughter, Ah Kum.
Q: Have you ever left the U.S. since you arrived here in K.S. 19 (1893)?
A: Yes, one trip to China; departed K.S. 30/2 (1904, Mar.)? SS "China." I returned to the U.S. C.R. 10/7 (Aug. 1921),[4] ss "Shinyo Maru," at San Francisco, and was admitted as the wife of a merchant, wife of

[2] Heungshan (Xiangshan) District was renamed Chungshan (Zhongshan) District in 1925 in honor of Dr. Sun Yat-sen, who led the 1911 Revolution that overthrew the Qing dynasty and founded the Republic of China. In 1965 the Wong Leung Do area separated from Chungshan District to become Doumen District. Today, Doumen District is a part of Xiangzhou District of Zhuhai City. For a history of Wong Leung Do people in the United States, see Him Mark Lai, "Potato King and Film Producer, Flower Growers, Professionals, and Activists: The Huangliang Du Community in Northern California," in *Chinese America: History and Perspectives, 1998* (San Francisco: Chinese Historical Society of America, 1998), pp. 1–24.
[3] See Chin Lung's affidavit of May 14, 1892 (pp. 17–19).
[4] The reckoning of dates since the establishment of the Chinese Republic in 1912.

Chin Lung, who was then a merchant of Sing Kee Co., San Francisco.

Q: Have you a cer. of identity?

A: Yes. (There is contained in the present file CI No. 36086, Leong Shee, Mer. Wife returning, ss "Shinyo Maru," 20437/2–6, 8.14.21. Same is retained in file and contains photo of the present applicant.)

Q: Why do you appear here today?

A: I want to depart for China on a laborer's return certificate.

Q: Are you married at this time?

A: Yes.

Q: How many times have you been married?

A: Once only.

Q: Will you name your husband?

A: Chin Lung – Chin Hong Dai.[5]

Q: Where is he at this time?

A: He is here today, with me.

Q: What is your present address?

A: 1210 Stockton St., S.F., Calif.

Q: With whom do you live there?

A: My husband and my children – one of my children lives there with me, a son, Chin Sow; also my husband lives there with me.

Q: What is your husband's occupation?

A: Merchant, Shang Hai Trunk Co., 1210 Stockton St., S.F., where I live.

Q: What is your present occupation?

A: Housewife.

Q: Do you follow any other occupation?

A: No.

Q: Can you read and write?

A: I can read and write Chinese, but not English.

Q: What will be your foreign address:

A: C/o Dok Jan Co., Macao, China; I don't remember the street or number. (Alleged husband states this applicant's address will be No. 16 Hung Shung San Street, Macao, China, Dok Jan Co.).

Q: Will anyone accompany you to China?

A: Yes, my son, Chin Sow, who lives with me in San Francisco (12017/ 37115).

Q: How many children have you ever had?

[5] A Chinese person maintained the same surname throughout his life but usually adopted a different given name when he started school, entered business, or married. Chin Hong Dai was the name taken by Chin Lung when he married.

A: 5 sons and 2 daughters.

Q: Name all your children, their ages, date of birth and whereabouts.

A: My oldest child is Chin Suey Kum, who died (changes). My oldest daughter is Chin Gum, who died shortly after she and I came to this country K.S. 19 (1893).

Q: Is Chin Gum whom you have just mentioned as your oldest daughter, the child who accompanied you to the U.S. in K.S. 19 (1893)?

A: Yes.

Q: Was that daughter born in China?

A: Yes.

Q: How many daughters have you had born to you, altogether?

A: Three.

Q: Name your second daughter?

A: Chin Suey Kum, about 35 or 36; I don't remember her birth date; she is now in China; she was born in the U.S., at San Francisco. Chin Suey Kan, 29; she is now in San Francisco, living in the Yet Sin Building, Stockton St., near Broadway; she is not married; she was born in San Francisco; she works on Market St., I don't know for whom; she embroiders handkerchiefs. I don't remember the date of her birth.

Q: Name your sons, the ages, dates of birth and whereabouts and where born?

A: Chin Wing, 34 or 35; I don't remember the date of his birth; he was born in San Francisco. He is now in San Francisco, in my husband's store, he is a member of the firm; he lives on Powell Street, with his wife. Chin Wah, 32, he is in the East; he is in New York city; he was born in San Francisco. Chin Foo, 26; he was born in San Francisco; I don't remember the date of his birth; he is now in my husband's store; he is a member of the firm; he is married and lives in the Yet Sin Building; my daughter who lives in that building lives there with him. Chin Gway, 26, born K.S. 30/4–11 (May 25, 1904), in San Francisco, and is now a member of my husband's firm; he lives on Powell Street, with his wife. Chin Sow, 23, born K.S. 33/10–13 (1907, Nov. 17); he was born in China, in Nom Song village, China. He is not married; he lives with me in San Francisco.

Q: Are you the mother of any other children?

A: No.

Q: On what do you base your right to depart for China and to return to the U.S.?

A: On the ground that my son Chin Sow is a resident of the U.S. and that I can return to him in this country.

Q: When did Chin Sow come to the U.S.?

A: C.R. 13 (1924), ss "Korea," at San Francisco.

Q: Did you testify for him at that time?

A: Yes.

Q: Under what status was he admitted at that time?

A: As the son of a merchant.

Q: Did your husband testify for him at that time?

A: Yes.

Q: Did you state that Chin Sow will accompany you to China?

A: Yes.

Q: Is Chin Sow here today?

A: No.

Q: Have you a photograph of Chin Sow with you at this time?

A: No.

Q: Who is this (showing photo of applicant, Chin Sow, attached to affidavit contained in file 23303/12–7, Chin Sow, mer. Son, ss "Korea Maru," May 4, 1924)?

A: My son, Chin Sow.

Q: Who is this (showing photo attached to same affidavit next to that of applicant in above mentioned case)?

A: My husband, Chin Lung.

Q: Is your husband Chin Lung going to remain in the U.S.?

A: Yes.

Q: Do you expect that he will be a resident of the U.S. upon your return to this country?

A: Yes, I expect that if he is living he will be in the U.S.

Q: Will you again state when you first arrived in the U.S.?

A: K.S. 19/3 (1893, April).

Q: Where were you married?

A: I was married in Nom Song village, HSD, China.

Q: Do you remember the date of your marriage?

A: No, I can't remember that.

Q: Do you recognize this affidavit and the photos attached thereto (showing affidavit of Chin Lung, dated May 14, 1892, which contains photo of the present applicant, and which affidavit is attached to arrival record of Leong Yee and child, Ah Kum, ss "China," April 18, 1893)?

A: Yes, that is the paper I had when I first came to the U.S.

Q: You are advised that that affidavit sets forth that you had been in the U.S. five or six years prior to October, 1889 – 9th month, K.S. 15, and you now state that you first came to the U.S. in K.S. 19 (1893). Can you explain why that affidavit should set forth such information?

A: I first came to the U.S. in K.S. 19 (1893). I don't know why that information is in the affidavit that I was in this country before K.S. 19 (1893).[6]

Q: Do you know that that affidavit also sets forth that your daughter, who accompanied you in K.S. 19 (1893) to the U.S., was born in the U.S., and you have stated today that she was born in China?

A: I don't know why; the fact is that that daughter was born in China.

Q: Had that daughter ever been in the U.S. before K.S. 19 (1893)?

A: No.

Q: Do you realize that you are making your statement today under oath?

A: Yes.

Q: Were you ever in the U.S. before K.S. 19 (1893)?

A: No.

Q: Do you ever recall being questioned by this Service, before, as to when you came to the U.S. the first time, and also that it was called to your attention that the affidavit just referred to sets forth that you were in the U.S. before K.S. 19 (1893)?

A: Yes, and I said that I had first come to the U.S. in K.S. 19 (1893).

Q: Do you remember when you testified to that effect?

A: Yes, in the case of Chin Sow.

Q: Do you remember being asked at that time where you were married?

A: Yes, and I said I had been married in China.

Q: You are advised that in order to permit your re-entry into the U.S. it will be necessary that your son, Chin Sow will have to return to the U.S. with you or prior thereto, in order that the grounds upon which you are basing your application shall then be existent. Do you understand?

A: Yes.

Q: You are further advised that should you remain away from the U.S. for a period longer than six months should your husband or your child not be a resident of the U.S. in the event of your reapplication for admission it would be necessary, in order to entitle you to admission to the U.S., that you be able to read in some language or dialect. Do you understand?

A: Yes.

Q: Who is this (showing photo of applicant, Chin Sow, 12017/37115, attached to Form 432)?

A: Chin Sow, my son.

---

[6] Great-Grandmother obviously does not remember that she had to lie in 1893 in order to get *mui tsai* Ah Kum into the United States.

Q: Have you anything further to state?
A: No.
Q: Who is this (indicating Chin Lung, alleged husband, who has been called into the room)?
A: My husband, Chin Lung.
Q: (to Chin Lung, alleged husband) Who is this woman?
A: My wife, Leong Shee. (Alleged husband dismissed.)
Q: Did you understand this interpreter (through interpreter J. Q. Moy)?
A: Yes.

Signed: [Leong Shee in Chinese characters] I certify that the foregoing is a true and correct record of testimony taken direct on the typewriter at the above described hearing.

H. F. HEWITT, typist

Source: Original document Leong Shee, case 12017/37232, Chinese Departure Case Files, San Francisco District Office, Immigration and Naturalization Service, Record Group 85, National Archives, San Bruno, California, reprinted in Judy Yung, *Unbound Voices: A Documentary History of Chinese Women in San Francisco* (Berkeley, CA: University of California Press, 1999), pp. 21–2, 25–31.

Questions to Think About

1.   How do women challenge and stretch the boundaries of social conventions in the Gilded Age?
2.   How do race, ethnicity, and class influence the ways in which women participated in public life during the Gilded Age?
3.   How do the responsibilities of mothering and motherhood affect women's lives during the Gilded Age?

Chapter 2   Reform and Revolt in the Modern Era, 1900–20

WORK

1 Maimie Pinzer, Letters to Fanny Howe, 1911

Maimie Pinzer (1885–1940) ran away from an abusive home in her mid-teens and supported herself intermittently through prostitution. Beginning in 1911, Pinzer developed a friendship with a wealthy social reformer, Fanny Howe, who encouraged her to reject the "sporting life." Pinzer, who had a business school education, describes the grueling nature of office work and her frustrations. Her frankness contrasts with the stereotypical image of a prostitute as a fallen woman, tempted to the high life by desire for frivolous luxury or as an unwitting victim of white slavery.

Broad Street, Philadelphia
January 7, 1911

My dear Mrs. Howe,

... I received your letter yesterday in the forenoon and in the afternoon took your note of introduction and went to see Mr. Morgan. He was very nice to me, but I do not think understood exactly how I was situated. I imagine he thought I was one of the many who think they are cheating the public by not writing for publication. I enlightened him, and he seemed very much relieved. He told me the conditions as they exist on any newspaper, and I knew then that I was not in for much. To give me a position with a salary was impossible; and the columns of the newspaper are open to anyone at the rate of $5.00 a column; and even the better and well-known writers scarcely get more than a

1/4 column, every other day or so, accepted by his paper. I told him I had no experience in that line, so had better not expect to do anything. If there was some way I could get onto the ropes, I've no doubt I could command a salary the same as other women do – but as he explained it, I had little or no chance. He was extremely kind and nice to me, and not in a patronizing way, either, but in a manner most flattering. I told him I would go down to see their advertising manager, and Mr. Morgan insisted that he go along, and he did, and I was introduced all around, and then he left me to talk with them and he returned to his office. Mr. Donnelly, the *Record* ad man, listened to all I had to say. I explained the system used by the *North American*, for whom I worked, and showed him how his ad columns could be increased by the use of their system. He seemed impressed and told me he would talk and think it over and would let me know. Of course, I can't tell whether it will bring a position, but I can only hope for the best and thank you very much for securing the assistance of Mr. Morgan. I intended to write you ere this, but I was busy day and night and I will tell you how.

When you were here, I don't know if I told you that I had been to see about doing some addressing of New Year's cards, for which a fine Spencerian hand was necessary. Addressing generally pays 75 cents a thousand envelopes, and only the most experienced can write almost a thousand in a day. So when I sent a sample of my best Spencerian hand, I received a reply saying that they would engage me for the two weeks preceding New Year's, at $5.00 a thousand. I thought that was almost too easy, and started in – only to learn that the $5.00 was for a thousand envelopes addressed in full, no abbreviations, and the average one was something like this:

Messrs. William A. Anderson, and Sons,

Milk Street, Boston, Massachusetts

c/o The United States Mercantile Company

Then the name had to be filled out on an engraved card. As each card cost 32 cents, an error meant the loss of that amount to the writer. So you know there couldn't be much speed, and that sort of writing takes so much time. The envelopes were 81/2 by 101/2, and the writing had to be twice the size of the above. At any rate, I soon learned my job and was no sinecure, and as they permitted men to work at night, I did too, and by not even getting up to eat luncheon or dinner, but bringing it with me, and working from 9:00 A.M. to 12:00 midnight for the week before Christmas and New Years I managed to earn $13.51. As my husband had no work in all that time, he borrowed money from Mr. Suiffen, Mr. Welsh's secretary, and I paid it with that money. So you can see I was kept busy and hated to lift a pen up except for that purpose. My arms ached at the shoulder, and even while I was glad to earn that money, I wouldn't do it again, for my eye burned all the time and I had headaches. . . .

Now I believe I've told you how things "are" with me, as you asked me to do in your letter. I don't know whether there is much else to write about. I, too, enjoyed your visit, although I felt embarrassed because I felt very small and insignificant, knowing that you knew me for what I am. I don't think I said or did anything to deceive you while you were here, but I think I would if I saw you often, for my pride would not permit me to be open and honest about the vile things I might do. I found it was awfully hard to be honest with you, for even though you do not moralize, I instinctively know by looking at you that you do not do things that are not clean and right. I didn't have any recent act to be ashamed of when I saw you but I felt very picayune, and doubt whether I could be as honest with you face to face as I am on paper. As yet I have stayed clean and decent..., and not for any object or purpose – just to be honest with you. But I am also going to be frank and tell you that possibly before this letter reaches you, I won't be. I hope you won't think I am crazy for writing you like this, but somehow I want to tell you, and perhaps you will be glad to know that I experience a great dread when I think of it, for I have kept absolutely straight since last March, almost a year....

Philadelphia, January 12, 1911
I WROTE YOU YESTERDAY AND HAVE ONLY A VAGUE IDEA OF WHAT THE letter was about. I know if I persist in writing you confused letters, you will think I am not entirely right in my mind. I don't know why my letters to you seem so disconnected and incoherent. Perhaps it is because I hesitate about calling a spade a spade, and yet I enjoy telling you about my affairs as I would tell them to myself. That must be the reason I get so frightfully bawled up.

I was very glad to get your letter. Do you know, when I try to recall just how you look, I can't seem to see anything but your crinkly golden hair. I wish I knew if you colored it or if it is so always. Now that I've written that, it sounds impertinent. I am writing just as I would talk if you were sitting here, and I don't think it would sound ugly if I asked it, and yet it does read silly, I know. I often wondered how an intelligent person of sound mind could keep a diary to record every small event, and thought. It seemed such a ridiculous thing, almost asinine. I think now that I have hit on the very reason why they do it, and what for. It must be that, while they are the only ones that see them, they are unconsciously addressing another person, a second self, who is interested in the minutest detail concerning the writers' life; and in writing down each thing, it sort of clears the mind each day and leaves it free for a new set of perplexities.

When I was in the hospital during the years of 1904–1905, when I lost my eye, I had all sorts of time for retrospection. Would I have been able to read, I would have had something constantly before my eyes, and my mind on anything else besides my personal troubles; but, without sight the thirty-two weeks I was in the Post Graduate Hospital in New York and eleven weeks in the Sydenham Hospital in New York and fourteen weeks in the German- town Hospital in this city, you may well imagine how busy my brain was with the past up to that time. And oh! what a jumble it all was. I can't begin to write you of what my thoughts were; but I know I had a half-formed idea of living better if I came out alive, blind or with sight. And I did, when I came out in the world again. I don't exactly know whether that was due to circumstances or desire on my part; at any rate, either the loss of the good looks or the time spent in retrospection subdued me very much. Before that, I had no care about anything; and afterwards I found I stopped to consider before going into things. Of course I was getting older, and that helped some. I lived very much more moderately and even married Mr. Jones, so that I would be obliged, in a certain sense, not to be too free about, and with, my manner of living. And yet I could not buckle down to cutting out entirely all the things I had summed up while in the hospital as being empty and not worthwhile. At times, I would go all over the thoughts that passed through my mind while in the various hospitals and would decide that I would keep my word to myself and cut it out. Of course, the attending luxuries that go with loose living I did not want to give up. But, summed all up, it is anything but a pleasant road to travel; and I saw how the few luxuries did not make up for the indignities offered me and the cautious way I had to live. As, for instance, I love women – that is, I would like to have women friends – but I can't have; or rather, I couldn't have. I avoided them, even though very often I would meet one who would want to be friendly, and even now, the habit is so strong in me that I never encourage any advances from them – much as I should like to – for I couldn't find any enjoyment in being on friendly terms with a woman who lived a sporting sort of life, and the others, I dreaded would find out, perhaps inadvertently, something about me, and perhaps cut me, and I couldn't stand that; so I always repel any advances they make – so much so, that Mr. Jones thinks I am rude about it. When we lived in Enid, Oklahoma, a small town of 12,000 people, I had an occasion to look up a lady who owned a Boston Terrier, and I took quite a fancy to her and she did to me. She had a very beautiful home and was very wealthy. For once, I permitted myself the luxury of accepting her invitations to little luncheons to be partaken only with her. She seemed to enjoy talking with me, and although everything I talked about was superficial and mostly lies, I too enjoyed going to her home. As we had been there almost six months when I met her, and I had never done anything wrong in the town, I hadn't much to fear, although I used to go to Oklahoma City about once a month to meet a man I knew there. So for six months I was very friendly with her and two other younger girls – the daughters of the local banker – when one day, like a bolt out of a clear sky, this lady's father (she was unmarried and about thirty-five years old – she kept house for her father) called to see me and in very terse language told me I must not continue my friendship with his daughter. It afterwards developed that a young man who called on one of these younger girls knew something ugly about me and told it to their father, who in turn told it to Mr. Kemble, who told his daughter. But she would not believe it at first, but must have later – for when her dog saw me on the street some time later and came to me, she called him away and cut me direct. At any rate, we left town the following week – although Mr. Jones was business agent for the carpenter's Union, receiving $25.00 a week without having to do any manual labor. I could not stand living there longer; and since then, with the exception of being "charming" to some friends of Mr. Welsh's who knew all about me, I haven't ventured to know any women except you – and that's different, of course.

When I was in the hospital in St. Louis in 1909, again I came to the conclusion that I would live right and perhaps be happy. I thought my mode of life explained why I was lying there all alone, without the visits of a human being other than the general nurse and no word from anyone – besides the letters from my husband, which are always the very kindest and affectionate. I would see all about me at the visiting hour people hurrying and scurrying to the various beds to see the other patients, bringing them fruit and flowers and magazines. I don't think I ever wanted anything in my life so much as I did some grapes while I was there, but I had no friends to bring or send them to me. Then the conviction was strong in me again that it was surely my fault that I was so friendless and that I would surely try living straight and start to make friends that were real. But, while I had that thought in my brain, I tucked it conveniently out of my road – and hadn't been out of the hospital three weeks before I went to San Antonio, Texas, with a circuit attorney of St. Louis who too had been ill in the St. Agnes Hospital when I was, and who had the same doctor. The doctor ordered the trip for his health and I went along, writing my husband some absurd story about my uncle Louis who lives thirty miles out of San Antonio sending me the ticket to go there. (Fact of the matter was, when I did go to this small town to visit my uncle whom I hadn't seen in ten years, he treated me as one would an acquaintance and never even asked me to stop for a meal.) At any rate, when I returned from San Antonio, went to Oklahoma City to join Mr. Jones, I was again thoroughly and heartily weary of my precarious way of living, for I had another belittling experience in San Antonio. And then I just sat down and waited.

For what, I didn't know, but I had an idea that I wasn't going to meet anyone and would just cut it all out. Then came Mr. Welsh's first letter; and no sooner was that correspondence started than I knew why, before that, I could only *think* to live decent. For I found that which is the reason people keep diaries. It records these thoughts, and once they are carefully taken apart and written, you can follow the lines of your thoughts more clearly; and then it is a clearing-house, and from one writing to the next, one's brain is cleared, ready to follow out the line of thought or perhaps start a new line of thought. In that way, Mr. Welsh helped me most, for I kept a sort of diary in my letters to him of my thoughts as they came to me each day. And then, when I felt I was responsible to a real live father for my actions, I was very careful as to what I did. And I never did anything (even the most ridiculous detail) that I didn't write to him of it; and I was happier than ever before in my life. And because I believed in him, he readily convinced me that I had a Father in Heaven; and when I think back to the first few weeks I was in the hospital last spring, I doubt whether it was really I who had such childlike faith in prayers. I haven't even the slightest atom of that left, but I wish I had. It was very comforting. In a measure I'm like a child for I love to show off, provided I have the right sort of an audience. I know when I procured the work at the *North American*, it was because I wanted to show everyone how clever I was; and then when Mr. Welsh left and I had no one to applaud, I quit being clever. You know, I've told you how hard I've looked for work. Well I have, in a halfhearted sort of a way and with the feeling: "Oh! What's the use – for I don't propose to get up at 6:30 to be at work at 8 and work in a close, stuffy room with people I despise, until dark, for $6.00 or $7.00 a week! When I could, just by phoning, spend an afternoon with some congenial person and in the end have more than a week's work could pay me." Doesn't that sound ugly – and it feels ugly – but they are my thoughts. I had them very persistently when I ceased writing regularly to Mr. Welsh, and you don't know how I miss writing my thoughts to him. I feel perhaps that is why I wrote you the day I was so very despondent. As yet, they are still thoughts –

Source: *The Maimie Papers*, eds. Ruth Rosen and Sue Davidson (Old Westbury, NY: The Feminist Press, 1977), pp. 5–7, 9–12. Copyright © 1977 by Radcliffe College. Reprinted with the permission of The Feminist Press, www.feministpress.org. All rights reserved.

2 A Negro Nurse, More Slavery at the South, 1912

The Independent Magazine *published autobiographical testimonies by a variety of working Americans who struggled to achieve the American dream. The Negro Nurse describes her work caring for children and doing housework in turn-of-the-century Georgia homes, the isolating and degrading conditions she experienced, and the challenges of mothering her own children. This passage underscores the limited work that African American women could find as servants in white homes. It also highlights how the possibilities of the domestic ideal for white, middle-class women were built on the denial of this ideal for African American women.*

[The following thrilling story was obtained by a representative of THE INDEPENDENT specially commissioned to gather the facts. The reporting is, of course, our representative's, but the facts are those given by the nurse. EDITOR.]

I am a negro woman, and I was born and reared in the South. I am now past forty years of age and am the mother of three children. My husband died nearly fifteen years ago, after we had been married about five years. For more than thirty years – or since I was ten years old – I have been a servant in one capacity or another in white families in a thriving Southern city, which has at present a population of more than 50,000. In my early years I was at first what might be called a "house-girl," or, better, a "house-boy." I used to answer the doorbell, sweep the yard, go on errands and do odd jobs. Later on I became a chambermaid and performed the usual duties of such a servant in a home. Still later I was graduated into a cook, in which position I served at different times for nearly eight years in all. During the last ten years I have been a nurse. I have worked for only four different families during all these thirty years. But, belonging to the servant class, which is the majority class among my race at the South, and associating only with servants, I have been able to become intimately acquainted not only with the lives of hundreds of household servants, but also with the lives of their employers. I can, therefore, speak with authority on the so-called servant question; and what I say is said out of an experience which covers many years.

To begin with, then, I should say that more than two-thirds of the negroes of the town where I live are menial servants of one kind or another, and besides that more than two-thirds of the negro women here, whether married or single, are compelled to work for a living, as nurses, cooks, washerwomen, chambermaids, seamstresses, hucksters, janitresses, and the like. I will say, also, that the condition of this vast host of poor colored people is just as bad as, if not worse than, it was during the days of slavery. Tho today we are enjoying a nominal freedom, we are literally slaves. And, not to generalize, I will give you a sketch of the work I have to do – and I'm only one of many.

I frequently work from fourteen to sixteen hours a day. I am compelled to by my contract, which is oral only, to sleep in the house. I am allowed to go home to my own children, the oldest of whom is a girl of 18 years, only once in two weeks, every other Sunday afternoon – even then I'm not permitted to stay all night. I not only have to nurse a little white child, now eleven months old, but I have to act as playmate, or "handy-andy," not to say governess, to three other children in the house, the oldest of whom is only nine years of age. I wash and dress the baby two or three times each day; I give it its meals, mainly from a bottle; I have to put it to bed each night; and, in addition, I have to get up and attend to its every call between midnight and morning. If the baby falls to sleep during the day, as it has been trained to do every day about eleven o'clock, I am not permitted to rest. It's "Mammy, do this," or "Mammy, do that," or "Mammy, do the other," from my mistress, all the time. So it is not strange to see "Mammy" watering the lawn with the garden hose, sweeping the sidewalk, mopping the porch and halls, helping the cook, or darning stockings. Not only so, but I have to put the other three children to bed each night as well as the baby, and I have to wash them and dress them each morning. I don't know what it is to go to church; I don't know what it is to go to a lecture or entertainment of anything of the kind; I live a treadmill life; and I see my own children only when they happen to see me on the streets when I am out with the children, or when my children come to the "yard" to see me, which isn't often, because my white folks don't like to see their servants' children hanging around their premises. You might as well say that I'm on duty all the time – from sunrise to sunrise, every day in the week. I am the slave, body and soul, of this family. And what do I get for this work – this lifetime bondage? The pitiful sum of ten dollars a month! And what am I expected to do with these ten dollars? With this money I'm expected to pay my house rent, which is four dollars per month, for a little house of two rooms, just big enough to turn around in; and I'm expected, also, to feed and clothe myself and three children. For two years my oldest child, it is true, has helped a little toward our support by taking in a little washing at home. She does the washing and ironing of two white families, with a total of five persons; one of these families pays her $1.00 per week, and the other 75 cents per week, and my daughter has to furnish her own soap and starch and wood. For six months my youngest child, a girl about thirteen years old, has been nursing, and she receives $1.50 per week but has no night work. When I think of the low rate of wages we poor colored people receive, and when I hear so much said about our unreliability, our untrustworthiness, and even our vices, I recall the story of the private soldier in a certain army who, once upon a time, being upbraided by the commanding officer because the heels of his shoes were not polished, is said to have replied: "Captain, do you expect all the virtues for $13 per month?" Of course, nothing is being done to increase our wages, and the way things are going at the present it would seem that nothing could be done to cause an increase of wages. We have no labor unions or organizations of any kind that could demand for us a uniform scale of wages for cooks, washerwomen, nurses, and the like; and, for another thing, if some negroes did here and there refuse to work for seven and eight and ten dollars a month, there would be hundreds of other negroes right on the spot ready to take their places and do the same work, or more, for the low wages that had been refused. So that, the truth is, we have to work for little or nothing, or become vagrants! And that, of course, in this State would mean that we would be arrested, tried, and dispatched to the "State Farm," where we would surely have to work for nothing or be beaten with many stripes!

Nor does this low rate of pay tend to make us efficient servants. The most that can be said of us negro household servants in the South – and I speak as one of them – is that we are to the extent of our ability willing and faithful slaves. We do not cook according to scientific principles because we do not know anything about scientific principles. Most of our cooking is done by guesswork or by memory. We cook well when our "hand" is in, as we say, and when anything about the dinner goes wrong, we simply say, "I lost my hand today!" We don't know anything about scientific food for babies, nor anything about what science says must be done for infants at certain periods of growth or when certain symptoms of disease appear; but somehow we "raise" more of the children than we kill, and, for the most part, they are lusty chaps – all of them. But the point is, we do not go to cooking-schools nor nurse-training schools, and so it cannot be expected of us that we should make as efficient servants without such training as we should make were such training provided. And yet with our cooking and nursing, such as it is, the white folks seem to be satisfied – perfectly satisfied. I sometimes wonder if this satisfaction is the out growth of the knowledge that more highly trained servants would be able to demand better pay!

Perhaps some might say, if the poor pay is the only thing about which we have to complain, then the slavery in which we daily toil and struggle is not so bad after all. But the poor pay isn't all – not by any means! I remember very well the first and last place from which I was dismissed. I lost my place because I refused to let the madam's husband kiss me. He must have been accustomed to undue familiarity with his servants, or else he took it as a matter of course, because without any love-making at all, soon after I was installed as cook, he walked up to me, threw his arms around me, and was in the act of kissing me, when I demanded to know what he meant, and shoved him away. I was young then, and newly married, and didn't know then that what has been a burden to my mind and heart ever since: that a colored woman's virtue in this part of the country has no protection. I at once went home, and told my husband about it. When my husband went to the man who had insulted me, the man cursed him, and slapped him, and had him arrested! The police judge fined my husband $25. I was present at the hearing, and testified on oath to the insult offered me. The white man, of course, denied the charge. The old judge looked up and said: "This court

will never take the word of a nigger against the word of a white man."
Many and many a time since I have heard similar stories repeated again and
again by my friends. I believe nearly all white men take, and expect to take,
undue liberties with their colored female servants – not only the fathers, but
in many cases the sons also. Those servants who rebel against such familiarity must either leave or expect a mighty hard time, if they stay. By
comparison, those who tamely submit to these improper relations live in
clover. They always have a little "spending change," wear better clothes,
and are able to get off from work least once a week – and sometimes
oftener. This moral debasement is not at all times unknown to the white
women in these homes. . . . The results of this concubinage can be seen in all
of our colored public schools in the South, for in most of our churches and
schools the majority of the young men and women are light-skinned mu-
lattoes. The real, Simon-pure, blue-gum, thick-lip, coal-black negro is passing away – certainly in the cities; and the fathers of the new generation of
negroes are white men, while their mothers are unmarried, colored women.

Another thing – it's a small indignity, it may be, but an indignity just the
same. No white person, not even the little children just learning to talk, no
white person at the South ever thinks of addressing any negro man or
woman as Mr., or *Mrs.*, or Miss. The women are called, "Cook," or
"Nurse," or "Mammy," or "Mary Jane," or "Lou," or "Dilcey," as the
case might be, and the men are called "Bob," or "Boy," or "Old Man," or
"Uncle Bill," or "Pate." In many cases our white employers refer to us, and
in our presence, too, as their "niggers." No matter what they call us – no
matter what we teach our children to call us – we must tamely submit, and
answer when we are called; we must enter no protest; if we did object, we
should be driven out without the least ceremony, and, in applying for work
at other places, we should find it very hard to procure another situation. In
almost every case, when our intending employers would be looking up our
record, the information would be given by telephone or otherwise that we
were "impudent," "saucy," "dishonest," and "generally unreliable." In our
town we have no such thing as an employment agency or intelligence
bureau, and, therefore, when we want work, we have to get out on the
street and go from place to place, always with hat in hand, hunting for it.

Another thing. Sometimes I have gone on the street cars or the railroad
trains with the white children, and, so long as I was in charge of the
children, I could sit anywhere I desired, front or back. If a white man
happened to ask some other white man, "What is that nigger doing in
here?" and was told, "Oh, she's the nurse of those white children in front
of her!" immediately there was the hush of peace. Everything was all right,
so long as I was in the white man's part of the street car or in the white
man's coach as a servant – a slave – but as soon as I did not present myself as

a menial, and the relationship of master and servant was abolished by my not having the white children with me, I would be forthwith assigned to the "nigger" seats or the "colored people's coach." Then, too, any day in my city, and I understand that it is so in every town in the South, you can see some "great big black burly" negro coachman or carriage driver huddled up beside some aristocratic Southern white woman, and nothing is said about it, nothing is done about it, nobody resents the familiar contact. But let that same colored man take off his brass buttons and his high hat, and put on the plain livery of an average American citizen, and drive one block down any thoroughfare in any town in the South with that same white woman, as her equal or companion or friend, and he'd be shot on the spot!

You hear a good deal nowadays about the "service pan." The "service pan" is the general term applied to "left-over" food, which in many a Southern home is freely placed at the disposal of the cook, or, whether so placed or not, it is usually disposed of by the cook. In my town, I know, and I guess in many other towns also, every night when the cook starts for her home she takes with her a pan or a plate or cold victuals. The same thing is true on Sunday afternoons after dinner – and most cooks have nearly every Sunday afternoon off. Well, I'll be frank with you, if it were not for the service pan, I don't know what the majority of our Southern colored families would do. The service pan is the mainstay in many a home. Good cooks in the South receive on an average $8 per month. Porters, butlers, coachmen, janitors, "office boys" and the like receive on an average $16 per month. Few and far between are the colored men in the South who receive $1 or more per day. Some mechanics do; as, for example, carpenters, brick masons, wheelwrights, blacksmiths, and the like. The vast majority of negroes in my town are serving in menial capacities in homes, stores and offices. Now taking it for granted, for the sake of illustration, that the husband receives $16 per month and the wife $8. That would be $24 between the two. The chances are that they will have anywhere from five to thirteen children between them. Now, how far will $24 go toward housing and clothing ten or twelve persons for thirty days? And, I tell you, with all of us poor people the service pan is a great institution; it is a great help to us, as we wag along the weary way of life. And then most of the white folks expect their cooks to avail themselves of these perquisites; they allow it; they expect it. I do not deny that the cooks find opportunity to hide away at times, along with the cold "grub," a little sugar, a little flour, a little meal, or a little piece of soap; but I indignantly deny that we are thieves. We don't steal; we just "take" things – they are a part of the oral contract, exprest or implied. We understand it, and most of the white folks understand it. Others may denounce the service pan, and say that it is used only to support idle negroes, but many a time, when I was a cook, and had the responsibility of rearing my three children upon my lone shoulders, many a time I have had occasion to bless the Lord for the service pan!

...

Ah, we poor colored women wage-earners in the South are fighting a terrible battle, and because of our weakness, our ignorance, our poverty, and our temptations we deserve the sympathies of mankind. Perhaps a million of us are introduced daily to the privacy of a million chambers thruout the South, and hold in our arms a million white children, thousands of whom, as infants, are suckled at our breasts – during my lifetime I myself have served as "wet nurse" to more than a dozen white children. On the one hand, we are assailed by white men, and, on the other hand, we are assailed by black men, who should be our natural protectors; and, whether in the cook kitchen, at the washtub, over the sewing machine, behind the baby carriage, or at the ironing board, we are but little more than pack horses, beasts of burden, slaves! In the distant future, it may be, centuries and centuries hence, a monument of brass or stone will be erected to the Old Black Mammies of the South, but what we need is present help, present sympathy, better wages, better hours, more protections, and a chance to breathe for once while alive as free women. If none others will help us, it would seem that the Southern white women themselves might do so in their own defense, because we are rearing their children – we feed them, we bathe them, we teach them to speak the English language, and in numberless instances we sleep with them – and it is inevitable that the lives of their children will in some measure be pure or impure according as they are affected by contact with their colored nurses.

Source: *Independent Magazine*, January 25, 1912, copyright 2004 University Library, the University of North Carolina at Chapel Hill.

CITIZENSHIP

3 Elizabeth Gurley Flynn, Women in Industry Should Organize, 1911

"Women in Industry Should Organize" argued forcefully in support of collective and direct action for and by women in industry. Its author, Elizabeth Gurley Flynn (1890–1964) was known through song and myth as Rebel Girl. She organized workers for the International Workers of the World between 1908 and 1917. This article appeared shortly after the tragic fire at the Triangle Factory in New York City that killed 146 immigrant women. Flynn asked male and female workers to unite as members of the working class; at

*the same time she exposed potential conflicts between women of the working
class and middle class.*

From the viewpoint of a revolutionary socialist there is certainly much to
criticize in the present labor organizations. They have their shortcomings of
so pronounced a character that many thoughtful but pessimistic workers
despair of practical benefit from assisting or considering them further. Yet
unionism remains a vital and burning question to the toilers, both men and
women.

...A labor trust of all workers, in all industries, regardless of skill,
nationality or sex; to obliterate all craft lines; to cast aside all binding and
traitorous contracts; to throw barriers down for the admission of all workers; such a union inspires the workers through its unity of the practical every
day needs with the ultimate revolutionary ideal of emancipation. Through it
we are able to live our ideals, to carry our revolutionary principles into the
shops, every day of the year: not to the ballot box one day alone.

Now as to women's relationships to the old and new unionisms. In the
final analysis, women's sufferings and inequalities, at least in the working
class, which is our only concern, are the results of either·wage slavery
directly or personal dependence upon a wage worker.

...Women to the number of seven million have been driven forth from
the home, by dire necessity, into the industrial arena, to be even more
fiercely exploited than their brother workers; they are constantly seeking
relief and release from the labor market on the marriage mart, which marks
woman the wage worker as a transitory being; and the social or co-operative spirit engendered in the factory is usually neutralized by the struggle for
husbands [living] outside. Multitudes of wives and mothers are virtually sex
slaves through their direct and debasing dependence upon individual men
for their existence, and motherhood is all too often unwelcome and enforced, while the struggle for existence even in the homes where love and
affectionate understanding cast their illuminating rays is usually so fierce
that life degenerates to a mere animal existence, a struggle for creature
comforts – no more and it is impossible for love to transcend the physical.
The mental horizon of the average housekeeper is exceedingly limited
because of the primitive form of labor in the household, the cooking,
cleaning, sewing, scrubbing, etc., for an individual family. How can one
have depth or mental scope when one's life is spent exclusively within the
four walls of one's individual composite home, and workshop, performing
personal service continually for the same small group, laboring alone and on
the primitive plan, doing work that could be better done by socialization
and machinery, were not women cheaper than machines today?

We are driven to the conclusion, after the admission of all these facts, that much more than the abstract right of the ballot is needed to free women; nothing short of a social revolution can shelter her cramping and stultifying spheres of today. Yet, I have a firm and abiding conviction that much can be done to alleviate the lot of the working class women today. I have never been one of those possessed of the audacity and hard-hearted courage to face a crowd of hungry strikers and console them with the hope that the next November they could vote the Socialist ticket and thereby strike a blow at freedom. Thoreau has said, "Even voting for the right, is doing nothing for it. It is only expressing to men feebly your desire that it should prevail." Likewise, I feel the futility, and know many other Socialist women must, through our appreciation of these sad conditions and our deep sympathy for our sister women of extending to them nothing more than the hope of an ultimate social revolution. I am impatient for it. I realize the beauty of our hopes, the truth of its effectiveness, the inevitability of its realization, but I want to see that hope finds a point of contact with the daily lives of the working women, and I believe it can through the union movement.

The only appeal that craft unions make to the wives of their membership is on the matter of the label.[1] But the small number of women shoppers who trouble to inquire about the label or the union affiliations of the clerks testify to the ineffectiveness of this appeal. Men unionists are not themselves stirred to great enthusiasm over the label on shoes, hats, overalls, cigars, etc. The reason is not far to seek – namely, that men steeped of craft interests and craft selfishness cannot be suddenly lifted to the plane of class interests and solidarity. How much less can we expect the women in the homes, many of whom know nothing of the significance of the label, to demand it on the countless purchases they make. No special efforts have ever been made seriously to interest the wives in what the men consider "man's affairs." Many a wife hasn't the remotest idea of what the union that John goes [to] every Friday night consists of, or at least her knowledge is grumbling expressed about John having to pay 50 cents a week to "that union." Stubborn insistence on the two hundred odd labels that mark union-made goods is difficult, sometimes as sacrificed from the point of view of personal comfort as an actual strike. Usually it means boycotting all the tradespeople for miles around, and it stands to reason that women who are not vitally and intelligently interested are not going to trudge miles searching for the union label.

---

[1]   A consumer movement that asked shoppers to buy only garments with union labels was a large movement among the middle class. Nonunion garments were often made in individual tenements and contained typhoid and tuberculosis germs, so buying union meant the products were free of disease as well.

But if one is willing to make a sacrifice for the sake of the union movement, one's ardor is dampened by a realization that demanding the union label usually means simply increasing the demand for some manufacturer's product to the exclusion of another. All too often the union label does not represent improved conditions, as witness the wage scale and price lists in the Wickert and Gardiner shoe factory in Brooklyn before the strike, lower than in the non-union shops which struck. And even where higher wages are paid for the production of union-made products, they are simply to one craft, not to all who handle the goods in the course of production, and the union dues of this craft are utilized to advertise the goods of the company. In short, the union label is open to suspicion and is a very weak weapon at best. Certainly not clean enough to appeal to women with as yet.

But more important than the label is the relation of the women to strikes. Many of the strikes of the Western Federation of Miners have been famous for the exceptional courage and fortune displayed by their women folk. Strikes of foreigners in the mining and steel districts of Pennsylvania have been the scenes of wonderful bravery among the women. Yet all strikes are not thus fortunately aided. Many a smooth-tongued agent of the employers has discovered on approaching the wives of strikers that he can induce them to influence their husbands. Many a striker has been taunted by his wife, who has been an eager listener to the emissary, that he is lazy, doesn't care about his family and that "Mr. Smith always treated you all right, will take you back to work," and so forth, ad infinitum. The meeting of the union may be enthusiastic, the speakers eloquent, convincing, and capable of stirring all that is stanch and courageous in man, but if when he trudges home he finds a desolate, poverty-stricken household, sees hardships visited on his family, and worst of all, finds that his wife is alienated through her lack of understanding – there comes a terrible reaction. No influence is more piercing, more subtle through the voices of his dear ones; the speakers, the union, the enthusiasm that was as wine in his blood fades before it. Yet the woman cannot be blamed, even if she helps to drive the husband to cowardice and treason to his fellows. All the instincts of maternity are aroused to protect her little ones, and she is in the grasp of a foe that "calls for something more than brawn or muscle to o'ercome" – namely – ignorance. Woman's influence is one of the strongest in the world, though we may scorn the idea of influence. But it must be made an educated influence and used to help on the battle that is for her and hers, if she but realized it. Every gain made by a union man means more of the necessities and some of the luxuries, for the family depending on him. There is the best of reasons from the view of enlightened selfishness why women should endorse and support the unions in their strikes.

Little need be said of the seven million wage-earning women. That union-ism is their one great weapon hardly admits of an argument. Even more than their brother toilers do these underpaid and overworked women need co-operative effort on their own behalf. Yet many of their experiences with the old unions have been neither pleasant nor encouraging. Strike after strike of cloak makers, shirt waist makers, dressmakers, etc. on the East Side of New York has been exploited by the rich faddists for woman's suffrage, etc., until the points at issue were lost sight of in the blare of automobile horns attendant on their coming and going. A band of earnest, struggling workers made the tail of a suffrage kite in the hands of women of the very class driving the girls to lives of misery or shame, women who could have financed the strike to a truly successful conclusion were they seriously disposed, is indeed a deplorable sight. But the final settlement of the many widely advertised strikers left much to be desired. A spontaneous revolt, a light with glowing enthusiasm and ardor that kept thousands of underfed and thinly clad girls on the picket line, should be productive of more than "a contract." Contracts binding dressmakers in one union, cloak makers in another, shirt waist makers in another, and so on through the list of clothing workers – contracts arranging separate wage scales, hours, dates of expiration, etc., mean no more spontaneous rebellions on the East Side of New York. Now union leaders arbitrate so that you may go back to your old job "without discrim-ination," the new concept of "victory," and if you dare to strike under the contract you will be fired from both shop and union for violation of it....

Women are in industry to stay. They cannot be driven back to the home. Their work left the home and they followed. They are part of the army of labor and must be organized and disciplined as such ... organized they are tenacious and true fighters. And the union factory girl of today is the helpful and encouraging wife of the union man of tomorrow. Mutual aid replaces suspicion, and distrust in the home and the benefit of mutual effort between women and men workers and husbands and wives should not be underesti-mated.

Then through intelligent criticisms and systematic efforts to remold the old – a new fighting union will come forth eventually to flower into the co-operative commonwealth.

Men and women workers unite.

Source: *International Worker*, June 11, 1911, reprinted in Rosalyn Fraad Baxandall, *Words on Fire: The Life and Writing of Elizabeth Gurley Flynn* (New Brunswick, NJ: Rutgers University Press, 1987), pp. 92–6.

4 Louis D. Brandeis and Josephine Goldmark, The Brandeis Brief, 1908

In the landmark Supreme Court case Muller v. Oregon, *principal investigators Florence Kelley and Josephine Goldmark of the National Consumer's League (NCL) and Louis Brandeis successfully argued that the state had the right under its police powers to regulate the maximum hours that women could work in factories and laundries, on the grounds that their reproductive roles entitled them to special protection. As executive director of the NCL, Kelley believed that protective labor legislation was an entering wedge to help reform the conditions under which everyone worked. Other reformers argued that accepting a special status based on biology undermined the ongoing struggle by women to attain equal rights and privileges under the law. Still others objected that* Muller *curtailed the rights of working women to make their own decisions. Despite its co-authorship, this brief bears the name of Louis Brandeis, a reform lawyer appointed to the Supreme Court in 1916.*

PART SECOND: THE WORLD'S EXPERIENCE UPON WHICH THE LEGISLATION LIMITING THE HOURS OF LABOR FOR WOMEN IS BASED

The Dangers of Long Hours

Causes

Physical differences between men and women. The dangers of long hours for women arise from their special physical organization taken in connection with the strain incident to factory and similar work.

Long hours of labor are dangerous for women primarily because of their special physical organization. In structure and function women are differentiated from men. Besides these anatomical and physiological differences, physicians are agreed that women are fundamentally weaker than men in all that makes for endurance: in muscular strength, in nervous energy, in the powers of persistent attention and application. Overwork, therefore, which strains endurance to the utmost, is more disastrous to the health of women than of men, and entails upon them more lasting injury.

[. . .]

Man and Woman. Havelock Ellis.

In strength as well as in rapidity and precision of movement women are inferior to men. This is not a conclusion that has ever been contested. It is in harmony with all the practical experience of life. It is perhaps also in harmony with the results of those investigators... who have found that, as in the blood of women, so also in their muscles, there is more water than in those of men. To a very great extent it is a certainty, a matter of difference in exercise and environment. It is probably, also, partly a matter of organic constitution. (Page 155.)

The motor superiority of men, and to some extent of males generally, is, it can scarcely be doubted, a deep-lying fact. It is related to what is most fundamental in men and in women, and to their whole psychic organization. (Page 156.)

There appears to be a general agreement that women are more docile and amenable to discipline; that they can do light work equally well; that they are steadier in some respects; but that, on the other hand, they are often absent on account of slight indisposition, and they break down sooner under strain. (Page 183.)

History of Factory Legislation. Hutchins and Harrison. 1903.

Women are "not only much less free agents than men," but they are physically incapable of bearing a continuance of work for the same length of time as men, and a deterioration of their health is attended with far more injurious consequences to society. (Page 84.)

[...]

The new strain in manufacture. Such being their physical endowment, women are affected to a far greater degree than men by the growing strain of modern industry. Machinery is increasingly speeded up, the number of machines tended by individual workers grows larger, processes become more and more complex as more operations are performed simultaneously. All these changes involve correspondingly greater physical strain upon the worker.

[...]

Report of the United States Industrial Commission, 1901.

It is brought out that in nearly all occupations an increasing strain and intensity of labor is required by modern methods of production.... The introduction of machinery and the division of labor have made it possible to increase greatly the speed of the individual workman.

[...]

Bad Effect of Long Hours on Health

The fatigue which follows long hours of labor becomes chronic and results in general deterioration of health. Often ignored, since it does not result in immediate disease, this weakness and anemia undermines the whole system; it destroys the nervous energy most necessary for steady work, and effectually predisposes to other illness. The long hours of standing, which are required in many industries, are universally denounced by physicians as the cause of pelvic disorders.

[...]

Massachusetts Legislative Documents. House, 1866, No. 98.

(Specific) cases are not necessary to show the injurious effect of constant labor at long hours.... There may be serious evils from constant and exhausting labor, that do not show themselves in any positive, clearly defined disease: while nevertheless the vital forces of the whole man, physical and mental, are very greatly impaired. (Page 35.)

Dr. Jarvis, physician of Dorchester, says:

"Every man has a certain amount of constitutional force. This is his vital capital which must not be diminished. Out of this comes daily a certain and definite amount of available force, which he may expend in labor of muscle or brain, without drawing on his vital capital. He may and he should work every day and expend so much force and no more, that he shall awake the next morning and every succeeding morning until he shall be threescore and ten, and find in himself the same amount of available force, the same power, and do his ordinary day's work, and again lie down at night with his... constitutional force unimpaired."

Judging by this standard, there can be no doubt of the serious injury often resulting from overwork, even when no palpable evidence appears. (Page 36.)

Dr. Ordway, practicing physician many years (in Lawrence), has no hesitation in saying that mill work, long continued, is injurious to bodily and mental health, and materially shortens life, especially of women. (Page 63.)

Reports of Commissioners on the Hours of Labor. Massachusetts Legislative Documents. House, 1867, No. 44.

Women are held under the present customs and ideas to at least five hours each half day of continuous work, often in the most tedious, minute, and monotonous employ. It is assumed ... that they have no lower limbs to ache with swollen or ruptured veins, no delicacy of nerve, or versatility of mind, to revolt from such severity of application. (Page 66.)

Massachusetts Bureau of Statistics of Labor. *Domestic Labor and Woman's Work*, 1872.

In the cotton mills at Fitchburg the women and children are pale, crooked, and sickly looking. The women appear dispirited, and the children without the bloom of childhood in their cheeks, or the elasticity that belongs to that age. Hours, 60 to 67 3/4 a week. (Page 94.)
   [...]

Age and Sex in Occupations. *Twentieth Century Practice of Medicine*, 1895, Vol. III. By Dr. James H. Lloyd.

Woman may suffer in health in various ways that do not affect materially her mortality – neurasthenia, the bane of overworked and underfed women, does not leave a definite trace on the mortality tables.
   Again, woman's ill health and drudgery in a factory may affect her progeny in a way that the statistician cannot estimate. (Page 326)

Journal of the American Medical Association, May 19, 1906. Fatigue. By Dr. Frederick S. Lee, Prof. Physiology, Columbia University, N.Y.

There are probably few physiologic functions that are not affected unfavorably by the prolonged and excessive activity of the muscular and the nervous systems. In such a condition the normal action of the tissues may easily give place to pathologic action.
   Fatigue undoubtedly diminishes the resistance of the tissues to bacteria, and also predisposes the individual to attacks from diseases other than bacterial. ... Only the assimilation and detoxication that normally come with rest, and best, rest with sleep, are capable of adequate restoring power.

The Hygiene, Diseases, and Mortality of Occupations. 1892.
J. T. Arlidge, M.D., F.R.C.P., Late Melroy Lecturerat Royal College.

Excessive exertion may operate either over a long period and produce its ill results slowly, or be sudden and severe. ... When such people are seized by some definite lesion, attention is so completely attracted to it that the antecedent overtoil laying the foundation for the malady is apt to be overlooked. (Page 16)
   Specific evil effects on childbirth and female functions. The evil effect of overwork before as well as after marriage upon childbirth is marked and disastrous.
   [...]

Report of Massachusetts Bureau of Labor Statistics, 1875.

It seems to be the back that gives out. Girls cannot work more than eight hours, and keep it up; they know it, and they rarely will, – and even this seems to "pull them down," so that it is extremely rare that a girl continues more than a few years at the business.

Mr. B ——, foreman of a large printing establishment, says: "Girls must sit at the 'case.'[2] I never knew but one woman, and she a strong, vigorous Irishwoman, of unusual height, who could stand at the case like a man. Female compositors, as a rule, are sickly, suffering much from backache, headache, weak limbs, and general 'female weakness.'"

Miss ——, for several years in charge of the female department of one of the largest offices in the country, testified: "One year is as long as one can work in a busy office without a good vacation. The confined position, constipation, heat, and dizzy headache, I think, are the most noticeable troubles of 'lady operators' who are 'grown up.' The hours are too long for such strained employment. From 8 A.M. to 6 P.M., with only an hour for dinner, makes too long a day for the kind of work." (Pages 90–92.)

Miss J ——, a lady compositor, says: "We cannot stand at the 'case.' It increases back and head ache, and weakness of limbs, as well as a dragging weight about the hips. I have been at this work five years, but have been frequently obliged to give up for vacations from peculiar troubles and general debility. I began to menstruate when fourteen; I am now twenty-two. I was well until I had set type for a year, when I began to be troubled with difficult periods, and have been more or less ever since. When I go away I get better, but, as often as I return to my work, I am troubled again. Have wholly lost color, and am not nearly as fleshy and heavy as when I began work. I have now a good deal of pain in my chest, and some cough, which increases, if I work harder than usual. I am well acquainted with many other lady compositors who suffer as I do."

Miss S ——, a lady long in charge of the "composing room" (female department) of a large printing establishment testifies: "I was myself a compositor, and have had scores of girls under me and with me, many of whom I have known intimately. I have no hesitation in saying that I think I never knew a dozen lady compositors who were 'well.' Their principal troubles are those belonging to the sex, and great pain in back, limbs, and head."

---

[2]   The tray or compartment in which metal type was stored.

Report of the Massachusetts Bureau of Statistics of Labor, 1884.

We secured the personal history of these 1032 of the whole 20,000 working girls of Boston, a number amply sufficient for the scientific purposes of the investigation. (Page 5.)

Long hours, and being obliged to stand all day, are very generally advanced as the principal reasons for any lack or loss of health occasioned by the work of the girls.... There appears, as far as my observation goes, quite a predisposition to pelvic disease among the female factory operatives.... The necessity for instrumental delivery has very much increased within a few years, owing to the females working in the mills while they are pregnant and in consequence of deformed pelvis. Other uterine diseases are produced, and, in other cases, aggravated in consequence of the same. (Page 69.)

Report of the California Bureau of Labor Statistics, 1887–1888.

Dr. F. B. Kane of San Francisco says: "Very many times my attention has been drawn professionally to the injury caused by the long hours of standing required of the saleswomen in this city, the one position most calculated to cause the manifold diseases peculiar to their sex, and direfully does Nature punish the disobedience of her laws."...

Report of the New Jersey Bureau of Statistics of Labor and Industries, 1902.

The weak, physical condition of the operatives, especially the females, is very noticeable....

The long hours of labor, frequently ten or twelve, and the foul air of the workroom is most marked in its effects upon the female operatives. In addition to throat and lung diseases, which are almost equally prevalent among both sexes, the sufferings of the female operatives from causes peculiar to the sex is very greatly aggravated by the conditions under which they work.

A physician of high standing whose practice is largely among the operatives of these mills is authority for the statement that a large majority of female mill workers are sufferers from some one or more of the organic complaints brought on or intensified by the conditions under which they work. If no such disease existed before entering the mill, it was almost sure to develop soon after beginning work; if it did exist before, it was aggravated to a degree that made them easy victims of consumption [tuberculosis].

[...]

Bad Effect of Long Hours on Morals

The effect of overwork on morals is closely related to the injury to health. Laxity of moral fiber follows physical debility. When the working day is so long that no time whatever is left for a minimum of leisure or home life, relief from the strain of work is sought in alcoholic stimulants and other excesses.

Massachusetts Legislative Document. House, 1866, No. 98.

Overwork is the fruitful source of innumerable evils. Ten and eleven hours daily of hard labor are more than the human system can bear, save in a few exceptional cases. . . . It cripples the body, ruins health, shortens life. It stunts the mind, gives no time for culture, no opportunity for reading, study, or mental improvement. It leaves the system jaded and worn, with no ability to study. . . . It tends to dissipation in various forms. The exhausted system craves stimulants. This opens the door to other indulgences, from which flow not only the degeneracy of individuals, but the degeneracy of the race. (Page 24.)

Relations between Labor and Capital. U.S. Senate Committee, 1883. Vol. I. Testimony of Robert Howard, Mule Spinner in Fall River Cotton Mills.

I have noticed that the hard, slavish overwork is driving those girls into the saloons, after they leave the mills evenings . . . good, respectable girls, but they come out so tired and so thirsty and so exhausted . . . from working along steadily from hour to hour and breathing the noxious effluvia from the grease and other ingredients used in the mill.

Wherever you go . . . near the abodes of people who are overworked, you will always find the sign of the rum shop.

Drinking is most prevalent among working people where the hours of labor are long. (Page 647.)

The Case for the Factory Acts. Edited by Mrs. Sidney Webb. London, 1901.

If working long and irregular hours, accepting a bare subsistence wage and enduring insanitary conditions tended to increase women's physical strength and industrial skill – if these conditions of unregulated industry even left unimpaired the woman's natural stock of strength and skill – we might regard factory legislation as irrelevant. But as a matter of fact a whole century of evidence proves exactly the contrary. To leave women's labor unregulated by law means inevitably to leave it exposed to terribly deteriorating influences.

The woman's lack of skill and lack of strength is made worse by lack of regulation. And there is still a further deterioration. Anyone who has read the evidence... will have been struck by the invariable coincidence of a low standard of regularity, sobriety, and morality, with the conditions to which women, under free competition, are exposed. (Page 209)

Dangerous Trades. Thomas Oliver, M.D. London, 1902.

It is frequently asserted that laundry women as a class are intemperate and rougher than most industrial workers. That they are peculiarly irregular in their habits it is impossible to deny; and the long hours, the discomfort, and exhaustion due to constant standing in wet and heat, discourage the entrance into the trade of a better class of workers is certain.... The prevalence of the drink habit among many of them, of which so much is said, is not difficult to account for: the heat of an atmosphere often laden with particles of soda, ammonia, and other chemicals has a remarkably thirst-inducing effect; the work is for the most part exhausting, even apart from the conditions, and the pernicious habit of quenching the thirst, and stimulating an overtired physical condition, with beer. (Page 672)
[...]

Bad Effect of Long Hours on General Welfare

The experience of manufacturing countries has illustrated the evil effect of overwork upon the general welfare. Deterioration of any large portion of the population inevitably lowers the entire community physically, mentally, and morally. When the health of women has been injured by long hours, not only is the working efficiency of the community impaired, but the deterioration is handed down to succeeding generations. Infant mortality rises, while the children of married working women, who survive, are injured by inevitable neglect. The overwork of future mothers thus directly attacks the welfare of the nation.

The State's Need of Protecting Woman

[...]

Report of the Massachusetts Bureau of Labor Statistics, 1871.

It is claimed that legislation on this subject is an interference between labor and capital.... But legislation has interfered with capital and labor both, in the demand for public safety and the public good. Now public safety and public good, the wealth of the commonwealth, centered, as such wealth is, in the well-being of its common people, demands that the State should interfere by special act in favor of...working women, and working children, by enacting a ten-hour law, to be enforced by a system of efficient inspection. (Page 567.)...

  [...]

Report of the New York Bureau of Labor Statistics, 1900.

The family furnishes the really fundamental education of the growing generation – the education of character, and the family life thus really determines the quality of the rising generation as efficient or nonefficient wealth producers. If a reduction in the hours of labor does promote the growth of a purer and better family life, it will unquestionably result in the production of greater material wealth on the part of the generation trained under its influence; nothing else in fact will so effectively diminish the vast number of criminals, paupers, and idlers, who, in the present generation, consume the people's substance. When one or both parents are away from home for twelve or thirteen hours (the necessary period for those who work ten hours) a day, the children receive comparatively little attention....

Hygiene of Occupations. Dr. Theodore Weyl. Jena, 1904.

Women bear the following generation whose health is essentially influenced by that of the mothers, and the State has a vital interest in securing for itself future generations capable of living and maintaining it. (Page 84.)...

Legislative Control of Women's Work. By S. P. Breckinridge.
Journal of Political Economy. Vol. XIV. 1906.

The assumption of control over the conditions under which industrial women are employed is one of the most significant features of recent legislative policy. In many of the advanced industrial communities the State not only undertakes to prescribe a minimum of decency, safety, and healthfulness, below which its wage earners may not be asked to go, but takes cognizance in several ways of sex differences and sex relationships....
In the third place, the State sometimes takes cognizance of the peculiarly close relationship which exists between the health of its women citizens and the physical vigor of future generations....It has been declared a matter of public concern that no group of its women workers should be allowed to unfit themselves by excessive hours of work, by standing, or other physical strain, for the burden of motherhood which each of them should be able to assume. (Page 107.)

The object of such control is the protection of the physical wellbeing of the community by setting a limit to the exploitation of the improvident, unworkmanlike, unorganized women who are yet the mothers, actual or prospective, of the coming generation. (Pages 108, 109.)

[...]

Report of the Maine Bureau of Labor Statistics, 1892.

Employers should realize that long hours at a severe tension are a cause of irritation among their employees, and they become ripe for almost any trouble, and trifles are often sufficient to precipitate violent strikes. The real cause of many of these strikes is overwork. (Page 11.)

The Effect of Women's Overwork on Future Generations

Report of the Massachusetts Bureau of Labor Statistics, 1871.

14. Progressive physical deterioration produced by family labor in factories. It is well known that like begets like, and if the parents are feeble in constitution, the children must also inevitably be feeble. Hence, among that class of people, you find many puny, sickly, partly developed children; every generation growing more and more so.

15. Connection between continuous factory labor and premature old age. It is a fact, patent to everyone, that premature old age is fully developed, in consequence of long hours of labor and close confinement. Very few live to be old that work in a factory. (Page 504.)

Proceedings of the French Senate, July 9, 1891. Arguments for a Ten-Hour Day for Women.

The woman wage earner, gentlemen, does not always live at the mill gates; she is therefore obliged to make a half or three-quarters' hour journey before she arrives; consequently she will leave home at half-past five in the morning, only to return at half-past eight or nine o'clock in the evening. Is that living? Under such circumstances can a woman truly care for her children and her home? (Page 581.)

Report of the Maryland Bureau of Industrial Statistics, 1896.

Once inside the walls of the factory a weary day's work of ten hours' duration is begun, with an intermission for lunch at noon....

When the day's work is at last over, the wearied crowd trooping from their place of employment hasten in all directions to their homes, which in many instances are in the extreme suburbs of the city. Once home, they swallow a hasty supper and soon retire to a needed and deserved rest, with no pleasant anticipations for the morrow.

What lives are these for future wives and mothers? Future generations will answer. (Page 52.)

Report of the United States Industrial Commission, 1901.

Factory life brings incidentally new and depressing effects, which those whose experience has been wholly agricultural do not appreciate. But the experience of States which have pushed their way from agricultural to manufacturing industries, and have found that their delay in protecting their factory employees has weakened the physical and moral strength of the new generation of working people, would seem to be an experience which the citizens of new manufacturing States should hope to avoid. (Page 788.) ...

The Case for the Factory Acts. Edited by Mrs. Sidney Webb.

It may be enough for the individual employer if his workpeople remain alive during the period for which he hires them. But for the continued efficiency of the nation's industry, it is indispensable that its citizens should not merely continue to exist for a few months or years, but should be well brought up as children, and maintained for their full normal life unimpaired in health, strength, and character.

... Industries yielding only a bare minimum of momentary subsistence are therefore not really self-supporting. In deteriorating the physique, intelligence, and character of their operatives, they are drawing on the capital stock of the nation. And even if the using up is not actually so rapid as to prevent the "sweated" workers from producing a new generation to replace them, the trade is none the less parasitic. In persistently deteriorating the stock it employs, it is subtly draining away the vital energy of the community. It is taking from these workers, week by week, more than its wages can restore to them. A whole community might conceivably thus become parasitic on itself, or, rather, upon its future. (Page 20.) ...

Infant Mortality. A Social Problem. George Newman, M.D. London, 1906.

A nation grows out of its children, and if its children die in infancy, it means that the sources of a nation's population are being sapped, and further that the conditions that kill such a large proportion of infants injure many of those which survive. Last year, 1905, there was a loss to the nation of 120,000 dead infants, in England and Wales alone, a figure which is almost exactly one quarter of all the deaths in England and Wales in that year. (Page 2.)

And this enormous sacrifice of human life is being repeated year by year and is not growing less. (Page 7.)

Nor is England alone.... The birth rate is declining in civilized nations with few exceptions; and the same may be said of the death rate. But the infant mortality rate, as a rule, is stationary or even increasing.

There are two features, however, which appear to be common to the high infant mortality districts, namely, a high density of population and a considerable degree of manufacturing industry. (Page 26.)

[. . .]

Source: Nancy Woloch, *Muller v. Oregon: A Brief History* (Boston and New York: Bedford/St. Martins, 1996), pp. 110–33.

5 Nannie Helen Burroughs, Black Women and Reform, 1915

Black suffragists were frequently excluded by members of the National American Woman Suffrage Association (NAWSA) which courted white southern women. Among those African American women who saw the ballot as key, Nannie Helen Burroughs (1879–1961) emerged as a formidable advocate of using the vote to redress a number of egregious problems most notably the sexual abuse of black women, lynching, economic discrimination, and political disfranchisement. She played an instrumental role in the organization and leadership of the Woman's Convention (1900), an auxiliary of the National Baptist Convention, and the National Training School for Women and Girls (1909). In the 1930s, when many African American leaders realigned with the Roosevelt Democrats, Burroughs remained loyal to the National League of Republican Colored Women. Her commitment to self-help and suffrage helped prepare a new generation of leadership in the second half of the twentieth century.

When the ballot is put in the hands of the American woman, the world is going to get a correct estimate of the Negro woman. It will find her a tower of strength of which poets have never sung, orators have never spoken, and scholars have never written.

Because the black man does not know the value of the ballot, and has bartered and sold his most valuable possession, it is no evidence that the Negro woman will do the same. The Negro woman therefore needs the ballot to get back, by the wise use of it, what the Negro man has lost by the misuse of it. She needs to ransom her race.... She carries the burdens of the Church, and of the school and bears a great deal more than her economic share in the home.

Another striking fact is that the Negro woman carries the moral destiny of two races in her hand. Had she not been the woman of unusual moral stamina that she is, the black race would have been made a great deal whiter, and the white race a great deal blacker during the past fifty years. She has been left a prey for the men of every race, but in spite of this, she has held the enemies of Negro female chastity at bay. The Negro woman is the white woman's as well as the white race's most needed ally in preserving an unmixed race.

The ballot, wisely used, will bring to her the respect and protection she needs. It is her weapon of moral defense. Under present conditions, when she appears in court in defense of her virtue, she is looked upon with amused contempt. She needs the ballot to reckon with men who place no value upon her virtue, and to mould healthy public sentiment in favor of her own protection.

Source: *Crisis*, August 1915, reprinted in *Through Women's Eyes: An American History with Documents*, eds. Ellen Carol Dubois and Lynn Dumenil (Boston and New York: Bedford/St. Martins, 2005), p. 428.

6 Sonya Levien, The Struggles of Immigrant Women, 1918

Born in Russia, Sonya Levien (1888–1960) worked in a feather duster factory after leaving school in the eighth grade. She loved to write and went to work at Success Magazine, *first in the office and then as an editorial assistant. In 1908 she earned a law degree from New York University by attending classes at night. Although she was admitted to the bar, she primarily made her living as a magazine editor. She belonged to the feminist Heterodoxy Club in Greenwich Village and briefly worked at the* The Woman's Journal, *under Alice Stone Blackwell. The following article, written when Levien was editing former President Theodore Roosevelt's essays for* The Metropolitan Magazine, *documents the complex relationships between immigrant women, social reformers, suffragists, and the federal government. In the aftermath of World War I, Levien moved to California and became one of the most highly paid female screenwriters in Hollywood.*

Those who aimlessly agitate for the betterment of the East Side immediately rouse the snake within my bosom – an ugly snake developed by slummers, charity investigators and adolescent uplifters. It dates back to the days when I played exhibit A. in the life of the University Settlement at a peculiarly rabid period of muckraking for the benefit of journalists. The East Side was milked dry and left a greater waste than ever. It was therefore with confusing emotions that I went from house to house with Col. Roosevelt and the other members of our party in an effort to do something for the starving babies in these days of stress.

The pinched faces of the mothers brought me to. The inalienable bond between us asserted itself, and instead of an interloper I saw myself as a deserter.

When I first came to this country and lived on the East Side, I naturally joined a group of agitators of socialists, anarchists, and single taxers, but the majority were Socialists. We signed ourselves "Yours for the Revolution", probably with the same glow as that of the Germans when they toasted to "Der Tag." But we were no patriots. Patriotism is a love and passion for one's country awakened by one's communal life. It is a holy emotion created by the noble relation of man to man. But when the controlling members of your communal life intimidate your spirit, poison your air and food, cripple your posterity and deaden your faith, it becomes difficult to take that communal life to your breast. To us patriotism meant loyalty to ward-healers, to a nation controlled by capitalists, a nation that sanctioned the despoilation of the working classes. I was brought up on Karl Marx and enumerable red pamphlets bound in parafin paper, and my suspicious mind saw the ravages of Capitalism all around me.

Yet my staunch belief in Socialism was not due to the red pamphlets I read or my association with the Group. Poverty had embittered young life for me. I had come here to the trumpet call of liberty. A feather-duster factory swallowed up my teens at four dollars a week. With all the cards of life stacked against us, and dissolution at the door I saw myself and my kind cling grimly to the sacred traditions of honesty and blind trust in God. Another period of illness or unemployment, and the charity organization would have its tenacles up on us. And when self-reliance and pride went there were those deadlier ghouls of the slums – disease and crime – always waiting, waiting.

In fact, as I examine the memories of my childhood they hold nothing of romance but only the fear of evil things, of restless nights in ill-smelling tenements, of yearning for spring in the country when the first buds appeared on the scraggy trees in Seward Park as I beheld them behind factory windows, closed and thick with feather moss; and above all, of an overwhelming desire for a public school education. If I would live I must escape from the East Side. If my body did not die, my mind and spirit would.

[...]

That those immigrants who are not utterly submerged by the struggle for bread often develop into the Bolsheviki, is the natural outcome of the

American policy. It is a policy no less inhuman than that of the Czar's. We would enlist the patriotism of the immigrants and at the same time strain their virtues beyond endurance. We thrust them into the fiercest kind of economic competition, and sap their energies and trust. The only national guaranty they have for safe living, is the security of the pen-house for disobedience.

There is greater hunger and suffering in the slums than when I lived there a dozen years ago, and that despite the many "first aids" developed since then. Wages have risen but not as rapidly as the cost of living. With the diminishing purchasing power of a workingman's wages, the present "<u>high wage</u>" cry is but a delusion. According to the U.S. Bureau of Statistics, within the ten years between 1907 and 1916 there has been an increase of wages amounting to 16% in the same period there has been an increase in the retail price of foods amounting to 62%. Almost half of the working-man's budget is spent on food. Considering that the other half has to be divided among rent, clothing, doctor's bills, education, fuel and what not, cleanliness and thrift and loyalty become sweated virtues. The risk of large families is soon discovered as one too great to take; as for decent fellowship, that also does not pay. Such is their struggle day in and day out.

That this nation is sincerely dedicated to working out the tenets of democracy they do not know. The only Americanism they know is that which falls from the lips of the sweatshop boss.

In times of peace we forget the nation's dependence upon its working-classes, in time of war we cannot. Especially at this time when the nation is demanding from them so much, more than from any other class.

The mothers of the East Side are giving up, proportionately, more sons to fight for this country than other mothers for the simple reason that they have more sons to give, and conscription leaves them no choice. And deeper is their sorrow because the exaltation of patriotism and sacrifice is not theirs.

A small dried-up and tear-stained old woman came to me soon after the roll-call of the first conscriptionists. Four sons out of eight had been drafted, two were called. Wouldn't I help her, she pleaded, kissing my hand as any peasant in Dvinak, from where she came, would do. She knew what taking soldiers by lottery meant, Her oldest was taken that way years ago in Russia and sent to the Caucauses, and never returned. She knew that some time it was possible to substitute another's life. She offered hers and wouldn't I use my influence with those in power to have it accepted.

I tried to explain that it wasn't a question of the public execution of her two sons.

She shook her hand. The world was the same all over. It was a little worse for her in this country. "Mamushka", she pleaded, her tears bathing my hands, "I am old and should be so happy to die. Please go and tell them."

America's destiny is now becoming thoroughly bound up with the lives of these people that have come here from other lands. We can no longer overestimate their ignorance to us in our plans for victory. To wrest their sons from them without giving them every possible opportunity to share in the nation's good, is as short-sighted as it is cruel.

Poverty is a serious element in the unassimilation of these people but ignorance is greater. We are already beginning to give awards of slices of democracy. Granting the vote to the N.Y. State women is a good example of the desire to begin somewhere. But how to relate this new privilege with greater leisure to assimilate the merits of citizenship, is even more important than the vote itself. Four hundred thousand alien women in N.Y. City alone will automatically become voters next November. Unlike their husbands, it will not be necessary for them to pass an examination of American History and its political institutions, in order to become citizens. When one mentions their voting next fall, they want to know what wrong they've done.

Now the Woman's Suffrage Party of New York is doing the finest work of its career in the effort they are making to educate these women to citizenship. But the women they must reach are too busy and tired to attend meetings. Thus it is with all such efforts. The milk station, the school that served luncheon to its undernourished pupils, and the children's clinic we visited, were doing services so humane, in ways so efficient and understanding that they must draw forth the most glowing of tributes. But all these were the effort of some kindly private endeavor. They could only reach a few. In fact, so small a percentage of the children who needed their care that their work was almost negligible when one considers the East Side as a whole.

The panacea? Shall we go on reviving utopian formulas as substitutes for experience, as social uplifters have done ever since they came into being? How to assimilate its immigrant population has been the speculation of America for the last decade.... My one cry is that the needs of these people should be the concern of the nation – no matter through what channels the needs are supplied. The federal government may not be able to prescribe the ultimate rules of conduct, but it is the only agency that can provide sufficient opportunities for these people to work out their own problems. One social reformer in politics is worth a hundred in charity organizations. There is incalculable force in suppression. All through the ages great emancipations have resulted from dreams let loose. The great dream and passion and energy of this age is the proletariat's dream of its control over its own destiny. It is the price it has put on its loyalty.

Source: Sonya Levien Manuscript Collection, Huntington Library (n.d.). Titled "Milk" HM 56283.

7 Crystal Eastman, Our War Record: A Plea for Tolerance, 1918

First founded in November 1914, the Woman's Peace Party of New York City, an exclusively female organization, adamantly opposed war as a strategy to resolve international conflict. In January 1918, eight months after America's entry into World War I, Crystal Eastman defended the actions of the Woman's Peace Party specifically with reference to the right of free speech. This pamphlet appeared shortly after the federal government used the Espionage Act (1917) to silence the anti-war magazine The Masses, *edited by Eastman's brother Max. Women became a strategic source of power for Woodrow Wilson as he sought support for his post-war vision that included a League of Nations.*

It is true that we opposed the entrance of this country into the war and used every honorable means at our command to prevent it. We believed that cooperation with other neutrals would have furnished a method of maintaining our joint rights without recourse to war, and at the same time a means with which to hasten peace negotiations in Europe. We especially urged that if a democracy is to go to war it should go by direct mandate of the people through a referendum. After war had become a fact, we further urged that conscription was no fit weapon for a democracy to fight its wars with, that forcing men to kill and to be killed against their will does violence to the vital spirit and essence of democracy.

However, once the war and conscription became the law of this land, our agitation against them ceased. Common sense as well as loyalty and the habit of obedience to law counseled this course. We have never in the slightest degree urged or suggested resistance to the selective service law nor followed any other policy of obstruction.

What then has been our position, what have we asked of our government during these critical months? Briefly this:

To begin with, we have insisted not merely upon the right, but upon the need for a full, free and continuous discussion in the press and on the platform of America's war aims and peace terms. We have urged this that the militarists and imperialists might be exposed, that ignorance might be destroyed, that we might be faithful to the declared ideals for which our armed forces are fighting, and that the whole world might know us as the enemies of German aggression but no less the friends of a German democracy.

We have at no time demanded an immediate peace or a separate peace. But, when revolutionary Russia first pronounced its simple, generous, practical peace formula – no forcible annexations, no punitive indemnities, free development for all nations, – we urged that our government should respond, stating its willingness to make peace on this formula. When the German Reichstag passed a resolution substantially endorsing this formula, we asked our government to welcome the resolution officially, and thus strengthen the hands of the German liberals who were struggling to make it the avowed policy of their government. When the President replied to the Pope, we rejoiced to find him clearly standing for the Russian formula and we advocated a further step, i.e., that our government should support the long unheeded request of Russia for a restatement of the Allied aims, – a policy now supported by the Marquis of Lansdowne.

Today we are still urging this step. But we also look ahead to the inevitable cessation of hostilities, to the peace conference which must come. We are urging that the ultimate agreement to be reached by the nations at that conference shall include Free Markets and Free Seas, Universal Disarmament, and A League of Nations, the obvious essentials of an enduring peace. And since we are wise enough to know that these ends cannot be achieved at a gathering of military personages and appointed diplomats, we are demanding direct democratic representation of the people of all countries at the peace conference.

This is our complete war record. We hold that there is nothing treasonable or unpatriotic or even emotional about it. On the basis of that record we ask protection from the government for our propaganda no matter how unpopular it may become. We ask tolerance from those who think our ideas are wrong. And from those who think our ideas are fundamentally right, whether they agreed with us about the question of entering the war or not, we ask friendship and loyalty and support.

Source: Cover Page for "Our War Record: A Plea for Tolerance," Woman's Peace Party of New York City, pamphlet, January 1, 1918, reprinted in *Crystal Eastman on Women and Revolution*, ed. Blanche Wiesen Cook (Oxford: Oxford University Press, 1978), pp. 264–5.

REPRESENTATIONS

8 Virginia Arnold Holding a Kaiser Wilson Banner, 1918

The National Woman's Party was created in 1916 by Alice Paul (1885–1977), Lucy Burns (1879–1966), and members of the Congressional Union for Woman Suffrage. In general, they used more militant tactics than NAWSA. Their members picketed the White House and while the Wilson administration

Figure 2.1

Source: Virginia Arnold [holding Kaiser Wilson banner]. Photograph: Harris & Ewing, Washington D.C. c.1917. Courtesy of the Library of Congress.

at first tolerated their demonstrations, by June of 1917 women protesters were arrested and imprisoned in harsh conditions. Public sympathy for the women grew as many of the suffragists, who regarded themselves as political prisoners, endured forced feeding. The poster is a direct reference to the president's criticism of the lack of rights under the German monarchy, against whom the United States declared war in April, 1917.

Source: Created August ?, 1918; National Woman's Party Records, Group I, Container I: 160, Folder: Pickets – Arrests and Imprisonment. Library of Congress, Manuscript Division, Digital ID mnnwp 160030. Available from www.archives. gov/exhibits/picturing_the_century/galleries/greatwar.html.

9 Women Rivet Heaters and Passers On, 1919

Some women seized the opportunities created by a shortage of manpower during World War I to take industrial jobs such as building ships at the Puget Sound Naval Yard. After the war, there was considerable economic dislocation. In February 1919, 60,000 workers with the Seattle Central Labor Council went on a sympathy strike with metal workers at the Seattle Shipyards. This was the first city-wide general strike and provoked fear of a Bolshevik Revolution in the United States. In this remarkable photograph that documents women industrial workers, there is no indication of the ongoing tensions. The focus is on the glorification of American labor.

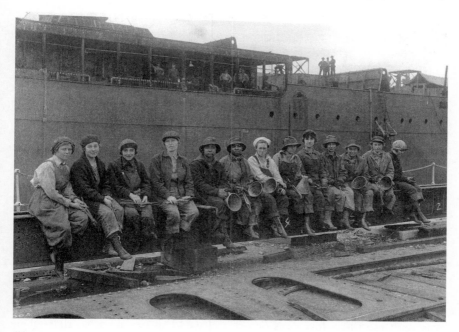

Figure 2.2

Source: Women Rivet Heaters and Passers On, Puget Sound Navy Yard, Washington, May 29, 1919. Courtesy of the National Archives.

DOMESTIC LIVES

10 Elinore Pruitt Stewart, The Homesteader's Marriage and A Little Funeral, 1912

Elinore Pruitt, a widow with a two-year-old daughter, moved to Wyoming to work as a housekeeper for Clyde Stewart, a cattle rancher. Shortly after her arrival, she decided to marry him and make a new life on this rugged frontier. In letters to a former employer in Denver, she wrote about her new life and some of the challenges of hard work, the death of her young son, and the growing love for her husband. Stewart's self-reference to the manipulative Becky Sharp, a popular character from William Thackery's 1847 novel Vanity Fair, *is intriguing. The* Atlantic Monthly *published the letters as a book in 1914.*

December 2, 1912.

DEAR MRS. CONEY, –

[...]

I have often wished I might tell you all about my Clyde, but have not because of two things. One is I could not even begin without telling you what a good man he is, and I did n't want you to think I could do nothing but brag. The other reason is the haste I married in. I am ashamed of that. I am afraid you will think me a Becky Sharp of a person. But although I married in haste, I have no cause to repent. That is very fortunate because I have never had one bit of leisure to repent in. So I am lucky all around. The engagement was powerfully short because both agreed that the trend of events and ranch work seemed to require that we be married first and do our "sparking" afterward. You see, we had to chink in the wedding between times, that is, between planting the oats and other work that must be done early or not at all. In Wyoming ranchers can scarcely take time even to be married in the spring-time. [...]

Well, there was no time to make wedding clothes, so I had to "do up" what I did have. Isn't it queer how sometimes, do what you can, work will keep getting in the way until you can't get anything done? That is how it was with me those few days before the wedding; so much so that when Wednesday dawned everything was topsy-turvy and I had a very strong desire to run away. But I always did hate a "piker," so I stood pat. Well, I had most of the dinner cooked, but it kept me hustling to get the house into anything like decent order before the old dog barked, and I knew my moments of liberty were limited. It was blowing a perfect hurricane and snowing like midwinter. I had bought a beautiful pair of shoes to wear on that day, but my vanity had squeezed my feet a little, so while I was so busy at work I had kept on a worn old pair, intending to put on the new ones later; but when the Pearsons drove up all I thought about was getting them into the house where there was fire, so I forgot all about the old shoes and the apron I wore.

I had only been here six weeks then, and was a stranger. That is why I had no one to help me and was so confused and hurried. As soon as the new-comers were warm, Mr. Stewart told me I had better come over by him and stand up. It was a large room I had to cross, and how I did it before all those strange eyes I never knew. All I can remember very distinctly is hearing Mr. Stewart saying, "I will," and myself chiming in that I would, too. Happening to glance down, I saw that I had forgotten to take off my apron or my old shoes, but just then Mr. Pearson pronounced us man and wife, and as I had dinner to serve right away I had no time to worry over my odd toilet.

[...] I had not thought I should ever marry again. Jerrine was always such a dear little pal, and I wanted to just knock about foot-loose and free to see life as a gypsy sees it. I had planned to see the Cliff-Dwellers' home; to live right there until I caught the spirit of the surroundings enough to live over their lives in imagination anyway. I had planned to see the old missions and to go to Alaska; to hunt in Canada. I even dreamed of Honolulu. Life stretched out before me one long, happy jaunt. I aimed to see all the world I could, but to travel unknown bypaths to do it. But first I wanted to try homesteading.

But for my having the grippe, I should never have come to Wyoming. Mrs. Seroise, who was a nurse at the institution for nurses in Denver while I was housekeeper there, had worked one summer at Saratoga, Wyoming. It was she who told me of the pine forests. I had never seen a pine until I came to Colorado; so the idea of a home among the pines fascinated me. At that time I was hoping to pass the Civil-Service examination, with no very definite idea as to what I would do, but just to be improving my time and opportunity. I never went to a public school a day in my life. In my childhood days there was no such thing in the Indian Territory part of Oklahoma where we lived, so I have had to try hard to keep learning. Before the time came for the examination I was so discouraged because of the grippe that nothing but the mountains, the pines, and the clean, fresh air seemed worth while; so it all came about just as I have written you.

[...]

As there had been no physician to help, so there was no minister to comfort, and I could not bear to let our baby leave the world without leaving any message to a community that sadly needed it. His little message to us had been love, so I selected a chapter from John and we had a funeral service, at which all our neighbors for thirty miles around were present. So you see, our union is sealed by love and welded by a great sorrow.

Little Jamie was the first little Stewart. God has given me two more precious little sons. The old sorrow is not so keen now. I can bear to tell you about it, but I never could before. When you think of me, you must think of me as one who is truly happy. It is true, I want a great many things I have n't got, but I don't want them enough to be discontented and not enjoy the many blessings that are mine. I have my home among the blue mountains, my healthy, well-formed children, my clean, honest husband, my kind, gentle milk cows, my garden which I make myself. I have loads and loads of flowers which I tend myself. There are lots of chickens, turkeys, and pigs which are my own special care. I have some slow old gentle horses and an old wagon. I can load up the kiddies and go where I please any time. I have the best, kindest neighbors and I have my dear absent friends. Do you wonder I am so happy? When I think of it all, I wonder how I can crowd all my joy into one short life. [...]

With much love to you, I am
"Honest and truly" yours,

ELINORE RUPERT STEWART.

Source: Elinore Pruitt Stewart, *Letters of a Woman Homesteader* (Boston: Houghton Mifflin, 1914), pp. 184–92.

11 Lutiant, Letter to a Friend, 1918

At the peak of the epidemic in Washington DC, volunteer nurses like Lutiant cared for soldiers dying from Spanish influenza. She recounted some of her experiences to a friend, an Indian woman like herself, back at Haskell Institute in Lawrence, Kansas. Lutiant presumably had little training in nursing but was willing, able, and above all, female. Her intimate reflections on her social life offer a glimpse of the responsibilities, perils, and pleasures of female civic duty to a nation that continued to define some Indians as wards, others as citizens, and yet others as both.

231–14th St. South East,
October 17, 1918

Dear friend Louise:
So everybody has the "Flu" at Haskell? I wish to goodness Miss Keck and Mrs. McK would get it and die with it. Really, it would be such a good riddance, and not much lost either! As many as 90 people die every day here with the "Flu". Soldiers too, are dying by the dozens. So far, Felicity, C. Zane, and I are the only ones of the Indian girls who have not had it. We certainly consider ourselves lucky too, believe me. Katherine and I just returned last Sunday evening from Camp Humphreys "Somewhere in Virginia" where we volunteered to help nurse soldiers sick with the Influenza. We were there at the Camp ten days among some of the very worse cases and yet we did not contract it. We had intended staying much longer than we did, but the work was entirely too hard for us, and anyway the soldiers were all getting better, so we came home to rest up a bit. We were day nurses and stationed in the Officers' barracks for six days and then transferred to the Privates' barracks or hospital and were there four days before we came back. All nurses were required to work twelve hours a day – we worked from seven in the morning until seven at night, with only a short time for luncheon and dinner. Believe me, we were always glad when night came because we sure did get tired. We had the actual Practical nursing to do – just like the other nurses had, and were given a certain number of wards

with three or four patients in each of them to look after. Our chief duties were to give medicines to the patients, take temperatures, fix ice packs, feed them at "eating time", rub their back or chest with camphorated sweet oil, make egg-nogs, and a whole string of other things I can't begin to name...

Repeated calls come from the Red Cross for nurses to do district work right here in D.C. I volunteered again, but as yet I have not been called and am waiting. Really, they are certainly "hard up" for nurses – even me can volunteer as a nurse in a camp or in Washington. There are about 800 soldiers stationed at Potomac Park right here in D.C. just a short distance from the Interior building where I work, and this morning's paper said that the deaths at this Park were increasing, so if fortune favors me, I may find myself there before the week is ended. I have a <u>very dear soldier friend</u> who is stationed there – Lieut. Cantril by name. He is not what one would call "handsome" but he is certainly <u>good-looking</u>, and on top of all that – he is a CATHOLIC. Sure like it for myself too. All the girls have soldiers here – Indian girls also. Some of the girls have soldiers and sailors too. The boys are particularly crazy about the Indian girls. They tell us that the Indian girls are not so "easy" as the white girls, so I guess maybe that's their reason.

Washington is certainly a beautiful place. There is so much to be said in favor of it, that if I started, I don't believe I should ever get through. Odile and I have to pass by the Capitol, the Union Station, the War Department, the Pension Bldg., and through the noted Lincoln Park every morning on our way to work. The Washington Monument (555 ft. high) is within walking distance of the Interior Department (where we work) and we walked there last evening after work. It certainly is high and we are planning to go up in the elevator some time to look over the city. We were going last evening, but the place is closed temporarily, on account of this "Flu".

The Aviation field is another very interesting place. Air-planes fly over the city at all hours of the day now, and sometimes so low that one can hear the noise of the machine.

Besides Aviators, we have hundreds of soldiers, sailors, Marines, French "Blue Devils" and even the National band of Italy in Washington. Douglas Fairbanks and Geraldine Farrar are here also on the fourth Liberty Loan campaign and I was privileged to take a chance to peep at them. Just yesterday, Douglas sold ONE MILLION DOLLARS WORTH OF BONDS FOR WASHINGTON. It was rumored that Washington was going to fail to reach its quota in Liberty Bonds on account of having so many deaths and sick people in the city, but the way "Doug" is selling 'em, it doesn't seem as if it will. A lot of the girls from the Office here go out to sell bonds but some of them don't make much of a success. One of the Indian girls, named Cathryne Welch, went out last week to sell bonds and she sold so many that she got excused from the Office for the rest of this week to do nothing but sell bonds. She is a very pretty girl – a high school graduate and one year normal. She has two brothers in the army – one is a Captain and the other a Sergeant. Maybe you remember seeing Capt. Gus Welch's picture in the K.C. Star – well that is her brother and he is "over there" now.

All the schools, churches, theaters, dancing halls, etc., are closed here also. There is a bill in the Senate today authorizing all the war-workers to be released from work for the duration of this epidemic. It has not passed the house yet, but I can't help but hope it does. If it does, Lutiant can find plenty of things at home to busy herself with, or she might accidentally take a trip to Potomac Park. Ha! Ha!

It is perfectly alright about the sweater. I don't expect you to be able to get it while you are quarantined, but will still be glad to have it if you can send it as soon as you are out of quarantine. It is rather cold in Washington, but not cold enough to wear winter coats yet, and my suit coat is a little too thin, so I figured out that a sweater would be the thing to have. Sometimes it is cold enough to wear a wrap while working, but of course it is out of question to work in a heavy winter coat. However, send it whenever you find it convenient to do so, and I will settle with you as promptly as possible.

Well Louise, if you are not dead tired reading this letter, I'll write another like it some other time. There is still a lot I could tell you about D.C. but it's nearing lunch time and I want to be right there on the dot, as I always am – to be sure.

Write again whenever you find it convenient to do so – always glad to hear the Haskell news from you.

Sincerely your friend.

Source: The National Archives, Central Plains Region, Kansas City, Record Group 75.

Questions to Think About

1. Compare the economic opportunities available to working women between 1900 and 1920.
2. Compare and contrast the strategies of women actively engaged in different reform movements between 1900 and 1920.
3. What do the two photographs appearing on pages 81 and 83 suggest about femininity in the public arena? Are these images of femininity consistent with other legal, political, and domestic perspectives on femininity in the period?

Chapter 3   Sex and Politics in an Age of Conservatism, 1920–33

WORK

1 Caroline Manning, The Immigrant Woman and Her Job, 1930

In 1920 Congress established the Women's Bureau within the Department of Labor in order to investigate and report on the needs of wage-earning women. Their agents gathered information about labor standards that affected women in factories. In 1930 the Women's Bureau began an investigation of immigrant women wage earners in Philadelphia and in the Lehigh Valley. These four case histories of Angelina, Minnie, Louise M., and Teresa M. reveal their limited opportunities even before the Great Depression cost many factory workers their jobs. In three of the four cases, the women worked to provide for their children.

Angelina

Thirteen years ago Angelina, then a girl of only 16, anxious to see the world, came with some neighbors to her cousin's in New York. She thought she knew what life in America would be like and only in a vague sort of way did she expect to work, but she supposed her money would buy beautiful clothes and that her life would be like that of the women in restaurant scenes in the movies. When, the day after she arrived, her cousin spoke quite emphatically about her going to work, she was surprised, but it was an even greater surprise when she found that she could not get the kind of work she wanted. She had started to learn dressmaking in Italy, but her cousin told her it was altogether different here, where each person makes but one special part of the dress and work is so scarce one has to take whatever can be found. So her cousin took her that day – her second in the United States – to an underwear shop and she was given pressing of corset covers, at 3 cents a dozen. Her first pay was $3.15. Adjustment to her work and her new life was difficult and she did not always succeed in keeping back the tears. She, who had come to this country to make and wear pretty clothes, never had a shirt waist that cost over $1 in the five years before she was married....

Then she had five happy years in her own home and forgot about work in the shop. But tragedy overtook the family and since 1922 her husband has been in a sanitarium and she is back again at her old job, the sole support of herself and two little children. There is no tone of complaint in her voice as she describes the routine of her day's work – preparing the breakfast, dressing the children and taking them to the neighbor's, and starting for the shop by 7 in the morning; then, after a long day at the machine, home again to prepare more food and care for the children.

Minnie

Another case of disillusionment was that of a young Jewish girl who had been induced to come to the United States by her sister. Unlike Angelina, who succeeded in taking care of herself and her children, Minnie has failed often to be even self-supporting. She arrived in August, 1921, and was immediately put to work in her brother-in-law's small store. She had had six years' experience in a store in Warsaw, but this was different. "I slaved here seven days a week. I was always in the store, early and late – sometimes more than 12 hours a day." For 10 months she endured it, grateful to her sister for work. Then the bottom dropped out and she became ill – first a patient in a hospital ward, then in a free convalescent home, and now in a boarding home for working girls. During much of the past two years she has been "on the city," as she expressed it, and she kept repeating "I must cover my expense." At the time of the interview she was making an effort in spite of homesickness and "many worriments" to be self-supporting by making lamp shades at $10 a week. Most of the girls in the shop were pieceworkers, but Minnie was not strong enough to hurry, so the boss gave her a "particular job" and paid her "straight," which she regards as a great advantage, as "piecework would kill me."

Once Minnie managed to go to night school for three weeks. She is sensitive about her lack of English: "Not very good language, so I can't hope for nice store job," although she feels she could do the work in a store better than anything else.

Louise M.

"Everybody else was going," so Louise M. a child of 14, left her poor home in Poland in 1905 to come with an uncle to the United States. For two years she tried her fortune in several housework jobs, but she was never satisfied, and as soon as she was 16 she went to a clothing factory and secured work as a sewing-machine operator. For six years she experienced the ups and downs in this industry – sometimes she waited in the shop for work and sometimes she waited at home; sometimes her pocketbook was empty, some weeks the pay envelope had $3, other weeks, $12. Probably her best job was pressing shirt waists, "folding and pinning them just as you buy them in the store," and for this she was paid at the rate of 15 cents a dozen. She was glad enough to give up this struggle for marriage and never expected to be a wage earner again.

But in the depression after the war the little fruit stand in which they had invested all their savings failed, and she returned to work – any kind of work, in a laundry on the mangle feed, in a restaurant kitchen, office cleaning. This last she particularly disliked. Her comments about it were: "Four car fares a day; that's too much. Marble floors. Just so much to scrub, and if you stopped five minutes you couldn't finish on time." She vowed she would not go back to that for $20 a week. At the time of the interview she was operating a drill press – a job that paid her $16 to $21 a week. She was delighted with the work and did not plan to give it up. "You feel different – you feel that you are just like everybody else. You ain't got to be ashamed. You feel like a different woman; you aren't near so tired." The joy in her job almost overshadowed the fact that this house was the first in which she had ever lived where there was no sink and no water, and she was happy that her earnings could provide the necessities. "You have to have plenty milk for the children. From week to week you just keep going."

Teresa M.

Although Teresa M. was only 12 years old when she came to America, she can not read English; however, she speaks it better than do most of her neighbors. In Hungary there were cigar factories near her home and she was glad to find them here and eager to get to work; so her father helped her to find a job as a roller in a cigar factory and there, except for the interruptions of childbearing, she has been during the last 20 years. Altogether, she estimates that she has lost about 4 years from work during her 14 years of married life. "My man made me stay home for babies," and there had been five, although only three are living.

In spite of the 20 years, most of which had been spent in only two shops she still was keen about working and was contented with her job. "I can always have my place. If I do not feel so good and stay home a day, I phone the boss and he says, 'All right, I'll get another roller in your place to-day but be sure you come back.' If we work, then the boss he likes."

Her husband also is thrifty and has one of the few steady jobs in a wire mill. There is an air of prosperity about their home and garden. Her husband could support the family, Teresa says, but they couldn't have things "nice" unless she worked; and she took the visitor to see the cellar, that had been cemented recently and paid for with her earnings – $200. There is electricity in the house, a washing machine, and modern plumbing.

The fact that her husband helps her with the housework, with the washings, and "sometimes he cook" makes it possible for Teresa to do two jobs. She says she could not do it "without my man, in everything he help," nor could the husband have such an attractive home if Teresa had not helped as a wage earner also.

She intends to continue working, hoping to be ready to meet adversity when it comes, for "everybody sick or old some day." She also hopes some day "to sit and rock on the porch like other ladies. I'll be old lady then."

Source: Reprinted by permission from *Immigrant Women: Revised, Second Edition*, ed. Maxine Schwartz Seller, (Albany, NY: SUNY Press, 1994), pp. 119–21. © 1994, State University of New York. All rights reserved.

2   Christine Galliher Describes her Participation in a Walkout Strike, 1929

Christine Galliher started working at the Bemberg–Glanzstoff textile mills in Elizabethton, Tennessee, when she was only 15 years old. Two years later, in April 1929, she went out on strike. When a second "spontaneous and complete walkout" resulted in a confrontation between labor and management, picketers and the National Guard, the violence brought national attention. The press reported on the "unladylike" behavior of two picketers arrested for disorderly conduct, Trixie Perry and Wild Bill. After six weeks Anna Weinstock, a federal conciliator, negotiated a settlement between the workers represented by United Textile Workers and the company. As the economic depression worsened, textile workers in mills across Tennessee, Georgia, and the Carolinas continued their protests, often spontaneous, that culminated in the General Strike of 1934. Many workers were never rehired and despite promises by the Roosevelt Administration, economic hardship

defined the region and its workers. Galliher refers to the time she spent at the
Bryn Mawr Summer School for Women Workers that promoted greater
opportunities for factory workers through the combined efforts of
middle-class and working-class women.

CHRISTINE GALLIHER:

The first time I had a job there [mills], I worked in winding. And then I had a bad leg and I was off from work with that, but when I went back down they hired me for North American, what they called Glanzstoff. The first time I went to work, though, I was fifteen. [...] I worked at both plants. At first I went to work at Bemberg, and I worked there maybe a year. But then I had a leg problem, and I was off a long time. But when I went back, see, I was sent down to North American to work. That's where I worked when we asked for the raise from $10.08 to $11.20, and we just quit work. And we'd never heard tell of a union! You see, we didn't know how big it was going to grow. It grew and grew and grew, and other departments came out. I was in inspection. And then Bemberg came out; both plants came out. There was five thousand people out. And we had asked for an $11.20 raise! [Laughter] [...] we all decided in that department if they didn't give us a raise, we wasn't going to work.

JACQUELYN HALL:

How did you all get together to decide that you were going to walk out if they didn't give you a raise? Did you meet after work?

CHRISTINE GALLIHER:

[...] And we didn't even know what a union was. We'd never heard tell of a union. But we just decided that we wasn't going to work for this wage. But as it happened, there was a carpenter and a union man, John Penix. He called someone that he knew in the labor movement, and they came here and organized, and it was just one big mess, and they just panicked, at that time they paid a flat scale. You started out at $8.96 a week; $10.08; $11.20. I don't know whether you got past $11.20 or not. [...] We didn't know a thing about a union. We just decided well, we just wasn't going to work for $10.08 a week. Fifty-six hours, they didn't seem to pay any attention to it. People had never been nowhere, and they'd never done anything. Maybe go to a movie on Saturday night. So I don't guess the hours made that much difference. I don't remember, except I know you'd get awfully tired.

[...]

JACQUELYN HALL:
What happened then when you walked out?

CHRISTINE GALLIHER:
It just got in a bigger and a bigger and a bigger mess. Other people kept joining us, first from North American and then Bemberg, because everybody wanted a raise anyway, until that John Penix got in touch with somebody in labor, and an organizer came here and organized. We were arrested twice, on those picket lines. It was over here on the old State Line Road. They brought out the National Guard.

In the meantime, my daddy cooked down there at the plant during that time. Some of them stayed in there, I reckon, to take care of the machinery and things that had to be looked after, and he cooked for them. [...]

After Mr. Penix got an organizer here, there was an old building they called the tabernacle. And it was setting right down here where you turn out to go out by the monument. It was a huge old building, rough building. And they'd always have revivals there of visiting evangelists. So they met there, and they elected their president and so forth and their committees to meet with other people involved, like management. [...]

It's right about where the new jail's been built now, or maybe a little bit over closer to the mountains.

But it was a huge building. There wasn't another building big enough to hold that many people marching, and they would march, march from the plants to town. They'd maybe meet down at the plant, and they'd all march. They didn't do anything rough. If there was any dirty work done, I didn't know anything about it. They probably did that at nights.

Women and men [on The Picket Line] ... I didn't go out too much on the picket line, because where I put my work in was at the office, people joining the union.

I believe [that I went to the Southern Summer School] during that strike. I worked for the union, and I met a lot of people – I couldn't tell you their names now – a lot of organizers, a lot of people that was connected with labor. And this old gentleman, a Mr. Handy, was in the pressmen's union, and he paid my tuition for the Southern Summer School.

[...], he might have come here on business. I just don't recall when I met that man, but he was a real old man, and he was interested in the labor movement. He had something to do with the Pressmen's Home in Nashville, Tennessee. He might have been on the board of directors or something. I suppose different people that was interested in the labor movement put up fellowships for each person that went. There were girls there from North Carolina, Maryland, Virginia, Florida, and Tennessee, I believe.

It was nice. They had public speaking, and English, I suppose. Boy, that really [unknown]. [Laughter] We had gym. But every evening, we always had group singing, and we enjoyed ourselves. We had a good time.

JACQUELYN HALL:
Were they trying to teach you how to be better union members?

CHRISTINE GALLIHER:
[The Summer School teachers were trying to teach us] Just to stand up for yourself and what you felt was right. Yes, that'd be right, better union members, and to maybe take a little more part in the union.
   [...]
Just say, "Well, now, you're all equal, regardless of whether it's an employer or an employee." Now I do remember that. And if you want something, ask for it. They tried to teach you how to go about it, asking for it and not be timid, especially with somebody that would be the boss or so-and-so above you. And you know, I had one foreman. I won't call his name; he's still living. He lives here in town [unknown], but he's had a rough time, too [Laughter], ever since his wife [unknown] went down. He built himself up from a little old [unknown]; he has pretty high pretensions [unknown]. But he'd look at you; if you'd go to the washroom, he'd stand there [unknown] big bully like [unknown] you know, look, that look. He'd look at you like he could run through you. Well, I just looked right back at him. And if I wanted to go to the washroom, I went to the washroom, [unknown] If you know what I mean.
   [...]
He never said a word, and I wouldn't say a word. And if my yarn was bad and I couldn't get off my production and it wasn't my fault, I'd tell him about it. He'd make an adjustment on it. But he was just the type of person that he had that look about him that would scare most people, intimidate them. There are some people like that; they may not intend to be that way.
   [The Strike and Summer School] matured you enough to stand pat for your rights or what you thought was right, and then we had channels to go through to get it. At the starting of it, we didn't have any channels, only just to go down and quit. And everybody started to quit. Well, boy, that was really a mess. I don't know what would have happened if that John Penix hadn't called in a labor organizer.

Source: Interview H-0314 Dave and Christine Galliher by Jacqueline Dowd Hall, Southern Oral History Program Collection, University of North Carolina (#4007), pp. 4–9, 17–20.

CITIZENSHIP

3 National Consumer's League, Why It Should Not Pass: The Blanket Equality Bill Proposed by the National Woman's Party, 1922

> *After the passage of the Nineteenth Amendment, Alice Paul (1885–1977) and members of the National Woman's Party devoted themselves single-mindedly to the passage of the "equal rights amendment" (ERA) formally introduced in Congress in December 1923. Other reformers feared "The Blanket Equality Bill" would undermine the protective legal status accorded industrial women. In this pamphlet, prepared in 1922 by the National Consumer's League (NCL), Florence Kelley (1859–1932) argued against the proposal on the grounds that it jeopardized protective labor legislation including minimum wage laws for women. The ERA did not pass but the Supreme Court struck down minimum wage laws for women in* Adkins v. Children's Hospital, 261 *U.S. 525 (1923) on the grounds that it violated the Due Process Clause of the Fifth Amendment to the Constitution. That decision was subsequently reversed in 1937.*

Sex is a biological fact. The political rights of citizens are not properly dependent upon sex, but social and domestic relations and industrial activities are.

All modern minded people desire that women should have full political equality, and like opportunity in business and the professions. No enlightened person desires that they should be denied the equal guardianship of their children – or that unjust inheritance laws, or discriminations against wives should be perpetuated.

Ostensibly the object of the blanket bill of the National Woman's Party is speedily to assure to all women the foregoing rights, and to free women from all surviving adverse statutes and judicial decisions.

The inescapable facts are, however, that men do not bear children, are free from the burdens of maternity and are not susceptible, in the same measure as women, to poisons characteristic of certain industries, and to the universal poison of fatigue.

These are differences so far reaching, so fundamental, that it is grotesque to ignore them. Women cannot be made men by act of the legislature, or by amendment of the federal constitution. The effort to enact the blanket bill in defiance of all biological differences recklessly imperils the special laws for women such as, for wives, for mothers, and for wage-earners. The "safeguarding clause," Section 4 of the bill, affords no adequate safeguard for these protective measures.

This is no matter of today or tomorrow. The inherent differences are permanent. Women will always need many laws different from those needed by men. Mere equality is not enough.

Blanket Bill for State Legislatures [A]

SECTION 1.   Women shall have the SAME rights, privileges and immunities under the law as men; with respect to

The exercise of suffrage;

Holding of office or any position under the government either state or local or for which government funds or subsidies are used; and with respect to remuneration for services in such office or position;

Eligibility to examination for any position affected by civil service regulations;

Jury service;

Choice of domicile, residence and name;

Acquiring, inheriting, controlling, holding, and conveying property;

Ownership and control of labor, services and earnings within and without the home; and power to recover damages for loss of such labor, services and earnings.

FREEDOM OF CONTRACT, including becoming a party in any capacity to negotiable instruments or evidence of indebtedness, or becoming surety or guarantor;

Becoming parties litigant;

Acting as executors or administrators of estates of decedents; Custody and control of children, and control of earnings and services of such children; Grounds for divorce;

IMMUNITIES or penalties for sex offenses;

Quarantine, examination and treatment of disease;

AND IN ALL OTHER RESPECTS.

SECTION 2.   No disabilities or inequalities on account of marriage shall exist unless they apply to both sexes.

SECTION 3.   This article shall be construed as abrogating in every respect the Common Law disabilities of women.

SECTION 4.   This act shall not affect laws regulating the employment of women in industry.

SECTION 5.   All acts and parts of acts in conflict with any of the provisions of this statute are hereby repealed.

The Courts alone can give final answers to legal questions raised by the blanket bill

It is a grave objection to the bill that it will, if enacted, clog the courts. Confusion and delay will ensue in the enforcement of existing laws, since the effect upon them of this law may be in doubt for years. Meanwhile, pending decision, the enactment of new protective measures in states which have none will be more difficult if not actually impossible by reason of the uncertainty.

Three danger spots in this bill are especially significant, viz:–

The word SAME in Line 1, Section 1;

The safeguarding clause, Section 4, and the repealing clause, Section 5.

The word SAME, used in Line 1 of the bill means "no more, no less, no different, identical." Under this restricting word the courts will be confronted by questions of which the following are samples:–

Marriage

1. Will wives have a legal claim to support from their husbands?
2. Can deserting husbands be brought back and compelled to support wife and child? (They can now, in many states). Upon what basis could the wife's claim rest if this law were in force?
3. The payment out of taxes, of pensions to wives or widows of civilian men is a special privilege of women. Shall widowers have pensions, or shall widowed mothers be deprived of theirs? Under the blanket law prescribing the SAME rights, privileges and immunities, will any third choice be possible?
4. Will the blanket law cancel the appropriations made by several states in 1922, in cooperation with the federal government, for the promotion of the welfare and hygiene of maternity and infancy? No identical appropriation for fathers is thinkable–maternity not applying alike to both sexes.
5. What becomes of the dower rights that women now have in many states?

Sex

6. What are IMMUNITIES for sex offenses? If immunities are to become a part of the law of the states, what will become of
   a. The penalties for seduction?
   b. The penalties for rape?

7.
   a. Will fathers become jointly responsible with mothers of illegitimate children? Or will neither be responsible?
   b. Will illegitimate children have the name of both father and mother?
   c. Will they inherit from both as legitimate children now do? Or from neither?

Freedom of Contract

8. If women are subjected to the SAME freedom of contract as men,–
   a. Will not women wage earners lose the statutory eight-hours day, rest at night, and one day's rest in seven, which they now have under statutes that, pro tanto, limit their freedom of contract?
   b. Could women get for themselves an eight hours law or a minimum wage commission, in a state where these do not yet exist, and where working men do not care to get them because they prefer for themselves negotiations backed by organizations and strikes?
   c. WHY should wage-earning women be thus forbidden to get laws for their own health and welfare and that of their unborn children? Why should they be made subject to the preferences of wage-earning men?
   d. Is not this of great and growing importance when the number of women wage-earners, already counted by millions, increases by leaps and bounds from one census to the next? And when the industries involving exposure to poisons are increasing faster than ever? And the over-work of mothers is one recognized cause of the high infant death rate? And of the rise in the mortality of mothers in child-birth?
   e. If there were no other way of promoting more perfect equality for women, an argument could perhaps be sustained for taking these risks. But why take them? Cannot every desirable measure attainable through the blanket bill be enacted in the ordinary way?

The Safeguarding Clause

"Section 4. This act shall not affect laws regulating the employment of women in industry." The wording of this clause differs from state to state.

Concerning legislative innovations the important point is not the promises made by the advocates, *but what the bill itself says*, and what experience has taught the people who will be affected by it to expect. Until the items of the blanket bill have been passed upon by the courts, what greater value than patent medicine advertisements can any claims for the safeguarding clause have?

The proponents point to the Wisconsin law enacted a year ago as having wrought no harm. But new laws are not like bombs. They do not explode. Women cap-makers can never forget that the Sherman law had been on the statute books for years, and wage-earning men and women had been assured that it could never apply to them. In the end, however, under a decision of the United States Supreme Court, that anti-trust law was the cause of the loss of the homes of hundreds of working class families in a single state and a single industry.

For women new to the field of legislation, however, the term "safeguarding clause" has an attractive sound. They do not know that, in the processes of enactment slow and circuitous, – or like a lightning flash in the closing hours of the session, nothing is more easily lost than a safeguarding clause.

The Repealing Clause

In Maryland, the blanket bill recently passed the House of Delegates without a repealing clause. If the bill were so enacted, would it (by implication) amend or repeal other laws? Opponents of the bill would argue that any attempted amendment of the existing law is futile without a clear statement of the laws to be changed and their wording as amended. Until the courts have spoken, who could know what the law actually is?

On the other hand, if the blanket bill *with* its sweeping repealing clause should pass unchanged, sooner or later the courts would have to decide whether any laws had been nullified and, if so, which ones. If it should then be held in spite of the safeguarding clause, as might readily happen, that the wage-earning women's protective laws had been repealed, the constructive work of years would in some states be undone.

The police power, it is true, would remain, but fresh legislation would be required to give it life. The police power does not act spontaneously. At best it is always passive.

As a part of a blanket bill, the effect of a sweeping repealing clause is incalculable. For an indefinite time it must inevitably endanger statutes recognized by the courts as needed for the health and well-being of wage-earning women.

The Challenge

When will the National Woman's Party answer our enquiry? Is it, as a Party, for or against protective measures for wage-earning women? Will it publicly state whether it is for or against the eight hours day and minimum wage commissions for women? Yes? or No?

It is not reasonable to reply, "we take no stand", when to the minds of wage-earning women the blanket bill is a deadly attack. The attack cannot be minimized by denying it.

Source: *Why It Should Not Pass: The Blanket Equality Bill Proposed by the National Woman's Party, May 1922* (New York: National Consumer's League, 1922), five pages, available at http://alexanderstreet6.com/wasm/wasmrestricted/era/doc21. htm.

4 Carrie Chapman Catt, Poison Propaganda, 1924

As pernicious rumors of a Bolshevik plot to undermine democracy at home circulated, accusations arose against a number of feminist social activists. To that end, the Spider Web Chart, published in 1924, targeted women reformers and organizations they supported. On behalf of the Women's Joint Congressional Committee, Carrie Chapman Catt (1859–1947) and Maud Wood Park investigated and discovered that a librarian in the Chemical Warfare Service of the War Department had compiled false information for circulation. In an article published in The Woman Citizen (May 31, 1924) Catt concluded that [some] industries published these lies aimed at the women's organizations in order to intimidate them and keep them from working towards the abolition of child labor and promoting education and peace.

Some time ago insidious comments upon all educational peace movements and their leaders began to appear in the press. In 1922 there was a wide-spread circularization of the newspapers with a fanciful declaration that the

"Law, not War" day celebrated in many cities was being financed by Moscow, and an especially virulent attack was made upon Mr. Libby, Quaker, of the National Council for the Prevention of War, who was promoting these demonstrations. Many papers reprinted the matter. In 1923 the American Defense Society sent out similar propaganda declaring that Russian communism and American efforts to promote peace were working hand in hand.

From time to time similar attacks have been made upon individuals, any individuals, who have appealed to public opinion on behalf of world peace. The charge has been implied in these stories that various women's organizations, well known and composed of highly honorable memberships, were being financed by Moscow because they were promoting peace sentiment.

On March 15 1924, the *Dearborn Independent* carried an amazing story, continued in the number of March 22, under the starting title "Are Women's Clubs Used by Bolshevists?" These articles asserted that the masses women within the many well-known organizations were being weakly played upon by a few women in "key positions" who were linked to world communism and its aim to overturn all governments. The second instalment [sic] was accompanied by a chart compiled from the Lusk report and connecting the highest and best organizations with socialist-pacifist activities. A definite attack was made upon the Women's Joint Congressional Committee, its seventeen component organizations and many of its members.

This Committee thereupon named a sub-committee, of which Mrs. Maud Wood Park was Chairman, to investigate the source of this attack, although its libelous character would have warranted a suit against Henry Ford, whose paper had published the articles. Quiet and efficient search revealed the astonishing source – the Chemical Warfare Bureau of our own government.

Things sometimes happen in this strange world that are so amazing one's senses are fairly paralyzed by the revelation. This is one of them. Here are women conducting themselves as they always have when they want something which can only be attained by political action, that is, speaking, arranging meetings, petitioning, reading, investigating, thinking, how to abolish war, the world's greatest crime. Yet, in this supposedly most tolerant republic in the world, boasting of its free speech and liberty for all, they suddenly discover that a department of their own government is systematically discrediting them by the distribution of false and libelous charges, which, because of their source, carry abnormal influence. These women, trying to attain their hopes through constructive, educational measures, are accused of being in conspiracy with communists whose aim is the overthrow of governments through revolution. For trying to teach men and women to think, the public is warned to beware of them. They are called Bolshevist – the world's present-day most damning condemnatory epithet – and the bills for distribution of these libels are quite clearly met by their own tax money! Is this America or Russia? Is this the twentieth century or the middle ages?

With facts in hand, the sub-committee of the Joint Congressional Committee did a very ladylike thing: it prepared a letter and took it in person to Hon. John W. Weeks, Secretary of War. The correspondence follows:

Washington DC
April 2, 1924.

My dear Mr. Secretary:
An attack has been made upon the Women's Joint Congressional Committee by means of a chart compiled and circulated by a subordinate in a bureau of the War Department, which is exceedingly irritating to the organizations comprising the Women's Joint Congressional Committee and to the twelve million women voters composing these organizations. They cannot understand why an employee of a government bureau should be permitted, with the knowledge of the head of that bureau, to attack the women's organizations of the country and the women voters in these organizations. They wonder where the funds come from whereby these attacks are made. The following is a statement of the objections which the organizations make to the chart above mentioned:

A. *The Purpose and Method of Organization of the Women's Joint Congressional Committee.*

The Women's Joint Congressional Committee, which is attacked in the chart, was organized in 1920. It is a clearing house for seventeen national women's organizations which have representatives in Washington for the purpose of keeping in touch with Federal legislation of interest to women. The committee, as such, initiates no policy and supports no legislation and no organization joining it is committed to any policy except that of cooperation, whenever possible. The members bring to it the endorsements of their organizations. After a measure has been endorsed by five or more member organizations of the committee, a sub-committee of representatives of endorsing organizations is organized, elects its officers and carries out a campaign of action for the enactment of the measure by the Congress.

An accurate list of the member organizations of the Women's Joint Congressional Committee in 1922–23, the year to which the chart refers, and of the sub-committees is appended.

B. *The Chart.*

This chart has for its caption the heading '*The Socialist Pacifist Movement in America Is an Absolutely Fundamental and Integral Part of International Socialism.*'

1. This heading is scurrilous, libelous and criminal as applied to the Women's Joint Congressional Committee, and we protest strongly against its use in this chart circulated with the knowledge of a branch of the government.

2. At the bottom of the chart appears the following verses:

> Miss Bolsheviki has come to town,
> With a Russian cap and a German gown,
> In women's clubs she's sure to be found,
> For she's come to disarm America.
>
> She sits in judgement on Capitol Hill,
> And watches appropriation bills,
> And without her O.K. it passes–Nil,
> For she's there to disarm America.
>
> She uses the movie and the lyceum too,
> And alters text-books to suit her view,
> She prates propaganda from pulpit and pew,
> For she's bound to disarm America.
>
> The male of the species has a different plan,
> He uses the bomb and firebrand,
> And incites class hatred wherever he can,
> While she's busy disarming America.
>
> His special stunt is arousing the mob,
> To expropriate and hate and kill and rob,
> While she's working on her political job,
> AWAKE! AROUSE!! AMERICA!!!

These verses are scurrilous and libelous and insulting to every woman voter in these women's organizations. We again protest in the strongest terms against the use of them in this connection.

3. In the third place the chart is false and inaccurate in listing the organizations which belong to the Women's Joint Congressional Committee. An accurate list is appended here. Of those listed on the chart the Women's International League for Peace and Freedom does not belong to the Women's Joint Congressional Committee. The Women's Council for World Disarmament does not belong and has never belonged to the Women's Joint Congressional Committee. Yet these two organizations are connected by lines with one of the Women's Joint Congressional Committee and both are included in

the list in the middle column of the chart of organizations belonging to the Women's Joint Congressional Committee. The intention to vilify is perfectly clear.

Again only seven, not all, of the member organizations of the Women's Joint Congressional Committee are participating organizations in the National Council for the Prevention of War. The General Federation of Women's Clubs is not a member of the National Council for the Prevention of War, the National Congress of Mothers and Parent-Teachers Association is not a member, the American Home Economics Association is not a member, the National Consumers' League is not a member, and the Girls' Friendly Society is not a member.

In addition to the heading and the verses, the second offense is in the list of women forming the border of the chart. Here is a list of names of women about whom scurrilous remarks criticizing their patriotism and citizenship are made. As to the truth of these remarks we have no evidence. If not true they are libelous. The point of interest before us is that these names are linked by lines with the Women's Joint Congressional Committee through the Women's International League for Peace and Freedom and the Women's Council for World Disarmament, when neither of these is a member of the Women's Joint Congressional Committee. The intention to vilify the Women's Joint Congressional Committee is perfectly clear and we protest against it.

C. *Author of Chart and Connections With General Fries.*

Investigation has revealed the fact that the author of the chart is known as Librarian of the Chemical Warfare Service of the War Department. When a request for the chart was made of her, the author stated that it must be referred to General Fries. When General Fries has been approached with requests for the chart, these have been referred to the author in several instances. Such a request is known to have been answered by letter from General Fries. The chart is said by the author to have been distributed to various official and private agencies. In other words, the Chemical Warfare Service of the War Department, a branch of the Government, is engaged in this contemptible attack on the women's organizations in the country.

D. *What We Request.*

1. We request a statement from General Fries to the effect that the chart is misleading in general and untrue in particulars and that the War Department has no information with which to support it.

2. We ask, further, that the files of the Chemical Warfare Service be examined and that copies of the above statement be sent to every person or agency or organization to whom the chart has been sent from the address of the Chemical Warfare Service.

We are sure that although this attack has been perpetrated by a subordinate in a bureau of the War Department immediate redress will be made to us. We should like to say, however, that if such redress is not made immediately by the War Department we intend to secure it in some other way. Twelve million women voters in these organizations do not propose to bear this scurrilous and contemptible attack by a subordinate in a government department without redress.

Sincerely yours,
MAUD WOOD PARK.
Chairman Special Committee, Women's
Joint Congressional Committee.

Apr. 16, 1924,

My dear Mrs. Park:

With reference to the letter from your Committee, dated April 2, 1924, complaining of the injustice done your organization by the circulation of a chart by a subordinate in the War Department, you are informed that all the charts complained of in the possession of the Chemical Warfare Service have been ordered destroyed. General Fries has been directed to inform all persons to whom these charts have been distributed from his office that there are errors in the chart and to request their destruction.

I regret that charts containing the errors pointed out by your Committee were circulated by any branch of the War Department.

Very sincerely,
(signed) JOHN W. WEEKS.
Secretary of War.

April 22, 1924.

Dear Mr. Secretary:

Permit us to thank you on behalf of the Women's Joint Congressional Committee for your letter of April 16th, stating that all of the charts to which we objected in the possession of the Chemical Warfare Service have been ordered destroyed and that General Fries has been directed to inform all persons to whom the charts were distributed of the inaccuracies and to request their destruction.

We presume that in informing these persons to whom the charts were distributed of the inaccuracies in them, General Fries will point out the particular inaccuracies to which we objected, that is, that the Women's Joint Congressional Committee is in no way connected with most of the persons to whose activities the Chemical Warfare Service has found objection, and that the caption and poem and other remarks have no bearing whatever on the Women's Joint Congressional Committee. It will be apparent to you that the mere statement that there are inaccuracies in the chart would not have the effect of disabusing the minds of the persons who have seen them of the erroneous impressions of the Women's Joint Congressional Committee which they have received. We therefore request an assurance from you that General Fries will make these specific statements.

We are glad, as we are sure that the representatives of the other women's organizations will be, that we can report your favorable reply to our conventions and that it will enable us to refute the slanders of any persons who hereafter claim to have the authority of the War Department in their unwarranted attacks on the Women's Joint Congressional Committee.

Very truly yours,
MAUD WOOD PARK,
Chairman Special Committee.

At this point, although the incident seems incomplete, probably both sides may "rest their case," the Government having apologized and promised withdrawal of the offending material. It is to be regretted that in its own defense the Joint Congressional Committee could only speak for itself and left the other women, charged by the chart with unpatriotic behavior, out in the cold. It now becomes necessary for them to take up cudgels in their own behalf.

Meantime, the scurrilous articles, somewhat shorn of their sharpest libels, have been reprinted from the *Dearborn Independent* in a leaflet by the Associated Industries of Kentucky (Louisville) and widely distributed by them. Just why should these industries publish this attack upon women? Clearly to intimidate them and prevent something they are sponsoring from becoming law. Is it the abolition of child labor, education or peace?

Women of America, don't get frightened; think. Don't be intimidated; act.

Source: *The Woman Citizen*, May 31, 1924, pp. 14, 32–3, available at http://womhist.alexanderstreet.com/wilpf/doc4.htm.

5 Eleanor Roosevelt, Women Must Learn to Play the Game as Men Do, 1928

Eleanor Roosevelt was appointed along with Molly Dewson to head the Bureau of Women's Activities for the Democratic National Committee in the spring of 1928 following almost a decade of activism on behalf of women and children. She had directed her prodigious energy and talent to writing, speaking, teaching, and organizing others and worked with reformers including Rose Schneiderman, Mary McLeod Bethune, and Carrie Chapman Catt. Her support for Al Smith in his presidential campaign and for her husband in his gubernatorial race informed her reflection on what women could learn from traditional and largely male party politics. The essay serves as a baseline for understanding how Roosevelt would change the role of First Lady (1932–45) and challenge others to reconsider the civil and political rights of the dispossessed.

Women have been voting for ten years. But have they achieved actual political equality with men? No. They go through the gesture of going to the polls; their votes are solicited by politicians; and they possess the external aspect of equal rights. But it is mostly a gesture without real power. With some outstanding exceptions, women who have gone into politics are refused serious consideration by the men leaders. Generally they are treated most courteously, to be sure, but what they want, what they have to say, is regarded as of little weight. In fact, they have no actual influence or say at all in the consequential councils of their parties.

In small things they are listened to; but when it comes to asking for important things they generally find they are up against a blank wall. This is true of local committees, State committees, and the national organizations of both major political parties.

From all over the United States, women of both camps have come to me, and their experiences are practically the same. When meetings are to be held at which momentous matters are to be decided, the women members often are not asked. When they are notified of formal meetings where important matters are to be ratified, they generally find all these things have been planned and prepared, without consultation with them, in secret confabs of the men beforehand. If they have objections to proposed policies or candidates, they are adroitly overruled. They are not allowed to run for office to any appreciable extent and if they propose candidates of their own sex, reasons are usually found for their elimination which, while diplomatic and polite, are just pretexts nevertheless.

In those circles which decide the affairs of national politics, women have no voice or power whatever. On the national committee of each party there is a woman representative from every State, and a woman appears as vice-chairman. Before national elections they will be told to organize the women throughout the United States, and asked to help in minor ways in raising funds. But when it comes to those grave councils at which possible candidates are discussed, as well as party policies, they are rarely invited in. At the national conventions no woman has ever been asked to serve on the platform committee.

Politically, as a sex, women are generally "frozen out" from any intrinsic share of influence in their parties.

The machinery of party politics has always been in the hands of men, and still is. Our statesmen and legislators are still keeping in form as the successors of the early warriors gathering around the campfire plotting the next day's attack. Yes, they have made feints indicating they are willing to take women into the high councils of the parties. But, in fact, the women who have gone into the political game will tell you they are excluded from any actual kind of important participation. They are called upon to produce votes, but they are kept in ignorance of noteworthy plans and affairs. Their requests are seldom refused outright, but they are put off with a technique that is an art in itself. The fact is that generally women are not taken seriously. With certain exceptions, men still as a class dismiss their consequence and value in politics, cherishing the old-fashioned concept that their place is in the home. While women's votes are a factor to be counted upon, and figure largely in any impending campaign, the individual women who figure in party councils are regarded by their male conferèes as having no real power back of them. And they haven't.

Men who work hard in party politics are always recognized, or taken care of in one way or another. Women, most of whom are voluntary workers and not at all self-seeking, are generally expected to find in their labor its own reward. When it comes to giving the offices or dealing out favors, men are always given precedence.

They will ask women to run for office now and then, sometimes because they think it politic and wise to show women how generous they are, but more often because they realize in advance their ticket cannot win in the district selected. Therefore they will put up a woman, knowing it will injure the party less to have a woman defeated, and then they can always say it was her sex that defeated her. Where victory is certain, very rarely can you get a woman nominated on the party ticket.

Of course there are women all over the United States who have been elected to high and important offices. There are three women in Congress; there have been two woman governors; and women sit in various State legislatures and hold State offices. In New York City one could cite several who have not only been elected but who have conducted themselves in office with ability and distinction. But does that indicate any equal recognition of share in political power? Infinitely more examples come to mind of women who were either denied a nomination or who were offered it only when inevitable defeat stared the party leaders in the face.

When, some years ago, it came to putting women on the Democratic State Committee in New York, only two outstanding men openly approved of the move. A number were willing, but a great many more were indifferent.

Governor Smith wanted women on the committee, believing they had something to contribute, and that they should have recognition for what they could do. Quite unlike Governor Smith, many other men come to mind who hold important positions of power in New York State. They deal with the women in a spirit of most deferential courtesy; but as many of us know, they heartily dislike the idea of women mixing in politics, are antagonistic to those who are active, and can be depended upon to do all in their power to render the women's influence negative.

Beneath the veneer of courtesy and outward show of consideration universally accorded women, there is a widespread male hostility – age-old, perhaps – against sharing with them any actual control.

How many excuses haven't I heard for not giving nominations to women! "Oh, she wouldn't like the kind of work she'd have to do!" Or, "You know she wouldn't like the people she'd have to associate with – that's not a job for a nice, refined woman." Or more usually: "You see, there is so little patronage nowadays. We must give every appointment the most careful consideration. We've got to consider the good of the party." "The good of the party" eliminates women!

When no women are present at the meetings, the leaders are more outspoken. "No, we're not going to have any woman on the ticket," declared one leader according to a report once made to me. "Those fool women are always making trouble, anyway. We won't have any we don't have to have, and if we have none, let's get one we understand."

It is a strong and liberal man, indeed, who speaks on behalf of the women at those secret conclaves, and endeavors to have them fairly treated.

To many women who fought so long and so valiantly for suffrage, what has happened has been most discouraging. For one reason or another, most of the leaders who carried the early fight to success have dropped out of politics. This has been in many ways unfortunate. Among them were women with gifts of real leadership. They were exceptional and high types of women, idealists concerned in carrying a cause to victory, with no idea of personal advancement or gain. In fact, attaining the vote was only part of a program for equal rights–an external gesture toward economic independence, and social and spiritual equality with men.

When the franchise was finally achieved, their interest was not held by any ambition for political preferment or honors. To learn the intricate machinery of politics and play the men's game left them cold. The routine of political office held no appeal. One of the most prominent of those early crusaders today gives her energies to campaigning for world peace. By nature a propagandist, it would be impossible to interest her in either of the major parties. Another woman, who donated hundreds of thousands of dollars to the cause, frankly admits she has never even cast a vote. She considers the situation, with women coping with men in the leading parties, utterly hopeless. Like many others, she regards suffrage as an empty victory, equal rights a travesty, and the vote a gesture without power.

An extreme point of view, in my opinion. There is a method – and not the one advocated by certain militants who hold aloof from party politics – by which, I believe, the end of a fair representation and share in control may be attained.

Personally, I do not believe in a Woman's Party. A woman's ticket could never possibly succeed. And to crystallize the issues on the basis of sex-opposition would only further antagonize men, congeal their age-old prejudices, and widen the chasm of existing differences.

How, then, can we bring the men leaders to concede participation in party affairs, adequate representation and real political equality?

Our means is to elect, accept and back women political bosses.

To organize as women, but within the parties, in districts, counties and States just as men organize, and to pick efficient leaders – say two or three in each State–whom we will support and by whose decisions we will abide. With the power of unified women voters behind them, such women bosses would be in a position to talk in terms of "business" with the men leaders; their voices would be heard, because their authority and the elective power they could command would have to be recognized.

Women are today ignored largely because they have no banded unity under representative leaders and spokesmen capable of dealing with the bosses controlling groups of men whose votes they can "deliver." These men bosses have the power of coordinated voters behind them. Our helplessness is that of an incoherent anarchy.

Perhaps the word "boss" may shock sensitive ears. To many it will conjure all that is unhealthy and corrupt in our political machinery. Yet when I speak of women bosses, I mean bosses actually in the sense that men are bosses. The term *boss* does not necessarily infer what it once did. Politics have been purged of many of the corruptions prevalent a quarter of a century ago. In neither of the political parties are there many, if any, such bosses, great or small, as were such common types in the heyday of Quay and Tweed. As things are today, the boss is a leader, often an enlightened, high-minded leader, who retains little of the qualities imputed by the old use of this obnoxious word, but who still exercises authority over his district. I therefore use the word, as it is the word men understand.

If women believe they have a right and duty in political life today, they must learn to talk the language of men. They must not only master the phraseology, but also understand the machinery which men have built up through years of practical experience. Against the men bosses there must be women bosses who can talk as equals, with the backing of a coherent organization of women voters behind them.

Voters who are only voters, whether men or women, are only the follow-ers of leaders. The important thing is the choosing of leaders.

We must be fair, and admit the blame for our present ineffectuality in politics does not lie wholly with the men. If we are still a negligible factor, ignored and neglected, we must be prepared to admit in what we have ourselves failed.

The trouble with many women is that they won't work. They won't take up their jobs as men do and put in seven or eight real working hours a day. They lack knowledge, and at that many won't take the pains to study history, economics, political methods or get out among human beings. If they take a volunteer political job, it is a thing of constant interruptions, with no sense of application, concentration, business efficiency or order. One of the reasons why men leaders so often do not consider as important what a woman says is that they do not feel sure she has been active among the mass of women voters and has learned what they want. In fact, many women do make the mistake of "talking out of a blue sky" instead of going about, mixing with women, and getting their point of view from close personal contact and practical experience. When a man leader says his following want certain things, the men higher up realize that he knows what he is talking about, and that he has gone through his district.

There are two classes of men in politics – those for whom it is a game or relaxation, and those for whom it is bread and butter. These latter are usually small office-holding politicians, bosses of small groups of men. At their head are men who are deeply interested for the good of their country as they see it, and who often for patriotic reasons hold government offices for a time. But you will find as a rule that their first interest is in some other career in which they have made a name, worked their best and hardest, and gained the wherewithal to live and support their families. Politics – public service – is something apart.

This attitude is comparatively rare, however, because most women work-ing in all political organizations are volunteers. Their motives for being volunteers may be mixed. I am far from claiming that as a sex we have a monopoly of disinterested desire to serve our country. Human nature is much the same in men and women. But the fact remains that the great mass of women working in political organizations all over this country are unpaid, and they are so far allowed to do the detail work which bores the men.

In the average home a woman's job is full of interruptions; and so, unless she sets out to methodize her life, she is apt to go through many wasted motions. Now many volunteer political workers come out of such unorgan-ized homes. When the children are small, if they have little help in their homes, the mothers cannot do outside work. But as the children grow up – or in rare cases before they are married – they may turn to politics as an outside interest. If they are women of means and have more help at home, they may still have led disorganized lives, for of necessity a home and children make unexpected demands.

I should not want the average woman, or the exceptional woman for that matter, who for one reason or another could not do a public job well, to take one at present. For just now a woman must do better than a man, for whatever she does in the public eye reflects on the whole cause of women. There are women in the United States I would gladly see run for any office. But if we cannot have the best I should prefer to wait and prepare a little longer until women are more ready to make a fine contribution to public life in any office they might hold.

An old politician once objected, "Don't you think these women lose their allure, that the bloom is just a little gone? Men are no longer interested?"

Frankly, I don't know. I imagine the answer is individual. It was once said that men did not marry women who showed too much intelligence. In my youth I knew women who hid their college degrees as if they were one of the seven deadly sins. But all that is passing, and so will pass many other prejudices that have their origin in the ancient tradition that women are a by-product of creation.

Remember, women have voted just ten years. They have held responsible positions in big business enterprises only since the war, to any great extent. The men at the head of big business or controlling politics are for the most part middle-aged men. Their wives grew up in an era when no public question was discussed in a popular manner, when men talked politics over their wine or cigars, and pulled their waistcoats down, on joining the ladies, to talk music, or the play or the latest scandal. Can you blame them if the adjustment to modern conditions is somewhat difficult?

Certain women profess to be horrified at the thought of women bosses bartering and dickering in the hard game of politics with men. But many more women realize that we are living in a material world, and that politics cannot be played from the clouds. To sum up, women must learn to play the game as men do. If they go into politics, they must stick to their jobs, respect the time and work of others, master a knowledge of history and human nature, learn diplomacy, subordinate their likes and dislikes of the moment and choose leaders to act for them and to whom they will be loyal. They can keep their ideals; but they must face facts and deal with them practically.

Source: Eleanor Roosevelt, "Women Must Learn to Play the Game as Men Do," *Red Book Magazine*, 50 (April 1928), pp. 78–9, 141–2, available through The Eleanor Roosevelt Papers Project at http://www.gwu.edu/~erpapers/documents/womenmustlearn.cfm.

REPRESENTATIONS

6 Betty Boop's Bamboo Isle, 1932

Betty Boop was a popular character in animated films in the late 1920s and 1930s. Betty Boop's Bamboo Isle *and* Minnie the Moocher *both released in 1932 portray her as a jazz age rebel. This particular image of Betty Boop fell victim to an industry self-censorship in the Hays Code. These codes had the approval of various women's clubs and civic organizations including the Parent-Teacher Association and the General Federation of Women's Clubs as well as the Catholic Legion of Decency.*

Figure 3.1

Source: Betty Boop in movie Bamboo Isle (1932).
Wikipedia – http://en.wikipedia.org/wiki/File:Betty_Boop.jpg

7 Ethel Waters, No Man's Mamma Now, 1925

"No Man's Mamma Now" announces joyfully the end of a marriage and the beginning of a woman's independence from the man who had dominated her life. Ethel Waters (1896–1977), like Bessie Smith (1892?–1937) and Ma Rainey (1886–1939) before her, celebrated female sexuality. Waters, Rainey, and Smith reveal the distinctly urban experience in contrast to their contemporary Zora Neale Hurston. Ironically, Hurston's writings, often identified with the Harlem Renaissance, represent a particular southern and rural experience.

You may wonder what's the reason for this crazy smile,
Say I haven't been so happy in a long while
Got a big load off my mind, here's the paper sealed and signed,
And the judge was nice and kind all through the trial.
This ends a five year war, I'm sweet Miss Was once more.

I can come when I please, I can go when I please.
I can flit, fly and flutter like the birds in the trees.
Because, I'm no man's mamma now. Hey, hey.

I can say what I like, I can do what I like.
I'm a girl who is on a matrimonial strike;
Which means, I'm no man's mamma now.

I'm screaming bail
I know how a fella feels getting out of jail
I got twin beds, I take pleasure in announcing one for sale.

Am I making it plain, I will never again,
Drag around another ball and chain.
I'm through, because I'm no man's mamma now.

I can smile, I can wink, I can go take a drink,
And I don't have to worry what my hubby will think.
Because, I'm no man's mamma now.

I can spend if I choose, I can play and sing the blues.
There's nobody messin with my one's and my twos.
Because, I'm no man's mamma now.

You know there was a time,
I used to think that men were grand.

But no more for mine,
I'm gonna label my apartment "No Man's Land."

I got rid of my cat cause the cat's name was Pat,
Won't even have a male fox in my flat,
Because, I'm no man's mamma now.

Source: Hazel V. Carby, "It Jus Be's Dat Way Sometime," in *Unequal Sisters: A Multicultural Reader in U.S. Women's History*, ed. Ellen Dubois and Vicki Ruiz (New York: Routledge, 1994), p, 338.

DOMESTIC LIVES

8 Margaret Sanger, Address of Welcome, 1925

Margaret Sanger (1879–1966) was arrested in 1916 for opening a birth control clinic in one of Brooklyn's most crowded immigrant neighborhoods, which violated the Comstock Law. Subsequently the law was revised and Sanger was an effective organizer and advocate for birth control throughout the 1920s. However, the revival of the Ku Klux Klan and the implementation of immigration quotas during the same decade heralded deep-seated divisions within the United States. As Sanger became interested in eugenics, the troubled relationship between birth control and eugenics raised serious questions for those who sought to protect the civil rights of the society's most vulnerable members and also promote women's ability to control fertility.

In the name of the American Birth Control League I welcome you to America and to the Sixth International Neo-Malthusian and Birth Control Conference. I am proud of this privilege. For the first time in the history of these United States men and women have come from other countries to these shores to consider the population problem. . . .

To delegates from all foreign countries, I wish to extend a welcome no less grateful. I want also to apologise – if I may do so without any disrespect – for the obstacles you have had to meet, the obstructions placed in your way by some of the rules and regulations of our American government. Not being familiar with all our customs, perhaps you do not know that the government of the United States has enacted laws aiming to exclude from this country all "undesirable" foreigners. These laws, like all such restrictive legislation, make it difficult for all foreigners to pass unmolested our famous Statue of Liberty. There is a *Quota* restriction. Only so many foreigners from each country are allowed to enter each month. No: this is not Birth

Control, though it is a crude method adopted by the United States to *control* our population. It is the latest method adopted by our Government to solve the population problem. And so you delegates from foreign countries have been made the innocent victims of an unsuccessful attempt of the American Government to cut down the number of "undesirable" citizens. I am glad that you have overcome these obstacles. As convinced Neo-Malthusians I knew you would. I welcome you to this Conference.

While the United States shuts her gates to foreigners, and is less hospitable than other countries in welcoming visitors to this land no attempt whatever is made to discourage the rapid multiplication of undesirable aliens – and natives – within our own borders. On the contrary: the Government of the United States deliberately encourages and even makes necessary by its laws the breeding – with a breakneck rapidity – of idiots, defectives, diseased, feeble-minded and criminal classes.

Billions of dollars are expended by our state and federal governments and by private charities and philanthropies for the care, the maintenance, and the perpetuation of these classes. Year by year their numbers are mounting. Year by year more money is expended. The American public is taxed – heavily taxed – to maintain an increasing race of morons which threatens the very foundations of our civilization. More than *one-quarter* of the total incomes of our States is spent upon the maintenance of asylums, prisons and other institutions for the care of the defective, the diseased and the delinquent. Do not conclude, however, that all of our feeble-minded and mentally defective are segregated in institutions. No, indeed! This is a free country, a democratic country, a country of universal suffrage. We can all vote, even the mentally arrested. And so it is no surprise to find the moron's vote as good as the vote of the genius. The outlook is not a cheerful one.

You, friends from foreign countries who have come here to our greatest city, must have noticed the intricate system of signals which regulates the crowded traffic in our streets and thoroughfares. By this system, the pedestrian is assured some degree of safety. But while the congestion of population in our American cities has forced upon us a system to regulate traffic in city streets and country roads, America as a nation refuses to open her eyes to the problem of biological traffic and racial roads. Biologically this country is "joy-riding" with reckless carelessness to an inevitable smash-up. Is it too late to prevent national destruction? This question we must face – and answer.

France is making a vain attempt to increase her population by awarding bonuses to those parents who will produce large families. The day is here when the Government of the United States should award bonuses to discourage large families. If the United States government were to expend some of its vast appropriations on a system of bonuses to decrease or to restrict the incessant and uninterrupted advent of the hordes of the unfit, we might look forward to the future of this country with less pessimism. If the millions upon millions of dollars which are now expended in the care and maintenance of those who in all kindness should never have been brought into this world were converted into a system of bonuses to unfit parents, paying them to refrain from further parenthood, and continuing to pay them while they controlled their procreative faculties, this would not only be a profitable investment, but the salvation of American civilization. If we could, by such a system of awards or bribes or whatever you choose to call it, discourage the reproduction of the obviously unfit, we should be lightening the economic and social burden now hindering the progress of the fit, and taking the first sensible step toward the solution of one of the most menacing problems of the American democracy. It is not too late to begin.

Source: *International Aspects of Birth Control: The Sixth International Neo-Malthusian and Birth Control Conference*, ed. Margaret Sanger (New York: The American Birth Control League, 1925), vol. 1, pp. 3–7. *Address of Welcome*, by Margaret Sanger, call number MS Am 2063 (647). By permission of the Houghton Library, Harvard University.

9 Alice Hamilton, Poverty and Birth Control, 1925

Alice Hamilton, MD (1869–1970) joined many other distinguished speakers at the Sixth International Neo-Malthusian and Birth Control Conference. Medical, eugenic, religious, and ethical aspects of birth control in the United States and abroad provided topics for discussion. Hamilton pioneered efforts in occupational health and specifically industrial diseases including work-related lead poisoning. Her comments on birth control are rooted in her scientific methods of problem solving.

It must have been some ten or twelve years after I came to live in Hull-House that I was suddenly asked one day in public whether I believed in Birth Control. Without stopping to think I answered at once that I most certainly did and then realized that this was the first time the question had ever been put to me or I had ever formulated my belief even to myself. The answer had been almost automatic, prompted by my daily experiences in a poor community, where I came in close contact with the lives of Italians, Irish, Slavs, Germans and Russian Polish Jews, and saw what unlimited child-bearing meant to them. I had pictures flash into my mind of the gradual slipping down of home standards and the loss of comforts, decencies, under the pressure of too many babies, coming too fast. I could think of promising boys and girls for whom a high school education had been proudly planned and a rise in the world; but who had been forced to leave school at fourteen and take any possible job, because there were so many mouths to feed that the father's wages would not suffice. I could think of dull, weary women, incapable of taking the part of mother as we think of that part, to the always increasing brood of children, who had to bring up themselves and their younger brothers and sisters because the one who should have done it had degenerated into a lifeless drudge. And so I found myself of a sudden an ardent advocate of a cause which till then I had hardly heard of; and all my experience since then has only confirmed and strengthened my adherence.

The reasons which are convincing to those of us who live among and know the poor are perhaps not the same as those which seem most urgent to others. We are not, for instance, moved much by the plea that the upper classes are being submerged by the lower and that the welfare of society demands a redressing of the balance. We know that ability and character are not a matter of class and that the difference comes from the unfair handicaps to which the children of the poor are subject and we would remedy matters by working for equality of opportunity for all children, instead of trying to encourage the propagation of one class and not of the other. The arguments for Birth Control which appeal most to us are based on the welfare of the women of the poorer classes and the welfare of their children.

A woman who starts her married life with a tiny flat and her wedding furniture and practically nothing more, has an enormous problem in budget making before her at the best, one which she usually handles with a skill that amazes me, when I think of her almost total lack of training except what she has had from her equally untrained mother. She can often, perhaps more often than not, make a very fair success out of it for the first years of her married life, while she is strong and the pressure is not too unendurable. She can even plan for better times and look forward to the time when her children will be educated and take good positions and more money will come in and life be somewhat easier.

But if the babies come year after year, she cannot, unless she is a very wonderful person – there are such in the poorest tenements – bear up under the continually increasing burden. The wedding furniture is traded for cheap and less bulky pieces, the children are put to bed in the living room, in the kitchen, anywhere, all attempt at prettiness and order is abandoned, later on even cleanliness may go. It is not that she does not still long for these comforts, she may be bitterly aware of their loss, but the task is too great for any woman and under the strain of childbearing she is no longer as strong as she was, she cannot make even the efforts she did when there were but two or three little ones. With each new burden she finds herself less able to shoulder any burden.

"What Could a Priest Know?"

She does not always submit to this increasing misery without a struggle. Birth Control is carried on in the tenements all the time, but it is not prevention of conception, *that* the women do not understand. It is in the form of abortion, which every woman can learn about if she wishes. Not long ago I invited a group of women to spend a Sunday afternoon with me at Hull-House, all of them married women with large families. The conversation turned very soon on abortions and the best method of producing them, and I was in consternation to listen to the experiences of these women, who had themselves undergone frightful risks and much suffering rather than add another child to the house too full already. These women were all Catholics, but when I spoke of that, they simply shrugged their shoulders. What could a priest know about a woman's life?

All the mistakes and crimes of society bear hardest on the children, and the greatest of all the injustices of civilized society is that which allows the children of one class to face life with less chance than the children of another class, less chance not only of health and happiness but even of life itself. And the larger the family of the poor man the less chance there is for the babies to survive the first year of life. I hesitate to use some figures I collected way back in 1909, but although I have diligently sought since then for more complete and better worked out statistics in this field I have not found them and I am obliged to fall back on a study of the birth rate and death rate under one year of age, in 1,600 poor families in Chicago.

In order to avoid conflicting factors, I compared the large families – eight children and over – with the small families – four children and under – of the same nationality, for all but three per cent of the families were foreign-born. In all, the result was the same, the rate of deaths per thousand births was far higher in the large family group than in the small. For instance, among the Jews the rate was 260 deaths per thousand births in large families – only 81 in small families. Among the Irish the two figures were 291 and 113, among the Slavs, 328 and 122, and among the Italians, 391 and 125. For all the 1,600 families, when divided into those with six children and more and those with four children and less, the rates were 267 deaths per thousand births for the former, 118 deaths for the latter.

Source: *International Aspects of Birth Control: The Sixth International Neo-Malthusian and Birth Control Conference*, ed. Margaret Sanger (New York: The American Birth Control League, 1926), vol. 4, pp. 181–4. *Poverty and Birth Control*, by Alice Hamilton, call number MS Am 2063 (615). By permission of the Houghton Library, Harvard University.

Questions to Think About

1. How did race, gender, class, and geography shape opportunities for women in the workforce between 1920 and 1932?
2. How did unresolved conflicts among politically engaged women affect the strategies of Alice Paul, Florence Kelley, Carrie Chapman Catt and Eleanor Roosevelt?
3. How did the revolution in manners and morals during the 1920s affect the ways that women embraced a more open discussion of female sexuality? Did race, class, ethnicity, or age affect this discussion?

Chapter 4   Work and Family in Times of Crisis, 1933–48

WORK

1 Jennie Matyas and the ILGWU, 1937

Labor activists attempted to organize workers in San Francisco's Chinatown throughout the 1930s. In 1937 a strike against National Dollar Store proved successful. Jennie Matyas worked for the International Ladies Garment Workers Union (ILGWU). She describes the events in a 1955 interview. Her analysis explains both the difficulties in organizing Chinese workers and why this particular event was different. Still, it took much more effort and the threat of jobs being sent overseas to China for white workers to accept Chinese workers in their shops.

Let me tell you how it started. Japan and China were at war. The Chinese people were organized very strongly to help the Chinese back home. Most of the Chinese here had relatives back home. They all felt very loyal to their home relatives and wanted to support them. China was very poor. Sending money back to China was a very serious matter with them.

There was one shop in Chinatown called the National Dollar Factory. The National Dollar is still in existence, but now it is in existency by its stores, its outlets. At that time, while the business of National Dollar was retail, they had this one factory on Washington Street near Kearny. The factory was finally torn down and it's being built into a church by Chinese volunteers.

Well, the people working for the National Dollar worked directly for a Chinese employer, Chinese workers working for a Chinese employer. The factory had about eighty or a hundred workers. Interestingly enough, the workers in the National Dollar factory found themselves underbid by other workers in Chinatown. They found that the work went to other Chinese contractors who did the work cheaper than they did.

There was no unionism anywhere, but the National Dollar factory, instead of having all of the work done by the workers in this large, rather nice factory, sent the work out to contractors where it could be done even cheaper. The workers began to feel very hurt over that. So they got together and formed an organization of some sort, not a union. They just got together in somebody's house and decided to write a letter to the owner of the factory. They never saw the owner, it was run by foremen, but all Chinese. They decided to supplicate the owner to remember that they needed money to send home to China and wouldn't he provide them with more work.

In the meantime, some of them came up to my office and met me and told me about it and asked whether we could do anything to help. Well, I thought heaven had opened up. I assured them that we would do everything in our power to help. By this time I understood that I'd better let the initiative be theirs always, and better just say that I was available and that our organization was very eager to help in any way possible. They didn't want anything more. They wanted to wait for the answer from this employer. They had given some address or another to which the employer was to write....

When these workers from the National Dollar Factory came to see me, they told me that they had hesitated a long time before coming to us because they thought we were a Communist union and they based their thinking on the fact that they knew this fellow and they had suspected that he was a Communist.

There was some pro-Communism and a good deal of anti-Communism. Much more anti- than pro-. The workers in general were much more anti-Communist and they didn't like to come anywhere near the union because they thought the union must be sympathetic somehow, but when they heard that this fellow was discharged, they began to think that perhaps we were all right....

Let me confess that when I first began to work with the Chinese, in spite of all my convictions and beliefs in non-discrimination, the Chinese were people I didn't really know. I hadn't known any Orientals and, without realizing it, I believe I was more influenced by the propaganda about smoking opium pipes than I knew....

I met with the Chinese in their homes a good deal, met them in restaurants after awhile, and always through an interpreter. There were a few who spoke English but the majority didn't. Not a word of English.

Well, finally they began to organize very strongly, and the employer found out that organization was going on. The man who was most active in trying to organize the other workers was an American-born Chinese whose wife didn't speak any English; she was a recent-comer to this country, but while he was American born, his English was not too understandable either. He was a fellow who was greatly respected by everybody in the shop....

In the meantime, this man who was so active in organizing, whose job was not making dresses, but fixing the machines for the dress operators, this man was demoted. His wages were not reduced, but he was given a job that took him away from being in constant contact with the workers. The workers felt so outraged by that. They felt that that was dishonest, that he was being punished, and they came to a meeting and advised me that that couldn't be. They wanted to strike right away....

We got nowhere at all and finally we declared a strike. That was an extraordinary thing in Chinatown. It was the first time, to my knowledge, that there ever was an organized strike of Chinese workers. Fortunately, it was a strike of Chinese workers against a Chinese employer. Here were workers demanding the right to organize and the employer saying "No." White or black or yellow, it didn't make any difference. The issues were the same and the methods to handle them were also the same.

Well, people who thought they knew Chinese tried to discourage me. They kept saying that there was no use, the Chinese were not dependable, the Chinese fought among themselves, they'd never stick to anything, they wouldn't do any picket duty. They tried to discourage me in every possible way.

But by this time, I had gotten to know the Chinese too and I learned to have tremendous respect for their character. I got to feel that if they said something, it was so. I accepted their word for anything they said and I learned also that people were just people, there were those who could be depended upon and those who couldn't be depended upon. But by and large, I was very satisfied that the Chinese were at least as good as the rest of us were. The fact that they happened to be Chinese was aside from the issue. They had their other characteristics, but from the point of view of dependability and integrity and all that, they were certainly as good as anybody else I knew.

The strike was finally declared and it will interest you to know that while I think we demanded something like $16 or $17 a week, I don't remember, actually the hope was that at least they would get $13.33 a week. That was the minimum wage for women in California for a forty hour week, after the $16 minimum had been interpreted as applying to a forty-eight hour week and so there was a proportionate cut. You would be shocked to know how many people worked for much less than $13.33 even. While the figure was brought down to $13.33 and while theoretically, no woman could work for less than $13.33 a week, there was a tremendous amount of chiseling and in shops where the appearances were that the employer wanted to be very law-abiding and pay the wage, there was a tremendous amount of kick-back....

No, you can't fight ... you go to the government and say, "I was employed but I wasn't getting $13.33." Well, they had to take it up and in the final analysis go to court. You can't go to court on behalf of nobody. There has to be a specific complaint. That's why we always point out and contend that the best law is valueless unless it can be properly policed, and unless the workers who use it can be properly protected. While there was a law that said that women cannot work more than eight hours a day and may not work for less than $16 a week for the forty-eight hours, there was no law to oblige the employer not to fire the worker who availed himself of the law. So that the law became a mythical affair actually....

We were out on strike for thirteen weeks, a terrifically long time. For one thing, it proved to everybody that they were very wrong about Chinese not sticking to their intention. Incidentally, this was the one strike I had in which I was able to turn almost everything over to the Chinese members themselves. They arranged their picketing schedules; they arranged who was to be on what shift. It was all very democratically done. They took turns, they lived up to it completely. The first shift had to meet at head-quarters at six o'clock in the morning. We were there and served coffee at six o'clock so that the workers could be on the picket line at seven o'clock in the morning. And these Chinese, who allegedly never get up until ten o'clock in the morning, were there on the picket line.

The whole city became tremendously interested. Everybody was anxious to help these Chinese workers in this Chinese strike and see to it that they won their fight. As a matter of fact, it was essential to picket the downtown stores, the retail business of the National Dollar Store. That involved the Department Store Employees' Union, which had just been organized and was very precarious too. But when the Chinese workers went on strike and the strike was official and was thoroughly endorsed by the Labor Council, because ... we were not yet out of the Labor Council. We were out of the AF of L and out of the CIO, I don't remember the exact chronology, but the Department Store Employees' Union called upon their employees in the National Dollar Store not to go through the picket line. The Department Store Employees' Union was threatened with a suit by the National Dollar Store because they had a contract for the sales people to work. When our people were on the picket line, the clerks refused to go through the picket line and they were supported financially by their union. It was a wonderful thing. Very inspiring. Here were white workers jeopardizing their jobs and their union to help these Chinese workers who were not in their industry, who were in manufacturing, not in selling. . . .

At the end of the thirteenth week, when we had a compromise offer of a settlement which would assure everybody their job and assure everybody the $13.33, I had the time of my life to get the workers to accept that settlement. They thought it was very insufficient, that $13.33 was way below what they ought to have. Some of the members upon whom I relied very greatly and who had become personal friends left the union because they thought the acceptance of such a settlement was a hurt to their pride, it was so much less than they had hoped to get. Others, the more rational among them, argued that if they had a union, bit by bit they'd be able to raise their standards, and anyhow, with a union contract, they'd be able to insist upon work being there and not going out. They would be certain of fair treatment in general and they'd have a right to a price committee to help make the price of the garments. They thought that while it was a modest beginning, it was a very decidedly good beginning. That finally prevailed after hours and hours and hours of discussion whether or not the agreement should be accepted. It prevailed, but some of my very best friends just quit the union altogether, and as a matter of fact, I never saw them again.

But the shop as a whole went back to work under a union agreement and for about a year they did well enough. They had work. Work was not sent to contracting shops, but the employer just couldn't take it evidently, and he decided to close the factory at the end of a year. . . .

I had tried very hard to get Chinese workers into the regular American shops. It wasn't too easy because many of them couldn't speak the language at all, but worse than that, in Chinatown they had machinery that was a little bit different from the machinery they had in the regular factories. For example, with the regular machines on which all the rest of us worked, the garments were pulled right from the person. In the Chinese shops, they were pulled horizontally, so that is a different machine altogether. I don't know how it happened, but that's how it is. And many of the workers were afraid to venture into the other factories, even if they could.

Little by little, we did succeed in getting them into other shops, but the race discrimination problem was not an easy one to overcome. Everybody pulled hard for the Chinese to win their fight, all the rest of our union was very sympathetic. Theoretically, we had overcome race prejudice among the other workers and among employers, but only theoretically. . . .

Source: Oral interview "Jennie Matyas and the I.L.G.W.U." by Corinne L. Gilb, conducted in 1955, Oral Histories Collection, Institute of Industrial Relations, University of California, Berkeley, available at Alexander Street Press, http://asp6new.alexanderstreet.com/was2/was2.object.details.aspx?dorpid=1000689757.

2 Emma Tenayuca, Pecan Shellers Strike, 1938

In January 1938 San Antonio pecan shellers, represented by the International Pecan Shellers Union and affiliated with the United Cannery, Agricultural, Packing, and Allied Workers of America (UCAPAWA), spontaneously went on strike following a cut in wages. Thousands of women working in miserable conditions cracking pecans for as little as 50 cents per 100 pounds initially looked to Emma Tenayuca, a popular and articulate leader of the local Workers Alliance. The strike ended with arbitration and higher wages for the shellers. In this lecture nearly 50 years after the event, Tenayuca recounted some of the influences on her labor activism.

The first thing I would like to do is thank you very, very much. During the thirties when I was working in San Antonio I never attached any importance to my work. I never kept newspaper clippings. Actually, I was too busy organizing and working.

I was born in San Antonio, and on my mother's side of the family I am a descendant of Spaniards who came to Texas and settled in one of the colonies on the Louisiana border. There was a mission established there. On my father's side, we never claimed anything but Indian blood, and so throughout my life I didn't have a fashionable Spanish name like García or Sánchez, I carried an Indian name. And I was very, very conscious of that. It was this historical background and my grandparents' attitude which formed my ideas and actually gave me the courage later to undertake the type of work I did in San Antonio. I had wonderful parents and wonderful grandparents.

I remember since I was about five watching the Battle of Flowers parade in front of Santa Rosa Hospital, right in front of the Plaza del Zacate. I also remember, and I was quite young, the election of Ma Ferguson. Here was the occasion for quite a discussion in my family between my grandfather and my mother's uncles. My father had voted for Jim Ferguson, even though Ferguson had been forced out or impeached for having taken some money from the University of Texas. My parents, my grandfather, and his family voted for Ma Ferguson and the reason for that was because she had stood up against the Ku Klux Klan in Texas.

I have a vision right now, a memory comes back to me of hooded figures. I also remember one particular circular, and it read "one hundred percent White Protestant Americans." That left me out. I was a Catholic and also I was a Mestiza, a mixture of Indian and Spanish. During the time I was growing up, it was very difficult to ignore the conditions in San Antonio. Ours was a close-knit family, and I didn't remember any discrimination, actually, until I started school. A lot of people found out that it was hard to push me around. But during the time that I was growing up here in San Antonio, my home, I had deep roots there and I felt a strong attachment with the past. I went to the mission when I was quite young. I remember we used to hold confessions on the eighth of December, which is the day of Our Immaculate Conception. I remember kicking up the dust and discovering my first Indian arrow, and that of course excited my imagination. My father taught me to fish in the San Antonio River, and it was that river that almost brought about my drowning. I was pulled out of that river with water rushing out of my nose and my mouth. I never learned to swim after that.

I witnessed a lot of discussion on topics such as Carranza and the Cristero Movement. I could not help but be impressed by the discussions inside of my family, my family circle. Also, the Plaza del Zacate was the type of place where everyone went on Saturdays and Sundays to hold discussions. If you went there you could find a minister preaching. You could also find revolutionists from Mexico holding discussions. I was exposed to all of this. I was also exposed to the nature of politics and to the form of corruption. I have mentioned this to some of you whom I know. I remember as a youngster attending a political rally with my father. Sandwiches were distributed and inside the sandwich was a five-dollar bill. I didn't get one, neither did my father. I would like you to know that.

Let me give you an idea of what it meant to be a Mexican in San Antonio. There were no bus drivers that were Mexicans when I was growing up. The only Mexican workers employed by the City Public Service and the Water Board were laborers, ditch diggers. I remember they used to take the leaves from the pecan trees and they would put them on their heads in order to go out and dig ditches. I came into contact with many, many families who had grievances, who had not been paid. I was perhaps eight or nine years old at the time. On one occasion while at the Plaza with my grandfather there was a family of poor migrant workers who came and a collection was made for them. I learned that while the family had harvested a crop, the farm owner who lived somewhere in the Rio Grande Valley had awakened the family at two or three in the morning, and he and his son ran the family from the land with shotguns. I remember this discussion at the Plaza on a Saturday and they decided to go down to the Mexican Consul and place charges against the farmer. People from the Plaza accompanied the family to the Mexican Consul. It turned out that the family was Texas-born. This made quite an impression on me as a seventeen-year-old, a recent graduate from high school.

One of the first groups of organized workers that I remember were women and it is with them that we saw the beginning of the breakup of the type of political organization that existed in San Antonio. And I saw those women herded and taken to jail. The second time that happened,

I went to jail with them. These were the Finck Cigar workers on strike. In both the Finck Cigar and pecan shelling strikes there was a desire to keep the Mexican population, the Mexican workers, as a reserve labor pool which could be used in case of strikes. There was poverty everywhere.

My city enjoyed the dubious reputation of having one of the highest tuberculosis rates in the country. My San Antonio also had the reputation of having one of the highest infant mortality rates. It was these things and also the fact that I had a grandfather who lost his money when the banks were closed in 1932 that made a deep impression on me. I think it was the combination of being a Texan, being a Mexican, and being more Indian than Spanish that propelled me to take action. I don't think I ever thought in terms of fear. If I had, I think I would have stayed home.

We had demonstrations of 10,000 unemployed workers demanding employment. We visited the mayor's office. We staged a strike at City Hall, and it was there that I was arrested. I went to jail many times. A nun friend used to write to me and tell me, "Emma, I have to read the papers to see whether you are in or out of jail."

I believe that what was done there and what had to be done was confronting the power structure. It was the struggles of the Workers' Alliance, the bringing in the people of mutual aid organizations, some of whom had been anarchists. I read all about the Wobblies and in my mind I also became an anarchist.

I had the idea of actually beginning with the Finck Cigar strike, of actually attacking the power structure, but at the same time doing it in such a manner that we did not get beaten up. We didn't go to jail too often you see. It was much easier for twenty or thirty of us to go to jail for three days or seventy-two hours. It was easier doing that than to fight. And we had many demonstrations in San Antonio. We have now a COPS (Citizens Organized for Public Service) organization, and I assure you that it is one of the most democratic and progressive organizations. And a very active organization too.

So in giving thanks I am thinking of the Finck Cigar strikers. I'm also thinking of the garment workers who went to jail and whose strikes were broken. I'm thinking also of men such as Maury Maverick, Sr., of San Antonio. I'm also thinking of the then Texas assistant attorney general, Everett Looney, who came to San Antonio and defended me on a charge of inciting to riot and therefore I was able to spend my twentieth, twenty-first, and twenty-third birthdays out of jail. I thank you very much.

Source: Emma Tenayuca, Speech before National Association for Chicano Studies, in *Chicana Voices: Intersections of Class, Race, and Gender* (Austin, TX: CMAS Publications, 1986), pp. 37–40.

3 Anna Mae Dickson, It's Something Inside You, 1930s

Anna Mae Dickson grew up in Grimes County, northwest of Houston, Texas, where sharecropping, segregation, and sexism dominated economic and social relations. For most of her life she was a domestic in private homes although she worked in a boarding house for a short while during World War II. Interviewed in her early sixties by freelance journalist Wendy Watriss, Dickson described her first job as a maid with a white family when she was in her teens. Her experiences exemplify a particular version of southern life for a poor, black female in the first half of the century.

... "I didn't have clothes like the other children at school because Mama wasn't really able to give them to me. I felt that if I went out and worked I could get some of the things I wanted. I wanted to get out in the world! It was an adventure to get away.

"I had wanted to be a secretary for a long time because once I saw the secretary to the high school principal and that seemed to be the most important job I saw a black woman have. But if you lived where I did you did domestic work or farming, even if you finished high school. If you married you worked for a chance to get on somebody's place that had real good land that you could farm and make good crops. For a black girl there wasn't anything like working at the stores. They weren't open to us at that time, in the late thirties. And I don't remember any registered nurses that was colored working in the hospital then. The only nursing that you did was taking care of people's children. It was easy to find a job baby-sitting, or somebody to cook for and houseclean. So that's what I did. And I didn't leave Navasota because I was scared to go to a big place like Houston. I worked for $2.50 and $3 a week back then in 1938. And by the end of the 1950s I was making $10 to $12 a week.

"I learned to take what opportunities I had. For a long time, for example, I wouldn't work for families that didn't have children because I found out there was more opportunity working in homes where there were children. If you were real good to the children and took care of them well you could do more things and the people would help you. I first got to know Houston because I worked for a family that had a little boy that took sick. They carried him to Houston to stay with his relatives and that little boy didn't want to leave me. So I went, too. The relatives saw how well I looked after that boy, and one day, to my surprise – because I wasn't getting very much from them – they took me to a big store and bought me some real fine underwear. It was the first time I ever had good underclothes.

"You could learn a lot about cooking in some homes. I'll never forget the first time I had to cook and serve a dinner by myself. I was thirteen. It was my first steady job – working summers between school. The lady was having fifteen people for Sunday dinner. She was having these little birds they call quail. I had never seen them before. Well, she showed me the recipe book, explained it to me, and said to have it ready when they came back from church. I was so scared I must have cried the whole time I cooked those birds! But I served them. And that lady didn't let anyone say anything bad about the food or the way I was serving it. I'll never forget that day. That lady taught me everything I know about cooking for white people.

"I felt like this in my work; I felt like if I were trustworthy and were kind to the people I was working for they would allow me more opportunity and help me. I found out it worked to the good. Like another family I worked for, they had a store. Now I always like to know what happens on the inside of things. And stores were important in those days because we got our credit and everything there. So I got this family to let me go and work in the store Saturday afternoons when I finished the meal at home. I'd hang up the garments that customers tried on so the clerk would be free to wait on them. They didn't hire colored girls as clerks then. But I'd watch how they did things, and I learned how those stores operate on the inside.

"Conditions changed from family to family. I've worked for people I would go back and work for anytime because they treated me as a member of the family. They didn't treat me like a servant. You'd try to find the people who seemed like they'd help you get ahead. But actually people chose us most of the time rather than we choosing them. You'd get jobs by somebody recommending you. So I've had to work for people that treated you like they didn't have any feelings for you. Some people, I don't care what you did, it was never right.

"Like this banker's wife, one day I was serving a lunch for her. She had all the bankers there, and she was the only woman. She had her meals served in courses. We had got to the dessert and coffee. I came in with the coffee cups – I used to be able to tote twelve cups of coffee on one hand and serve with the other. Well, I went in this day and it's a wonder I didn't scald two of those men and scald them good! When I set the first cup of coffee down, Mrs. Thompson hollered, 'Anna Mae, goddamnit, you're serving that coffee on the wrong side!' Boy, I just started to shake. One of the men just caught the tray and set it on the table.

"I went back in her kitchen, and I looked at the dishes stacked from one end of that room to the other. I took off her dainty little apron and her dainty little hat piece and folded them up in the drawer. Then I put on my old straw hat, and I walked out.

"When I went into a family I'd tell them the children had to obey me. One family I worked for had a little boy, and I guess he just hated black folks. He would spit on us and do things like that. I said to the lady, 'Now I want to tell you there's one thing I cannot tolerate: I cannot stand for anybody to spit on me. If he does that you may hate me for the rest of your life, but I will whip him good.'

"Well, one day I went to work, and I was wearing one of those blue uniforms. And, girl, when I ironed one I thought it shouldn't have a wrinkle in it anywhere! So I thought I was looking pretty cool that day. The lady was sick when I got to work, and she asked me to dress the little boy for school. I dressed him and brushed his hair. When I turned around he spit on the back of my dress. I grabbed him down in that bathtub and whipped him good with a rough towel he had there. His mother started yelling, 'Are you whipping him?' I said, 'I sure am!' She started to say something, and I said, 'Don't bother, I'm leaving anyway.' I left and never went back.

"Another time I was called a thief. You know that is something you never want on your record. Stealing is one thing I never did. I never even wanted to break anything.

"Well, I was working for this schoolteacher, Mrs. Reagon, and she had some beautiful pocket handkerchiefs. One Sunday she went to church and later on she couldn't find the handkerchief she took with her. She said, 'I know I came home with that handkerchief, Anna Mae. I know you got it.'

"Oh, my God, I just flipped! I started yelling at her, telling her what I thought, and you could hear me down the road! 'If I were stealing and I had to take a pocket handkerchief, I'd be a pretty poor thief,' I told her. 'What in the world would I do with one of your pretty little handkerchiefs, other than wipe my sweat with it? If I were stealing I certainly wouldn't take something that you'd miss right away.' I quit right then and there and walked out.

"Her daughter came up to the house before I left and said she would look for it because she didn't believe I took it. Sure enough they found it the next day in Mrs. Reagon's coat sleeve. Mrs. Reagon called me at home and said she and her husband would like me to come back to work. I said, 'I'm glad you have cleared my record, but you'll have to find yourself another Anna Mae, because this one won't be back.'

"When you grow up into something all your life, you don't always think about the negative side. Like coming in the door – all our lives we'd been going to the back door, so I never fretted much about it. But some things did bother me. Why could I go out the front door to sweep the porch but couldn't go through that front door for any other reason?

"Or you would go in the kitchen and make biscuits and rolls for people because they weren't buying bread in those days. Now you know you got to put your hands in it to make it. All right you'd make the bread and then after it would get brown and ready to eat, but they wouldn't want you to put your hands on it. And it was the same thing with meat. You could touch the meat before it was cooked, but after it was done, don't touch it! Oh, that would get me mad!

"But you'd go on because you needed the work. There were mornings I hated to go to work. I'd be saying to myself, 'Why don't they do their own work? I do mine, why don't they do theirs?' Then I'd get angry with myself – thinking about dropping out of school, thinking if I had gone on to school maybe I wouldn't have to be doing this kind of work. Wouldn't have to be going to the back doors to work.

"You did what you had to and didn't feel sorry for yourself. We just had to make a living and that was the only way to do it."

Source: Interview by Wendy Watriss in *Speaking for Ourselves: Women of the South*, ed. Maxine Alexander (New York: Pantheon Books, 1984), pp. 136–39.

CITIZENSHIP

4 *New York Times*, Women Will Form a Ferry Command, 1942

Women Airforce Service Pilots (WASPs) served as civil servants rather than as part of the United States military. The women who were accepted into this service had extensive flying hours and pilots' licenses. Many had been flying since they were 16. Several were college graduates and some were wealthy. Under the command of aviatrix Nancy Harkness Love, they ferried and tested planes but did not serve in combat. The WASPs were deactivated in December 1944 under pressure from male civilian pilots and veterans' groups and were not eligible for GI benefits until a Congressional act in 1977.

WASHINGTON, Sept 10 – The Army Air Forces today formed a Women's Auxiliary Ferrying Command, although withholding military recognition from the service.

A War Department announcement said that the command would begin with about fifty women, of whom ten would do administrative work and forty would fly airplanes.

The commander of the squadron will be Mrs. Nancy Harkness Love, 28-year-old pilot and the wife of Lieut. Col. Robert M. Love, Deputy Chief of Staff of the Air Transport Command. While Mrs. Love was referred to as "commander" and the group was designated as a "squadron," it was stipulated that the members will have only civil service status. They will be paid salaries of $3,000 a year.

The Air Transport Command ferries airplanes from factories to the Air Force fields here and abroad. While its regular members fly all types of planes, the women initially will be limited to handling training and Haison type of airplanes within the United States.

Requirements Are Given

Minimum requirements for candidates for admission were stated as including the following: Age between 21 and 35 years inclusive; high school education; commercial license with 200 horsepower rating; not less than 50 hours of certified flying time; American citizenship and cross-country flying experience.

Women pilots were asked to submit applications to the Air Transport Command, Army Air Forces, War Department, Washington. Applicants will be examined and engaged for probationary periods, during which they will be given special instruction.

Mrs. Love has been flying for twelve years and has logged more than 1,200 hours of flying time. She has passed tests qualifying her to handle planes with engines of 600 horsepower, is an expert in flying with instruments and also is rated to fly seaplanes.

She began flying while attending Milton Academy and continued to gain experience while attending Vassar College, organizing student flying clubs.

In 1935 Mrs. Love went to work for the Bureau of Air Commerce as one of a group engaged to place air markers in the principal cities of the country. By 1937 she was a test pilot for airplanes and, according to the War Department, contributed to "the development of the tricycle landing gear on safety planes, a gear now used on most medium and heavy bombers."

Mrs. Love first engaged in ferry operations as one of the original group of pilots who flew airplanes manufactured for Britain early in the war to the Canadian border.

5 Sue Kunitomi Embrey Describes her Experience as an Internee at Manzanar, 1940s

Sue Kunitomi, identified as a Nisei Activist for the Japanese American Project, documented life before, during, and after World War II from a uniquely female perspective. For a while, she worked as managing editor of the Manzanar Free Press, *published by the internees at a relocation camp where Japanese and Japanese Americans were sent in the spring of 1942. Her heightened awareness of politics, civil rights, and the injustices of internment frame her observations about the revolt at Manzanar in December 1942. Her interview is part of a project that commemorates how Japanese Americans endured the evacuation, detention, and restrictions of their civil liberties during the war years.*

I was born in Los Angeles, California, on January 6, 1923. My parents came from the same village in Okayama, which is in the southern part of Japan. My mother was a picture bride....

He [Father] was running a small business which he called a transfer and moving company. A lot of that was involved in Little Tokyo, where they moved people from one house to another, or into the city from the country. Toward the end of 1937 and 1938, many people started going back to Japan. Those who had come as immigrants worked to return home because of a real possibility of a war between the United States and Japan. So my father did a lot of packing and shipping and taking crates and boxes to San Pedro Harbor, where the Japanese ships came in. Many people took their American-born children with them. Toward the end of 1938, a week before Christmas, in fact, my father was returning home after delivering some flowers to a wedding out in the San Fernando Valley. We never found out what happened, but evidently the panel truck he was driving overturned, and he died of a skull fracture.

He died toward the end of 1938. So that left my mother with all these children. My two older brothers were working. But the rest of us were all in school.

...My father was not a very good businessman. He left a lot of uncollected bills, and she [Mother] went out and collected them. She would say, "You owe me this. My husband is dead. I've got to take care of my kids." This was the first time my mother actually left the house to do anything in terms of business, because she had been very involved in raising the kids....

I lived east of Little Tokyo and there was a little grammar school, the Amelia Street School, that went from kindergarten to the eighth grade and about 90 percent were Japanese kids. The rest of the students came from a few Chinese families and some Mexican American families. It was kind of an unusual school, and I guess I have always thought of school as being such a pleasant place. My kids tell me it isn't, and I am a little surprised. But we had a very good staff, I think, and they were always doing things. People say that things like Chicano studies or black studies are innovations in education. We had all that. You know, they used to bring Indians, and they'd have dances and we'd ask them questions. This was an elementary school. On May 5 there was Cinco de Mayo and Japanese Boys' Day, and they used to have people come in from the community or have kids from the school to do these programs. We actually had a cultural program all year round that emphasized the different ethnic groups. This was something that I found very unusual....

I graduated from high school in January of 1941. And there was talk at that time of the war starting....

Our next door neighbors decided to go back to Japan, and they had a small grocery store. My mother said she had always been business-minded and she would like to take a chance and buy the store from them and run it. I just happened to be the one that was not working. I'd just finished high school, so she said, "Why don't we try it? And after your sister finishes, if you want to do other things maybe you can go into that." So we bought the store in April of 1941, and our neighbors decided to go back to Japan. And of all places, they went back to Hiroshima, with a boy and a girl. The girl had already finished high school and the boy was still in high school, and I think they had a younger daughter. So, we borrowed some money and bought the store, and my mother and I ran it until April of 1942 when we sold it to be evacuated. My brothers were all working and my one brother was going to what was known at that time as Los Angeles Junior College. I sort of ran the store with my mother and so I didn't get back to school at all. Then we were sent to Manzanar, and then from Manzanar I went to Madison, Wisconsin toward the end of 1943....

In the beginning they wouldn't allow the Issei to take any kind of office because of the fact that they were classified as enemy aliens and the United States government was not supposed to have them do anything that might put them in jeopardy with their own country. But when the Issei began to feel they were not doing anything, the administration, the WRA [War Relocation Authority], began to change some of its policies and give some of the leadership to the Issei. But I think, generally, the camp itself, outside of the administration, was pretty much controlled by Issei.

I think they still did [held the real power]. People talk a lot about the Issei not being able to keep family control and all that, but I think when you come down to it the co-op was run more by Issei than Nisei, and most of the block leaders eventually became Issei, partly because the young ones were leaving. In the first year, I think, there was a lot of control by the Nisei and a lot of policy making going on behind the scenes. But when furlough time came and the young men left to go work in the fields and some to enlist in the Army, then there wasn't anyone left to take over except the Issei.

I had volunteered to help a couple of Catholic nuns who had come into camp and were going to live there and start a school because the school had not been organized. I guess I must have worked a couple of weeks without pay when I found out they were setting up this camouflage net factory and they were looking for workers. So I went and applied, and I worked there.

... You had to be a citizen to work there because we would be making camouflage nets for the United States Army and the administration had evidently signed some kind of contract. There was a lot of bickering about how much we were going to get paid and were we going to get paid, and we eventually did get paid. Then there was a lot of competition about which crew was going to make the most nets and win the watermelon or whatever they were giving away for prizes. Then the first group of furlough workers left, which meant that a lot of the staff people from the *Manzanar Free Press* were leaving, and so I thought it might be a good time for me to apply for a job there. So I applied at the *Manzanar Free Press* and they told me that I could probably get a job there....

... I know I didn't work very long at the camouflage net factory. I started out as a cub reporter on the *Free Press*.

I learned all the routine that went on in the newspaper field. One of the things we had to do was have it already laid out, and then the layout was picked up by someone like Bob Brown, the reports officer, or whoever was making a special trip into Lone Pine to deliver our final copy. It was printed in Lone Pine by the Chalfant Press. So none of us ever really got to see the printshop because we were in a military area and we couldn't get out of camp. Everything had to be typed and in final order. We had to make up the headlines and select the type we wanted from a type book and mark it for the printer so he would know exactly what was to be done. All the photographs would have to be in order with all the pages laid out. The printer did a fairly good job, I think, on every issue....

... I remember that there was a mimeograph machine around with a couple of operators. And then we got two additional typists to do the final draft. What they had to do was to type them in columns so the spacing would be accurate, do it on the typewriter, and then retype the whole thing in final draft....

... We did have, of course, a separate sports staff and then we had the business office part, the ones who collected advertising and took care of the money that came in for the advertising. We had a whole Japanese section and they did theirs on the mimeograph machine because there was no way to get Japanese type. Rather than photographs, they had sketches that one of the artists would do on a stencil. Then they would run it off so it would go inside the English section. We delivered the paper to everybody in camp.

... [The night of the riot] I remember that it was very cold that night, and I recall my mother, my sister and I were standing around that Coleman stove in our barrack when we heard all this noise. And we saw all these people walk by and it looked like a couple of hundred people in the crowd....

They came past our block, and I understand they came from the hospital which was way inland beyond 22. They came past our block and they were going to Block 19, and later I heard they were looking for someone in Block 19 that they were going to beat up, that they thought was proadministration. Whether he was with the pro-American group I don't know, and I don't even know who he was....

I understand that they went through everything, trunks and closets, looking for someone. Then from Block 19, which is right along the edge of the camp, and along a road and beyond that there's a strip of land and then the barbed wire fence and Highway 395. So they evidently went down that road toward the police station, and met the other groups that were coming from the other areas. The next thing I heard, my brother ran into the room and said that people had been shot....

He had thrown his badge and his cap away in the trash can along the way and run home because he didn't want to get involved. He had heard some shots and was very worried that some people had been either wounded or killed. I remember that my mother said that we'll all get shot now because people had protested. And then my younger sister's boyfriend, who had been observing, came running into the apartment saying some people had been killed. He was shaking from fear. We were saying, "Oh, what's going to happen?" You know, "What's going to happen next?" I don't know how soon after that but all the kitchen gongs began to ring, and they rang all night. I don't know what the purpose was, whether they were trying to get everybody to assemble or tell everybody to go inside and stay indoors or what....

I recall that jeeps were going up and down in camp. I wasn't sure whether they were just patrolling or were trying to break up the groups that were trying to meet or what, because my mother was so frightened that she wouldn't let any of us out. She said, "You just can't go out there because they may just shoot at you." By that time I guess it was just my two brothers, myself, my younger sister, my younger brother, and my mother. My oldest brother, who was married, was in a room across the next barrack, and my mother was even afraid to go out and see whether *he* was inside or not and safe! I guess, you know, if she thought that way, I probably figured all the Issei were thinking the same thing. You know, "the military is going to come in and shoot us all." That's all I remember of that night. You knew that somebody had been shot, and then days later different people told me different things about what happened if they were down there, and what they had seen....

I remember that we had an issue [of the *Free Press*] that was sent into Lone Pine on Friday, I think, or Saturday, and it was supposed to come out Monday. The riot happened Saturday night and all day Sunday, I guess, and the military police came in Sunday, so they impounded that issue. We never saw it. And I don't know whatever happened to it; I understood that the U. S. Army just impounded it. The thing I remember about that issue was that it was an anniversay issue, and the staff put "Remember Pearl Harbor" on the first page. I think that was the thing they didn't want distributed. Then there was a suspension of all work until Christmas just about, because the whole camp went into a state of mourning. I guess no one worked except the work crews that were delivering the oil for the stoves and the kitchen crews cooking the food. It was just those two things and the hospital, I guess, because I remember that no one would go to work. And we were told, "If you go to work, you're really going to get in trouble." Then they had the funeral for the two boys outside of camp, and nobody was invited except for possibly the representatives of the blocks and the family. One boy was seventeen. He was just a bystander. He got pushed by the crowd when the tear gas was thrown, and he died there on the spot....

His brother was in the U.S. Army somewhere back East. They had to call for him to get back, so the funeral was postponed until he came. My brothers knew the brother in the Army and also knew the young boy himself. My brothers told my mother but when she tried to remember who he was, she said she didn't remember him, "He's the one who came and laid the linoleum on our floor. He was on the work crew when they came, the one who died." And I think his brother came to see us when he came to camp, because my brothers knew him. I don't know who the other boy was. I don't know whether he was involved in the riot. I don't know whether he was also another bystander....

And evidently they got pushed by the crowd and then were shot....

I think the riot involved just a very small number of people.... They were still making adjustments from living by themselves in the city to being very crowded, living with strangers, having no privacy of any kind. And they had a lot of grievances about the food and about whether they were going to get paid. Some people hadn't even gotten paid, you know. Then there was the fact that the Issei weren't really recognized as adult leaders. I think there were so many grievances that they just sort of erupted at that time....

I think there was a lot of envy toward those who had these jobs as secretaries. Block 1 was the administrative block, and Block 1 also was a very popular place to eat because the cook there was very good. He made, with what he had available, some very unusual things which other block people were not able to eat because their cooks couldn't cook like he could. I remember working on the special editions for the paper; we would be there to maybe ten or eleven o'clock at night, and they would arrange for us to have a snack in the Block 1 mess hall. Some of these snacks were pretty fancy dishes. And the cook did it with what he had, and I think that that may also have been part of it, that everyone was vying to eat in Block 1, because the food was so bad elsewhere. For awhile people used to make the rounds. They put a stop to that because the food would run out in certain blocks. I remember, there was a man, an Issei, who was a very good friend of my father's who used to come around. He was a bachelor who lived in Block 1. He worked in the kitchen. He would bring my mother things like pancakes, and they were so good compared to the pancakes we were getting in our mess hall.

... it's funny how the different restrictions placed on you as a child and the social customs have a very strong influence. I felt guilty, although a lot of people were leaving camp at the time [1943]. A lot of my friends had left and had written to me saying, "Come out here, things are not that bad. At least you'll make a decent living." I still had a lot of mixed feelings. The big problem was that this Issei man I was talking about got very ill about a month before I left, and when he went into the hospital the diagnosis was that he had cancer of the stomach. He had told me that he was leaving Manzanar to go back to Japan, because he had no relatives here. He told me that he felt he had been abandoned by the United States government, that he had worked hard, you know, harvesting crops in California, and he said, "I gave forty years of my life to this country. I'm not a citizen, but now they've taken that away from me and I have nothing left, so I might as well go back to Japan and live with whatever relatives are left." So he had signed up for repatriation to Japan. And about that time I had decided that I just couldn't stay in Manzanar anymore. I was just ... I don't know. A lot of things were happening and I just felt I couldn't spend another year there.

I was finding myself, you know, being left behind when people were leaving from Manzanar, from the *Free Press* staff. And I guess, a lot of it had to do with having gone to this elementary school, because I really felt that there were areas where I could work if I weren't so restricted. Maybe a lot of it had to do with getting away from home, and possibly going somewhere I could at least find a job. And I was still thinking about going to college.

Two of my boyfriends got sent to other camps and I sort of gave up after that! (laughter) I also met a couple of MPs who were in the post office examining packages for contraband, and one of them happened to be from Long Beach, California. He had been all over – been to Europe, you know, and had lived in New York. Every time I'd see him, he'd tell me, "There's so many good things happening back there. There isn't the kind of prejudice you find in California. People are different. Go out there, and find these people, find a job and start a new life for yourself. Maybe your family can join you, because this is no place for you." So I was getting a lot of this from the Caucasians. I met a couple of teachers who were giving me encouragement, I guess because I was out a lot looking for stories and happened to have the kind of contacts that other people didn't have. I found myself in a position where I was pulled by the fact of my mother being a widow with her sons going out and going to the service. She was going to be left behind with my younger sister, my brother, and an older sister who had tuberculosis and who was in Olive View at the time. My brother was in Chicago, and he was sending me letters saying, "There are jobs, girls can find jobs here, and the pay is good, and you can live with me and we can send money back to Mother." So all of these things were happening, and this man was in the hospital dying of cancer of the stomach. My clearance came through, by the way, at that time. So Mr. Heath was the relocation officer at the time, and my sister was his secretary. So I was sort of in on some of the opportunities that were coming in. I went in, and I said, "Well, what am I supposed to do now? I got my clearance." He said, "Well, there's a YWCA in Madison, Wisconsin, offering a month's room and board until you find yourself a job and an apartment. If you want to stay there, they'll have room for you. Would you be willing to take it? They're doing it for two girls." So I thought, well, that would be a chance for me to get back on my feet. A month is a long time, and I can find a job there. And I had known some nurses who had gone to work in Wisconsin General Hospital there. They were sending letters. So I thought that would be a fairly good place to go. So I decided to go.

I had a lot of fears about going to college, and one of them, I think, still lingers. It's what my father said to me before he died. He said that as a woman and as a Japanese I have two strikes against me, and that I really shouldn't even consider college at all. And this was when I was leaving the eighth grade to go into high school and I was asking him all kinds of questions, like what he thought I should take. And, of course, what he said to me was typing, bookkeeping, and shorthand, so that at least I could make a living until I got married. You know, he was, I think, very practical. He had gone though a lot himself; nobody ever helped him when he came to the United States. He had to struggle and raised his family and had his business. And to him, it was a dream for me to even consider college.

Source: Interview with Sue Kunitomi Embrey by Arthur Hansen, August 24 and November 15, 1973, for California State University Oral History Program. Japanese American Project, Part I: Internees, ed. Arthur A. Hansen (Westport: Meckler, n.d.), pp. 97, 99, 101, 107, 116–7, 125–7, 130, 132–3.

REPRESENTATIONS

6 Rosie the Riveter, 1942

On the eve of World War II, women comprised one-fourth of all workers. The majority of these women supported themselves and their children and did not have a husband to help them. The Office of War Information stressed the opportunities that war work presented to American women like Mighnon Gunn in Cook County, Illinois. Created in July 1942, the Office of War Information cataloged this picture and caption in its overseas picture division in 1944.

Figure 4.1   Production. Aircraft Engines. Reconditioning used spark plugs for reuse in testing airplane motors, Mighnon Gunn operates this small testing machine with speed and precision although she was new to the job two months ago. A former domestic worker, this young woman is now a willing and efficient war worker, one of many women who are relieving labor shortages in war industries throughout the country. Melrose Park, Buick Plant.

Source: America from the Great Depression to World War II: Black and White Photographs from the FSA-OWI, 1935–1945, American Memory, Library of Congress; Ann Rosener, photographer, available at http://memory.loc.gov/cgi-bin/query/D?fsaall:26:./temp/~ammem_yzm2.

7 Still Image of Joan Crawford from *Mildred Pierce*, 1945

Mildred Pierce (Warner Brothers, 1945) is part psychological thriller, part murder mystery, and part woman's film. Six writers, most notably Catherine Tunney, worked on the screen adaptation of a James Cain novel. Joan Crawford's academy-award winning performance reflected the emotional complexity of the main character whose disappointment in an out-of-work husband leads to divorce and a roller-coaster ride of hard work, success, and glamour that culminates in her destruction as mother and businesswoman. Crawford projected multiple images of femininity in this role that revealed cultural tensions over women's proper place in the social order.

Figure 4.2

Source: *Mildred Pierce* Wisconsin Center for Film and Theater Research. Courtesy of Wisconsin Center for Film and Theater Research.

DOMESTIC LIVES

8 Tennessee Valley Authority, Office Memorandum
Re: Mattie and Jim Randolph, 1936

*The Tennessee Valley Authority (TVA) brought electricity to the region
and the potential for modern appliances that would ease the burden
particularly for rural women. Having already been displaced from their
first farm, Mattie Randolph and her husband Jim refused to sell their 14 acres
of land for $530. A caseworker from the Family Removal Section attempted
to negotiate with the Randolphs on several occasions. Her memorandum to
the legal division in Knoxville blames Mrs. Randolph for the impasse. An
alternative assessment of Mattie Randolph, however, emerges between the
lines in this passage.*

TENNESSEE VALLEY AUTHORITY

OFFICE MEMORANDUM

To: Mr. Alvin Zeigler, Legal Division, Tennessee Valley Authority, Knoxville
From: Greta Biddle, Family Removal Section, Norris
Date: January 9, 1936
Subject: TENNESSEE VALLEY AUTHORITY CONTACTS WITH MAT-
TIE AND JIM RANDOLPH TRACT NO. 566

(1)   Attitude antagonistic from beginning.
(2)   Tennessee Valley Authority offered to buy fourteen acres for $530
      [July 2 1934]
(3)   Randolphs refused to sell or consider selling.
(4)   Condemnation suit [filed 1/9/35].
(5)   Order of Possession granted Tennessee Valley Authority [1/11/35 or 8/
      10/35].
(6)   Refuse to allow Reservoir Clearance men to come on property.
(7)   Threatened man with shot guns.
(8)   University Relocation Division offered service in selecting new location.
      Randolphs refused to go look at another place or consider buying.
(9)   Family Removal Section of Tennessee Valley Authority offered to help
      in many ways. Randolphs flatly refused any assistance or to take
      seriously the threatening menace and danger of rapidly rising water.

(10)   Reluctantly submitted to the erection of a tent in case of flood but would not accept responsibility for it [Nov. 20 1935].

(11)   The Legal Section of Tennessee Valley Authority prepared papers for Mrs. Randolph. One document was the Randolph answer prepared for her in the condemnation suit against Tennessee Valley Authority leaving a blank for her claim and a place for her witnesses. She refused to accept it. They also offered her an order to approve the withdrawal of $475.00 leaving the rest in bank, allowing her freedom to come into court and to show the added value of her land. This was refused, answering to the effect "they had beaten her out and they might as well take it all" [Dec. 12 1935].

(12)   Unreasonable attitude demonstrated by Mrs. Randolph's proposal to remain permanently in home even after covered with water.

RANDOLPH, MATTIE & Jim – TRACT #NR 566

REASON FOR VISIT

(Biddle)
On December 10 Mr. Ziegler of the Legal Division stated that he had been requested to resort to legal methods, eviction, if necessary, in order to get "Mattie Randolph out." Mrs. Barber and Mr. Wilson requested that I go to see Mrs. Randolph before legal action was taken.
12/11/35

HOME

This family live in a two-room shack, one room serving as a living and bedroom, et al, which is of logs. A lean-to kitchen put together with planks has evidently been added on. The house is located in a narrow ravine, or hollow, on a steep bank of the Powell River. There are no windows in the dwelling, but a plank placed over a large space between the logs serves the purpose. A stove and three double beds, about four chairs, and a small table are in the one room; a stove and two tables in the kitchen. The house is in very bad condition, cold air coming through large cracks in the walls and holes in the floors. There are many spaces in the roof where the sky can be seen. The cowshed is under the house. There are no toilet facilities, and during the worker's visit, Wanda, the four-year-old, proceeded to use the front porch for this purpose.

FAMILY

Mattie, Jim, and six of their seven children live in this two-room house. Mrs. Randolph, a rather small, stocky, fiery, brown-eyed woman, is evidently the dominating member of the family. Jim, her husband, is a quiet, easy-going fellow, having little to say on any family problem, even when asked "What do you think?" by his wife. The six children seemed happy, but why or how is the question. They were dirty, needed more warm clothes, they had no play things at all. Wanda, the four-year-old, was quite excited when the worker showed her that chips of kindling could be used for blocks and houses and bridges can be built with them.

This family was accepted on relief April, 1934 and received aid until Mr. Randolph was transferred to [work relief FERA], September, 1934. At this time he presented a doctor's certificate showing he had diabetes and heart trouble, so Mrs. Randolph, though pregnant, started working October, 1934, and did sewing on a sewing project through April, 1935. Her baby was born in June, 1935. [FERA] records give this family a bad recommendation for cooperation, industry, or resourcefulness. They state Mrs. Randolph has always been a bad housekeeper. However, the case worker, in her most recent entry, said that the Randolph home was the cleanest on her last visit that she had ever seen it. It would seem to the worker that Mrs. Randolph has really been "cleaning up" for her visits from the TVA officials and has been enjoying somewhat the notoriety she has gained and the trouble she has caused. Mrs. Randolph has rheumatism and is really not strong, owing to the birth of seven children during the past fifteen years. The girl seven is cross-eyed and has a skin trouble over her body. The children have gone to school very little and the family belongs to no church. The mother uses snuff or tobacco, as does the thirteen-year-old daughter. The latter is an expert spitter. It is evident that this family has a very low standard of living.

HISTORY

This family, or rather "Mattie, herself", has been called the A-1 bluffer and problem case for the TVA. The family's attitude has, from the beginning of TVA, been one of antagonism. They have never shown any willingness to cooperate with any person connected with TVA. Mrs. Randolph told worker on first visit, "I'll stay here until the water comes up and float down with it when it does." The crux of the problem is the fact that Mattie, who really owns the land, feels the TVA should pay her more than $530 for her fourteen acres of land. She also felt the appraisers "had taken advantage of her and Jim." According to the story she told, the other people around her had bought off the appraisers, but she and Jim didn't say a word to them when they came by their place. The visitor then said, "Well, you really don't feel you were so underpaid for your own land, but that you didn't get what you thought you should in comparison with what other folks got." She answered, "That's it."

RELATIVES

Mrs. Randolph's mother, Nan Wallace, her stepbrother, Clarence Wallace, and her own fifteen-year-old boy, live about two miles from the Randolph home, address Route 3, LaFollette. Another brother, Roscoe, lives in Indiana. Her father, _____ Heatherly, is a former reservoir family and moved to Blount County. It is doubtful if any help could be given by these relatives, but they should be contacted. Mr. Randolph has no kinfolk that could aid.

EMPLOYMENT

This family formerly lived at Westbourne and Caryville, both coal mining camps. Mr. Randolph worked at the coal companies in both places. In 1926 they worked on the farm of H. [C.] Irwin. Here they sharecropped, and according to Mrs. Randolph, she was able to buy "twenty-five to thirty acres" from Mr. Irwin. (Mrs. Randolph still claims Mr. Irwin gave her this amount and that the TVA is paying for only fourteen acres). The Randolphs moved to their river front shack in 1930, and evidently from 1930 to 1933 they got along quite well, cultivating about three acres in corn, beans, and potatoes, putting out a few fruit trees, building a fence or two. In 1933 or 1934 Mr. Randolph evidently lost all spirit to work, the domination in his home becoming irritating. He then asked for relief and family has gotten bi-monthly grocery orders until last summer, when unemployables were cut off (Mrs. Randolph having a new-born babe, Mr. Randolph claiming he was too sick to work).

PROBLEM

The big problem in this family is a psychological one. Mrs. Randolph, as said before, is a very domineering, tyrannous, blustering soul. She has been accused of threatening several TVA men with a shotgun. Her stubborn, obstinate manner has possibly put up a strong wall to any possible success-ful contacts. Another problem is the fact that neither she nor any of her family have any idea as to the meaning of the TVA, why it came in and broke up her community, why they moved her neighbors away, why they closed the gates of the "darn dam" and backed up the water over her garden just at the time she wanted to pick her beans, but they didn't fool her, as she said with her hands on her hips, for she just took her shoes off, waded down in the water, and picked the beans anyway. In her mind, the TVA had ruined a good farming country, coming in there and upsetting everything. She furthermore stated that the water wouldn't be up for two or three years and she saw no reason for moving now. These facts and beliefs have, to some extent, been mishandled by some folk, for when a positive creature goes in and tells Mrs. Randolph, "You bluffed everybody in the TVA, but you're not going to bluff me," this only increases the antagonism and belligerent attitude. She furthermore claims to have been told that "she was going to be kicked off over two years ago" and then she retorts, with chin in air, "I'm still here." Mrs. Randolph has been "egged on" by some neighbors and others to believe she can get more money from the TVA and she is doing her durndest to get more, but no one has explained to her that she is going about it in the wrong way.

RESOURCES

This family could draw out $530 from the bank for their land, but Mrs. Randolph says "If they want to beat me out of it, they might as well take it all. I ain't going to take a cent of it." They have about 25 chickens, two pigs, two cows, one bull, and one calf. Other than material resources, there is a real lack of family capabilities to achieve any progress. They have had very limited experiences, do not want a better place to live, or electric lights, or a bath room, or any other high-falutin thing. Their real needs are great, but their desires have been thwarted.

PLANS FOR MOVING

This family absolutely refuses to even talk of moving. However, the worker made a friendly, informal contact on first visit and asked Mrs. Randolph to be thinking of any way visitor could be of help in working out her problems, which visitor believed Mrs. Randolph felt keenly. Worker left family, promising to return the next week and help them in any way they might suggest.

Source: Tennessee Valley Authority, Office Memorandum, Subject: Tennessee Valley Authority Contacts with Mattie and Jim Randolph, tract m. 566, available at http://www.archives.gov/southeast/exhibit/8.php.

9 Eudora Welty, To Play Dolls, 1936

Growing up female in Jackson, Mississippi, reportedly the poorest state in the Union, in the mid-1930s posed challenges for white and black. "To play dolls" reveals some of the imaginary world of these young girls captured in the candid snapshot taken by Eudora Welty (1909–2001) in 1936 and chosen by her for publication as part of an album in 1971. Welty traveled throughout her home state as a publicity agent for the Works Progress Administration. The people she met also inspired many of her characters in her prize-winning stories.

Figure 4.3

Source: Eudora Welty, *One Time, One Place: Mississippi in the Depression. A Shapshot Album* (New York: Random House, 1971), p. 46. © Eudora Welty/ Corbis.

10 Letters from Polly to William Crow, 1944 to 1945

Polly Crow and her young son Bill moved from Pensacola, Florida to Louisville, Kentucky, after her husband was shipped to Europe in the summer of 1944. In Louisville she lived with her mother and sought work in a defense plant. Before the war she had worked as a bookkeeper for the telephone company. The letters that she sent to her husband describe the challenges of work and family that many women war workers encountered when taking on new jobs and responsibilities.

Pensacola, June 8, 1944

Darlin':

... After I get settled in Louisville I'm thinking seriously of going to work in some defense plant there on the swing shift so I can be at home during the day with Bill as he needs me – would like to know what you think of the idea, if you can write. Of course, I'd much rather have an office job but I couldn't be with Bill whereas I could if I worked at nite which I have decided is the best plan as I cain't save any thing by not working and I want to have something for us when you get home so you can enjoy life for awhile before going back to work and Bill and I want all of your time too for awhile so's we can all three make up for lost time.

Gotta scoot as I have several more chores to do.

I love you, Darlin', Polly

Louisville, June 12, 1944

Darlin':

You are now the husband of a career woman – just call me your little Ship Yard Babe! Yeh! I made up my mind that I wanted to work from 4:00 p.m. 'till midnight so's I could have my cake and eat it too. I wanted to work but didn't want to leave Bill all day – in the first place it would be too much for Mother altho' she was perfectly willing and then Bill needs me. This way Mother will just have to feed him once and tuck him in which is no trouble at all any more as I just put him in bed and let him play quietly until he's ready to go to sleep and he drops right off.... I finally ended up with just what I wanted. Comptometer [calculator] job – 4:00 till mid-nite – 70 cents an hour to start which amounts to $36.40 a week, $145.60 per month, increase in two months if I'm any good and I know I will be. Oh yeh! At Jeffersonville Boat and Machine Co. I'll have to go over to Jeffersonville, Ind. which will take about 45 minutes each way. Hope I can get a ride home each nite as that's the only feature I dislike but I'm not gonna be a sissy. If I can't get a ride, I'll get tags for our buggy and probably use it ... If I don't need it for work I may not get them but will just have to see how things work out. Want to take Bill out swimming a lot this summer so I may need it for that....

Opened my little checking account too and it's a grand and a glorious feeling to write a check all your own and not have to ask for one. Any hoo, I don't want it said I charged things to 'em and didn't pay it so we don't owe anybody anything and I'm gonna start sockin' it in the savings and checking too so's we'll have something when our sweet little Daddy comes home.

Good nite, Darlin'

I love you, Polly

Louisville, June 13, 1944

Darlin':

Just got home from work at 12:30 a.m. Got a ride both ways with one of the girls in the office who lives about ten blocks from here – certainly am glad cause I didn't go for the idea of coming home alone. Like my job fine and it was great fun to get going on a comptometer again. I'm figuring the pay checks as everyone with Jefferson Boat is paid by the hour so that makes plenty of work. I haven't sat in one position and an erect one at that for so long that it was rather hard to do so I made several trips to the water fountain mainly for the exercise. We have 30 minutes for lunch at 7:15 and go across the park to a little cafe which slings out pretty good hash. At about 9:30 we all give the boss, Mr. Toby, a nickel and he goes and gets all a good old ice cold coke which is most refreshing. Haven't counted the office force but there must be about 20 of us in the nite shift. They seemed very generous with my work last nite and couldn't get over the most legible figures I made. They must be used to sloppy jobs or something. I turned over as much work as the other girls and didn't make one single error which they couldn't get over.... Will write you before I go to work each day so's I can tuck me in just as soon as I get home so I get plenty of good old shut eye.

I dreamed this morning that you'd come home on furlough but had to return shortly 'n you were in civilian clothes and had received 4 of ten boxes we'd sent you. I was so glad to see you I almost popped, then I woke up. Shucks.

Good nite, Darlin'

I love you terribly, Polly

Louisville, June 17, 1944

Darlin':

...The gals all got paid last nite. Course I didn't as the week runs from Tuesday to Tuesday. They collect 10 cents from every one and the one whose check numbers show the best poker hand wins the pot, some stuff, eh?

Maybe I'll accidentally win once in a while. Talk about wolves! Baby, the swing shift is overrun with 'em, no one seems to think or care about whether you're married or not, as it evidently makes no difference. However, it does to me....

I love you like H –
Baby, Polly

Louisville, Nov. 6, 1944

Darlin':

...Have an appointment to take the car in Thursday morning to get it simonized. Have to have it in by 10:00 a.m. and it will be ready about 5:00 p.m. so I'll have to pick it up as I don't want to leave it there overnite. The strip of rubber padding came off the right door so I want to get that fixed also. Will cost about $7.00 but I figured I'd better get it done to protect the finish as it hasn't been done since you left. About time, wouldn't you say? Had 6 qts. of anti-freeze put in it yesterday and it's a good thing I did as it was 26 degrees at 7:00 a.m. and everyone will probably make a mad rush for it now. Have used all my gas coupons now up to Dec. 21st and cain't figure how I did it as I've never run short before. I guess the leak must have lost a lot before I discovered it.... That's where my money goes! But I want to take good care of the buggie.... After the simonize job, I shouldn't have to spend any more on it for awhile any hoo. Tiz worth every penny to have it ready whenever we want to go....

"Tiz time to go"
Good nite, Darlin'
I love you, Polly

Louisville, Nov. 9, 1944

Darlin':

...The union came in to-nite. Join or else! The gals have all been in a stew since the maids and porters got their raises as they now make more than we do. A fine thing, uh! yeah! We were ready to take up the scrub jobs around in place of ours. They all, of course, belong to the union, soooo, all the office employees all over the yards joined and we had to too. I always said I'd never join one but I sat right here and did. We, of course, are all supposed to get a raise out of it so I figured I wouldn't be losing any thing if we did, so if we don't then I can always get a job elsewhere. I like it here and like the hours so I don't want to quit and am out for every penny I can get while the gettings good, right? We now have about $780.00 in the bank and 5 bonds which sho looks good to me and as soon as I get the buggie in good shape and all the Xmas extras over then I can really pile it away....

Good nite, Darlin'
I love you, Polly

Louisville, Dec. 5, 1944

Darlin':

There's rumors out that by March 1st there will be no more nite shift in any part of Jefferson Boat as work will be completed by then and they're letting men go over in the yards at the rate of 50 a week and expect to have 5,000 gone by March 1. If it's true then I suppose my greatly enjoyed working career will come to an end, as you know we build L.S.T.s [Landing Ship Tanks, used primarily for invasion purposes] for the Navy and I cain't understand how they can cut down like that with the war still going on. One of the boys in New Caledonia wrote his wife that they heard on the radio that the war with Germany will be over in two months and the war with Japan over by the 1st of June. She wrote him tonite asking from what source the announcement came and if it was just a prophecy. Have you all heard any such sentiments? Twould be wonderful if it is really true but I certainly won't count on it. They would probably find a place for me on the day shift, if I wanted it but I couldn't do that as Bill needs me too much and it would be too hard on Mother to care for him all day. I have enough savings piled up to last me several months and I know if I don't get it done before you return I never will. However by the time I get all finished and you aren't home by then, or at least have hopes of returning soon thereafter, I'll start pounding the pavements again as I gotta save all the money I can now while the getting is good, but I'll just hope and pray each nite that you will be home by next summer at the latest....

I love you,
Darlin', Polly

Louisville, Jan. 30, 1945

Darlin':

Thought for a while this a.m. I would have to take Bill to work with me, or stay at home. He was evidently dreaming a bad dream and awakened just as I was getting up. He wanted me and no one else would do and while I ate breakfast, he clung onto me like he'd never let me go. We finally convinced him that I was just going to work until 10:00. Going out into the snow at 7:00 a.m. and catching buses wasn't half bad and I really enjoyed it. I was the only one out on our street, and lots of the houses had lights on which looked very welcoming. I liked the feeling of not depending on some one else to get me to and from work. However if I get a regular ride, I'll take it too sometime for it seems like I don't have any time with Bill at all. Got home at 6:00 this afternoon as I had to stop and get the groceries for tomorrow. By the time we ate, did the dishes, I washed out a few things, mended the fur coat again and bathed us both, it was time to go to bed. Bill and I are sitting in bed writing you but he is having a horrible time getting enough stationery, as he has already had three sheets and is yelling for more. Yet, he even scribbled on this [V-Mail] as you can see. He gets a bigger kick out of writing Daddy than anything else he does. I'm going to teach him to say his little prayers for you each nite. Good nite, Darlin'.

I love you forever, Polly
Mailed your package.

Louisville, Feb. 27, 1945

Darlin':

Finished my first day's work at Du Pont's and quit all day long – yeh! isn't that a heck of a start. After being accustomed to modern streamlined offices it was a come down to see the make-shift affair in which I'll work. The worse part is – in the middle of the room is the rest room – a tiny affair just barely large enough to hold a basin and johnny and is used by both men and women – no latch on the door and you either have to hold it shut with one hand and if you need both hands then hold your breath and hope no one comes in on you. They're building our office tho' and it's to be ready in several weeks – don't know if I'll stick it out long enough to see it or not. Then they want to work 12 hours on Monday, Tuesday, and Wednesday – 9 each on Thursday and Friday and off all day on Saturday. If you work the 12 hours you get home the best way you can and that definitely isn't for me so when I first heard the plans I went to the supervisor and told him that I would work the 9 hours a day for 6 days a week as was explained to me when I took the job and if they were changing the hours I'd just have to quit – he told me to just go ahead and work the hours I'd planned on. The cafeteria is choice tho' – that is after we finally made through gobs of mud for almost a block until we get to it but then we can take as long to eat as we want – that's the only good thing I can say about it. Yeh! If it wasn't for the almighty dollar I wouldn't show up tomorrow.

...Some thing of ours is always broken and I sho wish you'd hurry home to fix everything for us....

Good nite, darlin'
I love you terribly, Polly

Louisville, April 3, 1945

Darlin':

...The boss called us all together yesterday afternoon and said when the news of victory came the plant would shut for the rest of the day but if the news came at nite we were to report the next morning as usual. He went on to explain that this plant is making a product which is ... used or to be used in the Pacific and will continue in full force after the European victory. Every one is expecting the exciting news any minute but I'm beginning to believe it is already over and they just aren't releasing the news yet for fear everyone will go wild with celebrating. I'm not gettin' enthused tho' until I know for true that the word is official....

Gotta go to work.

I love you terribly, Darlin', Polly

Louisville, July 24, 1945

Darlin':

... There was another article about the burden on the railroads here in the States since the redeployment started and to lessen the burden the Army is changing the redeployment program and sending the men directly to the Pacific instead of thru the States on furlough – sure hope you aren't being knocked out of a furlough for that reason. Guess I'll just hope to keep on waiting and tearing my hair each time the mail man passes me by.

... Think I'll wash the buggie and wax it – since I'm not a workin' gal any more I have to pinch our pennies and I'll try anything once too.

I love you terribly, Darlin', Polly

Source: *Since you Went Away: World War II Letters from American Women on the Home Front*, ed. Judy Barrett Litoff and David C. Smith (New York: Oxford University Press, 1991), pp. 146–53.

Questions to Think About

1. How did women of color empower themselves during the Great Depression and World War II?
2. How did the Great Depression and World War II change the roles of women in the workplace?
3. How did the Great Depression and World War II challenge traditional definitions of women in the family?

Chapter 5   The Second Sex in America, 1948–68

WORK

1 Michael Wilson, *Salt of the Earth*, 1954

The strike against the Empire Zinc Company in New Mexico and an injunction prohibiting the miners from striking set the stage for the dramatic Salt of the Earth (1954), a fictionalized treatment of the events. The film was produced by Paul Jarrico, written by Michael Wilson and directed by Herbert Biberman, all blacklisted by the major Hollywood studios in the aftermath of the House Un-American Activities Committee (HUAC) Hearings in 1947. As narrated by the central character Esperanza Quintero, actress Rosaura Revueltas, this story reveals the strength of the women who, in defying their husbands to sustain their families, went out on the picket line. Their action caused a rupture in traditional gender roles among Mexican Americans

---

FADE IN:
EXT., PICKET LINE. LONG PANORAMIC SHOT, MORNING.
This panorama should be as sweeping a vista as the first scene of the picket line. We get the sense of women streaming toward the picket post from four points of the compass. Some arrive in ancient cars, others walk by way of the road or foot paths or the railroad tracks. There are so many women on the line that even though they march two abreast they overlap the road.

ESPERANZA'S VOICE: And so they came, the women...they rose before dawn and they came, wives, daughters, grandmothers. They came from

Zinc Town and the hills beyond, from other mining camps, ten, twenty, thirty miles away...

CLOSER VIEW: THE PICKET LINE.
The women march in an orderly, determined fashion. There is no gaiety. Teresa and Mrs. Salazar are in charge. They are as bold and self-assured as two drill sergeants. Most of the women are dressed for the occasion – wearing shirts, jeans and sneakers or saddle shoes.

ESPERANZA'S VOICE: By sun-up there were a hundred on the line. And they kept coming – women we had never seen before, women who had nothing to do with the strike. Somehow they heard about a women's picket line – and they came.

MEDIUM LONG SHOT: MINERS ON HILLSIDE.
On the steep wooded slope above the picket post the varsity squats on its collective haunches. The men smoke, watching the picket line with mingled awe and apprehension.

ESPERANZA'S VOICE: And the men came too. They looked unhappy. I think they were afraid. Afraid the women wouldn't stand fast – or maybe afraid they would.

THE HILLSIDE. ANOTHER ANGLE, HIGHER UP THE SLOPE.
Several miners stand here with their families. They, too, look unhappy. Jenkins and his wife are among them.

ESPERANZA'S VOICE: But not all the women went to the picket post. Some were forbidden by their husbands. (*A pause.*) I was one of these.

CLOSE GROUP SHOT: THE QUINTERO FAMILY.
Standing apart from the others, near a clump of juniper. Luís stands beside his father, whose uneasy frown is directed at the picket line. Estella stands beside her mother, who holds the baby Juanito in her arms. Esperanza keeps gazing at the picket line off scene, never at Ramón.

ESPERANZA: It's not fair...I should be there with them. After all, I'm the one who got the women the vote.
RAMON (*stubbornly*): No.
ESPERANZA: But the motion passed. It's...it's not democratic of you to...
RAMON (*interrupting*): The union don't run my house. (*After a long pause.*) Those Anglo dames stirred you up to make fools of yourselves – but you don't see any of *them* down there.
ESPERANZA (*squinting, peering*): Yes, I do. There's Ruth Barnes.

RAMON: She's the organizer's wife. She's got to be there.
ESPERANZA: No, she *wants* to be there. (*Looking off*) And there's Mrs. Kalinsky.
RAMON (*pointing off scene*): There's Jenkins' wife. You don't see her on no picket line.
ESPERANZA (*quietly*): Anglo husbands can also be backward.
RAMON: Can be *what?*
ESPERANZA: Backward.

He glances quizzically at her. She keeps staring at:
THE PICKET LINE FROM THEIR ANGLE.

ESPERANZA'S VOICE (*plaintively*): Can't I even put in an appearance?
RAMON'S VOICE: In heaven's name, woman, with a baby in your arms?

BACK TO FAMILY GROUP.

ESPERANZA: The baby likes to be walked. It helps him burp.

Ramón shakes his head. He looks at:
THE SHERIFF'S CONVOY. LONG SHOT.
    Some fifty paces beyond the picket line we can see two open trucks and two sheriff's cars. The trucks are loaded with men.
EXT., SHERIFF'S CAR. MEDIUM SHOT.
    Superintendent Alexander, Chief Foreman Barton, the Sheriff and the deputy Vance are standing beside the car. Alexander is in a petulant mood, but the Sheriff and Vance seem amused by the situation. Three pretty Mexican-American girls pass by on their way to the picket line. Vance whistles at them. As they move out of the scene Vance calls:

VANCE: Hey, girls! Wait a minute! Don't you wanta see my pistol?
ALEXANDER: Shut up. (*As the Sheriff chuckles*) What's so amusing? They're flaunting a court order.
SHERIFF (*grins*): Not so sure about that. Letter of the Law, you know. All the injunction says is no picketing by miners.
ALEXANDER (*furious*): Whose side are you on anyway?
SHERIFF: Now don't get excited, Mr. Alexander. They'll scatter like a covey of quail.
BARTON (*impatiently*): Well, let's get at it – before another hundred dames show up.
SHERIFF (*rouses himself, calls*): All right, boys.

WIDER ANGLE: THE CONVOY.
Drivers and deputies climb into the cab of each truck. Barton, Vance and two other deputies get into the lead car. Vance holds up his tear gas gun.

VANCE: What about these?
SHERIFF: Forget it. They'll scatter like quail.

Barton starts the motor. He waves at the truck drivers and the other sheriff's car. They wave back. The convoy starts up, gathering speed rapidly.

FULL SHOT: MINERS ON THE HILL-SLOPE.

They spring to their feet, tense.

FULL SHOT: THE PICKET LINE.

The women stop marching, turn in unison to face the oncoming convoy.

FULL PANNING SHOT: THE CONVOY hurtling toward the picket line.

CLOSE SHOT: FACES OF MINERS.

They groan involuntarily.

CLOSE SHOT: FACES OF WOMEN PICKETS,

steady, unflinching.

THE SHERIFF'S CAR FROM THEIR ANGLE, horn blowing, speeding directly at them, looming bigger, closer.

FULL SHOT: THE PICKET LINE.

At the last split second, Barton jams on his brakes, and the car skids. The women have not moved.

CLOSE SHOT: WOMEN AND CAR.

The car skids into the picket line. A woman is swiped by the front fender, flung onto the road.

FULL SHOT: THE PICKET LINE.

We hear a collective gasp from the women. Then they scream. Two women run to their injured sister. The others swarm around the car. The deputies are trying to get the doors open. The women begin to rock the car. Finally the deputies manage to get out. They flail the women with their fists, their gun stocks. But there are four women to each deputy, and they cling to the men, grabbing at their weapons.

MEDIUM SHOT: THE FIRST TRUCK.

The Anglo scabs standing in the back of the truck react in fear and consternation. But they stay where they are.

MEDIUM LONG SHOT: MINERS ON HILLSIDE.

A group of them start coming down the hill. We can see Charley and Frank gesturing, trying to restrain them – but the miners come on.

BACK TO THE PICKET POST.

Vance kicks out at woman who is trying to tear off his cartridge-belt, sends her sprawling. He backs off, panic-stricken, and fires a tear gas shell into a mass of women pickets. The exploding shell disperses them momentarily. The women fan out, coughing and choking.

THE PICKET POST, SHOOTING FROM HILL ABOVE.

At Mrs. Salazar's command, the women form into two platoons; the larger group remains on the road, blocking the convoy, despite the fact that other deputies open fire with tear gas; but another line has formed at the side of the road, facing the miners bent on entering the fray.

CLOSER ANGLE: THE SECOND PICKET LINE.

As the miners coming down the slope reach the road, Mrs. Salazar waves them back angrily, yells in Spanish:

MRS. SALAZAR: Get back! Get back! Stay out of this!

FIRST MINER (*desperately*): But they're beating up my wife!

WOMEN (*simultaneously in English and Spanish*): It'll be worse if you get in it. Then they'll start shooting...
They'll throw you in jail!
We can take care of ourselves...
You're not needed here...
Get back! Get back!

The men fall back, nonplussed by the vehemence of the women.

BACK TO PICKET POST. LONG SHOT FROM HILLSIDE.

Other deputies have come running from the rear of the convoy to support the four outnumbered deputies. The scabs remain in their trucks. But the wind is blowing the wrong way, and the tear gas drifts back toward the trucks. The scabs begin to cough. A couple of them jump over the tail-gate of the first truck and run. That starts a panicky rout. Other scabs tumble out of the trucks and run back down the road to escape the tear gas.

CLOSE GROUP SHOT: THE QUINTERO FAMILY

Staring at the action. Esperanza can't stand it any longer. She hands the baby to Ramón and is gone before be realizes her intent.

HIS VIEW: ESPERANZA

running diagonally down the slope toward the picket post. In the distance we see deputies still battling the women. The deputies seem to have lost their heads. They lash out viciously at any woman who confronts them, in a vain attempt to scatter the women and clear the road.

CLOSER ANGLE: THE PICKET POST.

Luz Morales is climbing Vance's back, clinging to his arms. Another woman clutches at his gun hand, trying to prevent him from drawing his pistol. Esperanza comes running up. She stops for a second, slips off her right shoe. Vance knocks the other woman down, pulls his revolver from his holster. Esperanza whacks him over the wrist with her shoe, knocking the weapon out of his hand. Luz digs into his hair with both hands.

BACK TO RAMON ON HILLSIDE,

helpless, speechless, holding the baby. Suddenly he runs out of scene. Luis grabs Estella's hand, follows.

ANOTHER PART OF THE HILL: THE LOWER SLOPE.

Charley and Frank are watching the action. Ramón comes running into scene.

RAMON: Why are you standing there? Do something!
CHARLEY (*looking o.s.*): Relax.
RAMON: But women are getting hurt! We've gotta take over!
CHARLEY: They're doing all right.
FRANK (*grins, looks at baby*): Anyway, looks like you've got your hands full.

Completely frustrated, Ramón looks down at the tiny bundle in his arms. Then he looks off at:

THE PICKET POST: LONG SHOT FROM RAMON'S ANGLE.

We can see Barton calling his men off. He jumps in the car, turns it around. Several deputies climb aboard as he drives off. The others retreat on foot, leaving the two abandoned trucks. The women re-form their lines, and begin to sing "The Union Is Our Leader."

Source: Herbert Biberman, *Salt of the Earth: The Story of a Film* (Boston: Beacon Press, 1965), pp. 351–5.

2 *Los Angeles Times,* Classified Advertisements, 1960

The National Organization for Women (NOW) fought for women's civil rights in the workplace by challenging sex-segregated advertisements such as those in the text below and by advocating equity in pay. Founded in 1966, NOW's effective use of the mass media and tactics such as lobbying, petitions, boycotts, and rallies echoed earlier efforts of feminists that had culminated in the Nineteenth Amendment. Partly a result of their efforts, the United States Census Bureau revised 52 job titles in 1972.

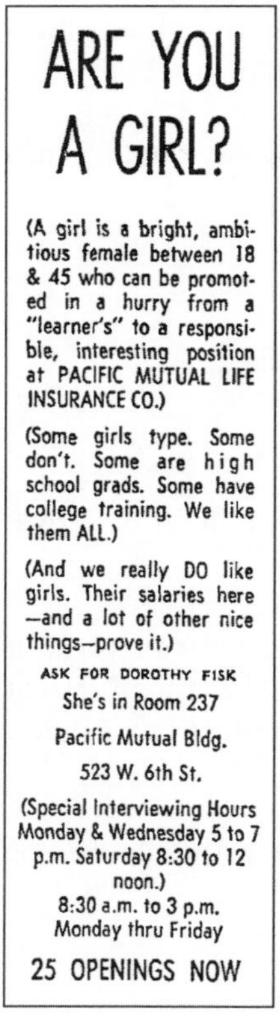

ARE YOU
A GIRL?

(A girl is a bright, ambitious female between 18
& 45 who can be promot-
ed in a hurry from a
"learner's" to a responsible, interesting position
at PACIFIC MUTUAL LIFE
INSURANCE CO.)

(Some girls type. Some
don't. Some are high
school grads. Some have
college training. We like
them ALL.)

(And we really DO like
girls. Their salaries here
—and a lot of other nice
things—prove it.)

ASK FOR DOROTHY FISK
She's in Room 237
Pacific Mutual Bldg.
523 W. 6th St.

(Special Interviewing Hours
Monday & Wednesday 5 to 7
p.m. Saturday 8:30 to 12
noon.)
8:30 a.m. to 3 p.m.
Monday thru Friday

25 OPENINGS NOW

Figure 5.1

Source: *Los Angeles Times*, Classified Advertisement.
March, 1960.

3 Betty Friedan, The Sexual Sell, 1963

Research for The Feminine Mystique *(1963) exposed a broad-based
discontent with the social division of labor particularly among white
middle-class women who were housewives. Inspired by an alumnae survey
of her Smith College 1943 classmates, Betty Goldstein Friedan identified a
general malaise women experienced when home-making and volunteer
work left them unfulfilled. "The Problem with No Name" helped define
a significant aspect of the women's movement, later called "second wave."
Friedan's academic background in economics and labor and her work as
a labor organizer and journalist affected how she framed her essay. In the
following excerpt from a chapter called "The Sexual Sell" Friedan
explained an important part of the dynamic that propels the feminine
mystique forward.*

Some months ago, as I began to fit together the puzzle of women's retreat to home, I had the feeling I was missing something. I could trace the routes by which sophisticated thought circled back on itself to perpetuate an obsolete image of femininity; I could see how that image meshed with prejudice and misinterpreted frustrations to hide the emptiness of "Occupation: house-wife" from women themselves.

But what powers it all? If, despite the nameless desperation of so many American housewives, despite the opportunities open to all women now, so few have any purpose in life other than to be a wife and mother, somebody, something pretty powerful must be at work. The energy behind the feminist movement was too dynamic merely to have trickled dry; it must have been turned off, diverted, by something more powerful than that underestimated power of women.

There are certain facts of life so obvious and mundane that one never talks about them. Only the child blurts out: "Why do people in books never go to the toilet?" Why is it never said that the really crucial function, the really important role that women serve as housewives is *to buy more things for the house*. In all the talk of femininity and woman's role, one forgets that the real business of America is business. But the perpetuation of house-wifery, the growth of the feminine mystique, makes sense (and dollars) when one realizes that women are the chief customers of American business. Somehow, somewhere, someone must have figured out that women will buy more things if they are kept in the underused, nameless-yearning, energy-to-get-rid-of state of being housewives.

A thinking vice-president says: "Too many women getting educated. Don't want to stay home. Unhealthy. If they all get to be scientists and such, they won't have time to shop. But how can we keep them home? They want careers now."

"We'll liberate them to have careers at home," the new executive with horn-rimmed glasses and the Ph.D. in psychology suggests. "We'll make home-making creative."

Of course, it didn't happen quite like that. It was not an economic conspiracy directed against women. It was a byproduct of our general confusion lately of means with ends; just something that happened to women when the business of producing and selling and investing in business for profit – which is merely the way our economy is organized to serve man's needs efficiently – began to be confused with the purpose of our nation, the end of life itself. No more surprising, the subversion of women's lives in America to the ends of business, than the subversion of the sciences of human behavior to the business of deluding women about their real needs. It would take a clever economist to figure out what would keep our affluent economy going if the housewife market began to fall off, just as an economist would have to figure out what to do if there were no threat of war.

It is easy to see why it happened. I learned *how* it happened when I went to see a man who is paid approximately a million dollars a year for his professional services in manipulating the emotions of American women to serve the needs of business. This particular man got in on the ground floor of the hidden-persuasion business in 1945, and kept going.

Properly manipulated ("if you are not afraid of that word," he said), American housewives can be given the sense of identity, purpose, creativity, the self-realization, even the sexual joy they lack – by the buying of things. I suddenly realized the significance of the boast that women wield seventy-five per cent of the purchasing power in America. I suddenly saw American women as *victims* of that ghastly gift, that power at the point of purchase. The insights he shared with me so liberally revealed many things....

The dilemma of business was spelled out in a survey made in 1945 for the publisher of a leading women's magazine on the attitudes of women toward electrical appliances. The message was considered of interest to all the companies that, with the war about to end, were going to have to make consumer sales take the place of war contracts. It was a study of "the psychology of housekeeping"; "a woman's attitude toward housekeeping appliances cannot be separated from her attitude toward homemaking in general," it warned.

On the basis of a national sample of 4,500 wives (middle-class, high-school or college-educated), American women were divided into three categories: "The True Housewife Type," "The Career Woman," and "The Balanced Homemaker." While 51 per cent of the women then fitted "The True House-wife Type" ("From the psychological point of view, housekeeping is this woman's dominating interest. She takes the utmost pride and satisfaction in maintaining a comfortable and well-run home for her family. Consciously or subconsciously, she feels that she is indispensable and that no one else can take over her job. She has little, if any, desire for a position outside the home, and if she has one it is through force or circumstances or necessity"), it was apparent that this group was diminishing, and probably would continue to do so as new fields, interests, education were now open to women.

The largest market for appliances, however, was this "True Housewife" – though she had a certain "reluctance" to accept new devices that had to be recognized and overcome.

The second type – The Career Woman or Would-Be Career Woman – was a minority, but an extremely "unhealthy" one from the sellers' standpoint; advertisers were warned that it would be to their advantage not to let this group get any larger. For such women, though not necessarily job-holders, "do not believe that a woman's place is primarily in the home."

The moral of the study was explicit: "Since the Balanced Homemaker represents the market with the greatest future potential, it would be to the advantage of the appliance manufacturer to make more and more women aware of the desirability of belonging to this group. Educate them through advertising that it is possible to have outside interests and become alert to wider intellectual influences (without becoming a Career Woman). The art of good homemaking should be the goal of every normal woman."

The problem – which, if recognized at that time by one hidden persuader for the home-appliance industry, was surely recognized by others with products for the home – was that "a whole new generation of women is being educated to do work outside the home. Furthermore, an increased desire for emancipation is evident." The solution, quite simply, was to encourage them to be "modern" housewives. The Career or Would-Be Career Woman who frankly dislikes cleaning, dusting, ironing, washing clothes, is less interested in a new wax, a new soap powder. Unlike "The True Housewife" and the "Balanced Homemaker" who prefer to have sufficient appliances and do the housework themselves, the Career Woman would "prefer servants – housework takes too much time and energy." She buys appliances, however, whether or not she has servants, but she is "more likely to complain about the service they give," and to be "harder to sell."

It was too late – impossible – to turn these modern could-or-would-be career women back into True Housewives, but the study pointed out, in 1945, the potential for Balanced Housewifery – the home career. Let them "want to have their cake and eat it too ... save time, have more comfort, avoid dirt and disorder, have mechanized supervision, yet not want to give up the feeling of personal achievement and pride in a well-run household, which comes from 'doing it yourself.' As one young housewife said: 'It's nice to be modern – it's like running a factory in which you have all the latest machinery.'"

The manipulator's services became increasingly valuable. In later surveys, he no longer interviewed professional women; they were not at home during the day. The women in his samples were deliberately True or Balanced Housewives, the new suburban housewives. Household and consumer products are, after all, geared to women; seventy-five per cent of all consumer advertising budgets is spent to appeal to women; that is, to housewives, the women who are available during the day to be interviewed, the women with the time for shopping. Naturally, his depth interviews, projective tests, "living laboratories," were designed to impress his clients, but more often than not they contained the shrewd insights of a skilled social scientist, insights that could be used with profit.

By the mid-fifties, the surveys reported with pleasure that the Career Woman ("the woman who clamored for equality – almost for identity in every sphere of life, the woman who reacted to 'domestic slavery' with indignation and vehemence") was gone, replaced by the "less worldly, less sophisticated" woman whose activity in PTA gives her "broad contacts with the world outside her home," but who "finds in housework a medium of expression for her femininity and individuality." She's not like the old-fashioned self-sacrificing housewife; she considers herself the equal of man. But she still feels "lazy, neglectful, haunted by guilt feelings" because she doesn't have enough work to do. The advertiser must manipulate her need for a "feeling of creativeness" into the buying of his product.

The question of letting the woman use her mind and even participate in science through housework is, however, not without its drawbacks. Science should not relieve housewives of too much drudgery; it must concentrate instead on creating the *illusion* of that sense of achievement that housewives seem to need.

To prove this point, 250 housewives were given a depth test: they were asked to choose among four imaginary methods of cleaning. The housewives spoke up in favor of this last appliance. If it "appears new, modern" she would rather have the one that lets her work herself, this report said. "One compelling reason is her desire to be a participant, not just a button-pusher."

This fascinating study incidentally revealed that a certain electronic cleaning appliance – long considered one of our great laborsavers – actually made "housekeeping more difficult than it need be." From the response of eighty per cent of those housewives, it seemed that once a woman got this appliance going, she "felt compelled to do cleaning that wasn't really necessary." The electronic appliance actually dictated the extent and type of cleaning to be done.

Should the housewife then be encouraged to go back to that simple cheap sweeper that let her clean only as much as she felt necessary? No, said the report, of course not. Simply give that old-fashioned sweeper the "status" of the electronic appliance as a "labor-saving necessity" for the modern house-wife "and then indicate that the modern homemaker would, naturally, own both."

No one, not even the depth researchers, denied that housework was endless, and its boring repetition just did not give that much satisfaction, did not require that much vaunted expert knowledge. But the endlessness of it all was an advantage from the seller's point of view. The problem was to keep at bay the underlying realization which was lurking dangerously in "thousands of depth interviews which we have conducted for dozens of different kinds of house-cleaning products" – the realization that, as one housewife said, "It stinks! I have to do it, so I do it. It's a necessary evil, that's all." What to do? For one thing, put out more and more products, make the directions more complicated, make it really necessary for the housewife to "be an expert." (Washing clothes, the report advised, must become more than a matter of throwing clothes into a machine and pouring in soap. Garments must be carefully sorted, one load given treatment A, a second load treatment B, some washed by hand. The housewife can then "take great pride in knowing just which of the arsenal of products to use on each occasion.")

Capitalize, the report continued, on housewives' "guilt over the hidden dirt" so she will rip her house to shreds in a "deep cleaning" operation, which will give her a "sense of completeness" for a few weeks. ("The times of thorough cleaning are the points at which she is most willing to try new products and 'deep clean' advertising holds out the promise of completion.")

Concentrate on the very young teenage girls, this report further advised. The young ones will want what "the others" want, even if their mothers don't. ("As one of our teenagers said: 'All the gang has started their own sets of sterling. We're real keen about it – compare patterns and go through the ads together. My own family never had any sterling and they think I'm showing off when I spend my money on it – they think plated's just as good. But the kids think they're way off base.'") Get them in schools, churches, sororities, social clubs; get them through home-economics teachers, group leaders, teenage TV programs and teenage advertising. "This is the big market of the future and word-of-mouth advertising, along with group pressure, is not only the most potent influence but in the absence of tradition, a most necessary one."

As for the more independent older wife, that unfortunate tendency to use materials that require little care – stainless steel, plastic dishes, paper napkins – can be met by making her feel guilty about the effects on the children. ("As one young wife told us: 'I'm out of the house all day long, so I can't prepare and serve meals the way I want to. I don't like it that way – my husband and the children deserve a better break. Sometimes I think it'd be better if we tried to get along on one salary and have a real home life but there are always so many things we need.'") Such guilt, the report maintained, can be used to make her see the product, silver, as a means of holding the family together; it gives "added psychological value." What's more, the product can even fill the housewife's need for identity: "Suggest that it becomes truly a part of *you*, reflecting *you*. Do not be afraid to suggest mystically that sterling will adapt itself to any house and any person."

The women who sew, this survey discovered, are the active, energetic, intelligent modern housewives, the new home-oriented modern American women, who have a great unfulfilled need to create, and achieve, and realize their own individuality – which must be filled by some home activity. The big problem for the home-sewing industry was that the "image" of sewing was too "dull"; somehow it didn't achieve the feeling of creating something important. In selling their products, the industry must emphasize the "lasting creativeness" of sewing.

But even sewing can't be too creative, too individual, according to the advice offered to one pattern manufacturer. His patterns required some intelligence to follow, left quite a lot of room for individual expression, and the manufacturer was in trouble for that very reason; his patterns implied that a woman "would know what she likes and would probably have definite ideas." He was advised to widen this "far too limited fashion personality" and get one with "fashion conformity" – appeal to the "fashion-insecure woman," "the conformist element in fashion," who feels "it is not smart to be dressed too differently." For, of course, the manufacturer's problem was not to satisfy woman's need for individuality, for expression or creativity, but to sell more patterns – which is better done by building conformity.

Time and time again, the surveys shrewdly analyzed the needs, and even the secret frustrations of the American housewife; and each time if these needs were properly manipulated, she could be induced to buy more "things." In 1957, a survey told the department stores that their role in this new world was not only to "sell" the housewife but to satisfy her need for "education" – to satisfy the yearning she has, alone in her house, to feel herself a part of the changing world. The store will sell her more, the report said, if it will understand that the real need she is trying to fill by shopping is not anything she can buy there.

Another survey reported that there was a puzzling "desexualization of married life" despite the great emphasis on marriage and family and sex. The problem: what can supply what the report diagnosed as a "missing sexual spark?" The solution: the report advised sellers to "put the libido back into advertising." Despite the feeling that our manufacturers are trying to sell everything through sex, sex as found on TV commercials and ads in national magazines is too tame, the report said, too narrow. "Consumerism," is desexing the American libido because it "has failed to reflect the powerful life forces in every individual which range far beyond the relationship between the sexes." The sellers, it seemed, have sexed the sex out of sex.

How to put the libido back, restore the lost spontaneity, drive, love of life, the individuality, that sex in America seems to lack? In an absent-minded moment, the report concludes that "love of life, as of the other sex, should remain unsoiled by exterior motives ... let the wife be more than a housewife ... a woman ... "

The manipulators and their clients in American business can hardly be accused of creating the feminine mystique. But they are the most powerful of its perpetuators; it is their millions which blanket the land with persuasive images, flattering the American housewife, diverting her guilt and disguising her growing sense of emptiness. They have done this so successfully, employing the techniques and concepts of modern social science, and transposing them into those deceptively simple, clever, outrageous ads and commercials, that an observer of the American scene today accepts as fact that the great majority of American women have no ambition other than to be housewives. If they are not solely responsible for sending women home, they are surely responsible for keeping them there. Their unremitting harangue is hard to escape in this day of mass communications; they have seared the feminine mystique deep into every woman's mind, and into the minds of her husband, her children, her neighbors. They have made it part of the fabric of her everyday life, taunting her because she is not a better housewife, does not love her family enough, is growing old.

If that gifted girl-child grows up to be a housewife, can even the manipulator make supermarket stamps use all of her human intelligence, her human energy, in the century she may live while that boy goes to the moon?

Never underestimate the power of a woman, says another ad. But that power was and is underestimated in America. Or rather, it is only estimated in terms that can be manipulated at the point of purchase. Woman's human intelligence and energy do not really figure in. And yet, they exist, to be used for some higher purpose than housework and thing-buying – or wasted. Perhaps it is only a sick society, unwilling to face its own problems and unable to conceive of goals and purposes equal to the ability and knowledge of its members, that chooses to ignore the strength of women. Perhaps it is only a sick or immature society that chooses to make women "housewives," not people. Perhaps it is only sick or immature men and women, unwilling to face the great challenges of society, who can retreat for long, without unbearable distress, into that thing-ridden house and make it the end of life itself.

Source: Betty Friedan, *The Feminine Mystique* (New York: Norton, 1963), pp. 206–32 passim.

CITIZENSHIP

4 Dorothy Kenyon and Phyllis J. Shampanier, *Hoyt v. Florida*, 1961

In 1957 Gwendolyn Hoyt grabbed her son's broken baseball bat and beat her husband to death in their Florida home. She was tried before a jury, found guilty of murder, and sentenced to 30 years at hard labor. Dorothy Kenyon, an attorney for the American Civil Liberties Union, wrote in support of Hoyt's appeal that the exclusion of women from the jury deprived her of equal protection of the law guaranteed by the Fourteenth Amendment. The text below offers a compelling argument as to why a Florida law requiring women to volunteer for jury service should be declared unconstitutional. The Florida Supreme Court upheld Hoyt's conviction, and it was three more years until Crook v. White *(1966) established equal jury service for women.*

What of the Rights of Women under the Amendment?

It is a violation of the equal protection guaranteed by the Fourteenth Amendment for a Negro to be tried before a jury from which members of his race or color are systematically excluded, in whole or in substantial part. It is equally a violation for members of other races or color, and even for members of sharply differing economic categories.

What then of women who, if they are excluded, as Mr. Justice Douglas said in *Bollard* v. *United States*, 329 U.S. 187 (1946), would leave "only half of the available population" to be "drawn upon for jury service?" What is the reason compelling enough to justify their absence from this important "phase of civic responsibility" and "diffused impartiality?" How can we have a true cross section of the community to draw upon without women? Where is that equality of protection guaranteed by our Constitution if a woman defendant accused of a dreadful sex murder must be judged only by men?

These questions have been answered, as we have seen, and almost always against women, in the past. But the past is past and we are dealing with the present. As was said in *Brown* v. *Board of Education*, 347 U.S. 483, "We cannot turn the clock back to 1868 when the Amendment was adopted.... We must consider public education in the light of its full development and its present place in American life throughout the nation."

The same reasoning surely applies to women who too have had to fight a slow and painful battle during the last century and a half for recognition and status not very different from that of the Negro slaves....

The Reasons Stated for Excluding Women from Jury Service are no longer Compelling or Valid

One of the remaining legal disabilities is this classification of women into a separate category for jury service, a category that seems to have outlived its time and purpose.

This consideration for the woman homemaker, that relatively small group of women of child-bearing age with small children to take care of at home, is admirable. But their numbers do not begin to include all women, the bulk of whom, who have no such special responsibilities, could be drawn upon just as men are now for this vital service. Furthermore, the hardship that jury service might subject them to could easily be prevented through the broad discretionary power of the judge to excuse in such cases. In fact it is unthinkable that a judge would not be eager to excuse mothers of children under such circumstances. To exempt all women in order to protect these few seems unrealistic and uncalled for.

In the U.S. today women comprise 33% of the total labor force, 36% of all women and girls over fourteen are members of the labor force, 55% of them are married and more than 30% of all married women work. Fifty percent of all girls marry before they are 20. The average age of a woman when her last child enters school is 32. Her normal life expectancy is 73.7 years (as compared with a life expectancy for men of 67.2). In other words only 11 years out of the average married woman's nearly 53 years of adult life (or 20%) are needed for or given over to babysitting. With a population steadily extending its life span, women already are more numerous than men by about three million and outliving them by six and one half years each, it is clear that our older citizens are becoming more numerous and more female, all the time and the number of younger women with babies in the home less and less.

Judge Hobson, in his dissenting opinion in the case at bar, *supra*, put it well when he said:

> "No valid reason exists for limiting jury service to women who volunteer. Trial Judges have the same broad discretion to excuse women with pressing duties at home used to excuse men with pressing business commitments. Moreover, since the advent of woman suffrage and the entry, in this era of modernity, of untold numbers of American women into all fields of business and professional life, the reason given for excluding them from jury service no longer exists."

The Fact of their Exclusion works a Positive Injustice not only to them but to Persons other than Themselves

Not only are the reasons stated for the exemption of women no longer compelling or valid; there are other reasons for calling it unreasonable. Their exemption works a real hardship on the male juryman upon whom a greater burden of service is placed than would otherwise be the case. It deprives the conscientious woman citizen of the chance to feel that she too is performing her duty and makes it more difficult for her to do so. And lastly, it does great injustice to the female defendant (as in the case at bar) who so badly needs the diffused impartiality of a jury drawn from all segments of our society, emphatically including women.

There are thus really three rights affected by jury service. One is the right of men to have women share this onerous duty of citizenship with them. Another is the right of the fully emancipated, fully enfranchised woman citizen to exercise this important right and obligation of citizenship. It is a belittlement of her accomplishment in overcoming that long time sex defect of hers to suggest, even by implication, that even in this day and age she is perhaps still not qualified or capable of performing this simple act of good citizenship on the same terms as men. It is a genuine humiliation and degradation of her spirit. Not all women feel this way but some do and they constitute some of our most conscientious citizens. The third right is perhaps the most important. That is the right of the woman accused of crime to have her case heard by a jury composed of the broadest possible cross section of the people making up her community, her neighbors and her peers, so that its impartiality may be insured by the wideness and diffusion of the interests it represents. In such a cross section, can anyone doubt that women play an enormously important part?

For years men said that some cases were not "fit" for women to hear. They had in mind of course cases involving sex offenses. But nothing could have been more shortsighted or snobbish. For, as the *League of Women Voters* observed many years ago, "*such a trial concerns other persons more vitally than it does the jurors and one of these persons principally involved is always a woman or a girl. That fact in itself would seem to prove without further comment why there should be women on the jury no matter what may be the evidence that has to be produced to reach a verdict fair to the litigants and fair to the community.*" (Emphasis supplied.)

In the case at bar the defendant is a woman and her crime is one of those dreadful marital tragedies which women have known about for centuries and in respect to which they certainly have every bit as great experience and capacity for understanding as men. Does it not shock our sense of fair play that, because a few young women with small babies at home might find it inconvenient to come to court to hear her case (and of course they would not have to because the Judge would excuse them), this woman should be deprived of even one single woman on her jury?

The Time to Act is now – the Florida Law should be Declared Unconstitutional and Jury Service Opened up to Women Everywhere on the same terms as Men

The United Nations has brought a change into women's lives too. The words of the Charter, "Fundamental Freedoms for All without Distinction as to Race, Sex, Language, or Religion," are being translated into living deeds. The defect of sex is in process of being swept away on a worldwide scale at last. Only ten countries in the entire world now refuse voting rights to women, and in two of them the vote is refused to men as well. Women are being brought out of their long-enforced segregation; the Moslem veil, the purdah of India, all are being abandoned; and women are beginning to mingle with men in the affairs of the world. The responsibilities of citizenship are being granted to them practically everywhere on the same terms as men. Should we in the United States be more backward than the rest of the world in integrating our women?

Source: Brief of the Florida Civil Liberties Union and the American Civil Liberties Union, Amici Curiae, *Hoyt v. Florida*, 368 U.S. 57 (October 1961), available at Alexander Street Press.

5 Casey Hayden and Mary King, A Kind of Memo, 1965

Casey Hayden and Mary King, two young white activists in the Student Nonviolent Coordinating Committee (SNCC), co-authored "A Kind of Memo" in 1965. Inspired by Ella Baker and her wish to see people take responsibilities for their own actions, Hayden and King raised philosophical issues about female liberation in both a personal and political context, and the place for this discussion within a movement that sought to redress racial and class oppressions. In developing the idea of caste as a way to locate female oppression, Hayden and King sought ways to address a developing rift between black and white women that threatened to splinter the grassroots movement.

November 18, 1965

We've talked a lot, to each other and to some of you, about our own and other women's problems in trying to live in our personal lives and in our work as independent and creative people. In these conversations we've found what seem to be recurrent ideas or themes. Maybe we can look at these things many of us perceive, often as a result of insights learned from the movement:

- Sex and caste: There seem to be many parallels that can be drawn between treatment of Negroes and treatment of women in our society as a whole. But in particular, women we've talked to who work in the movement seem to be caught up in a common-law caste system that operates, sometimes subtly, forcing them to work around or outside hierarchical structures of power which may exclude them. Women seem to be placed in the same position of assumed subordination in personal situations too. It is a caste system which, at its worst, uses and exploits women.

This is complicated by several facts, among them: 1) The caste system is not institutionalized by law (women have the right to vote, to sue for divorce, etc.); 2) Women can't withdraw from the situation (a la nationalism) or overthrow it; 3) There are biological differences (even though those biological differences are usually discussed or accepted without taking present and future technology into account so we probably can't be sure what these differences mean). Many people who are very hip to the implications of the racial caste system, even people in the movement, don't seem to be able to see the sexual-caste system and if the question is raised they respond with: "That's the way it's supposed to be. There are biological differences." Or with other statements which recall a white segregationist confronted with integration.

- Women and problems of work: The caste-system perspective dictates the roles assigned to women in the movement, and certainly even more to women outside the movement. Within the movement, questions arise in situations ranging from relationships of women organizers to men in the community, to who cleans the freedom house, to who holds leadership positions, to who does secretarial work, and to who acts as spokesman for groups. Other problems arise between women with varying degrees of awareness of themselves as being as capable as men but held back from full participation, or between women who see themselves as needing more control of their work than other women demand. And there are problems with relationships between white women and black women.
- Women and personal relations with men: Having learned from the movement to think radically about the personal worth and abilities of people whose role in society had gone unchallenged before, a lot of women in the movement have begun trying to apply those lessons to their own relations with men. Each of us probably has her own story of the various results, and of the internal struggle occasioned by trying to break out of very deeply learned fears, needs, and self-perceptions, and of what happens when we try to replace them with concepts of people and freedom learned from the movement and organizing.
- Institutions: Nearly everyone has real questions about those institutions which shape perspectives on men and women: marriage, childrearing patterns, women's (and men's) magazines, etc. People are beginning to think about and even to experiment with new forms in these areas.

- Men's reactions to the questions raised here: A very few men seem to feel, when they hear conversations involving these problems, that they have a right to be present and participate in them, since they are so deeply involved. At the same time, very few men can respond nondefensively, since the whole idea is either beyond their comprehension or threatens and exposes them. The usual response is laughter. That inability to see the whole issue as serious, as the straitjacketing of both sexes, and as societally determined often shapes our own response so that we learn to think in their terms about ourselves and to feel silly rather than trust our inner feelings. The problems we're listing here, and what others have said about them, are therefore largely drawn from conversations among women only – and that difficulty in establishing dialogue with men is a recurring theme among people we've talked to.

- Lack of community for discussion: Nobody is writing, or organizing or talking publicly about women in any way that reflects the problems that various women in the movement come across and which we've tried to touch above. Consider this quote from an article in the centennial issue of *The Nation:*

However equally we consider men and women, the work plans for husbands and wives cannot be given equal weight. A woman should not aim for "a second-level career" because she is a *woman;* from girlhood on she should recognize that, if she is also going to be a wife and mother, she will not be able to give as much to her work as she would if single. That is, she should not feel that she cannot aspire to directing the laboratory simply because she is a woman, but rather because she is also a wife and mother; as such, her work as a lab technician (or the equivalent in another field) should bring both satisfaction and the knowledge that, through it, she is fulfilling an additional role, making an additional contribution.

And that's about as deep as the analysis goes publicly, which is not nearly so deep as we've heard many of you go in chance conversations.

The reason we want to try to open up dialogue is mostly subjective. Working in the movement often intensifies personal problems, especially if we start trying to apply things we're learning there to our personal lives. Perhaps we can start to talk with each other more openly than in the past and create a community of support for each other so we can deal with ourselves and others with integrity and can therefore keep working.

Objectively, the chances seem nil that we could start a movement based on anything as distant to general American thought as a sex-caste system. Therefore, most of us will probably want to work full time on problems such as war, poverty, race. The very fact that the country can't face, much less deal with, the questions we're raising means that the movement is one place to look for some relief. Real efforts at dialogue within the movement and with whatever liberal groups, community women, or students might listen are justified. That is, all the problems between men and women and all the problems of women functioning in society as equal human beings are among the most basic that people face. We've talked in the movement about trying to build a society which would see basic human problems (which are now seen as private troubles), as public problems and would try to shape institutions to meet human needs rather than shaping people to meet the needs of those with power. To raise questions like those above illustrates very directly that society hasn't dealt with some of its deepest problems and opens discussion of why that is so. (In one sense, it is a radicalizing question that can take people beyond legalistic solutions into areas of personal and institutional change.) The second objective reason we'd like to see discussion begin is that we've learned a great deal in the movement and perhaps this is one area where a determined attempt to apply ideas we've learned there can produce some new alternatives.

Source: Casey Hayden and Mary King, "A Kind of Memo," November 18, 1965, reprinted in *Liberation* (April 1966) and republished as Appendix 3 of Mary King, *Freedom Song: A Personal Story of the 1960s' Civil Rights Movement* (New York: William Morrow, 1987).

6 Fannie Lou Hamer, Testimony Before the Credentials Committee at the Democratic National Convention, 1964

Fannie Lou Hamer's testimony before the Credentials Committee of the Democratic National Convention in August 1964 dramatized the meaning of citizenship in a nation still in the midst of coming to terms with the Fourteenth and Fifteenth Amendments. Television brought her to the nation's attention, but it was Hamer's questioning of America that so eloquently challenged the exclusion of African Americans. Her words underscored much of her struggle to register voters in rural Mississippi, where she had confronted the Ku Klux Klan, poverty, and party politics.

Mr. Chairman, and to the Credentials Committee, my name is Mrs. Fannie Lou Hamer, and I live at 626 East Lafayette Street, Ruleville, Mississippi, Sunflower County, the home of Senator James O. Eastland, and Senator Stennis.

It was the 31st of August in 1962 that eighteen of us traveled twenty-six miles to the county courthouse in Indianola to try to register to become first-class citizens.

We was met in Indianola by policemen, Highway Patrolmen, and they only allowed two of us in to take the literacy test at the time. After we had taken this test and started back to Ruleville, we was held up by the City Police and the State Highway Patrolmen and carried back to Indianola where the bus driver was charged that day with driving a bus the wrong color.

After we paid the fine among us, we continued on to Ruleville, and Reverend Jeff Sunny carried me four miles in the rural area where I had worked as a timekeeper and sharecropper for eighteen years. I was met there by my children, who told me that the plantation owner was angry because I had gone down to try to register.

After they told me, my husband came, and said the plantation owner was raising Cain because I had tried to register. Before he quit talking the plantation owner came and said, "Fannie Lou, do you know - did Pap tell you what I said?"

And I said, "Yes, sir."

He said, "Well I mean that." He said, "If you don't go down and withdraw your registration, you will have to leave." Said, "Then if you go down and withdraw," said, "you still might have to go because we are not ready for that in Mississippi."

And I addressed him and told him and said, "I didn't try to register for you. I tried to register for myself."

I had to leave that same night.

On the 10th of September 1962, sixteen bullets was fired into the home of Mr. and Mrs. Robert Tucker for me. That same night two girls were shot in Ruleville, Mississippi. Also Mr. Joe McDonald's house was shot in.

And June the 9th, 1963, I had attended a voter registration workshop; was returning back to Mississippi. Ten of us was traveling by the Continental Trailway bus. When we got to Winona, Mississippi, which is Montgomery County, four of the people got off to use the restaurant and two people wanted to use the washroom.

The four people that had gone in to use the restaurant was ordered out. During this time I was on the bus. But when I looked through the window and saw they had rushed out I got off of the bus to see what had happened. And one of the ladies said, "It was a State Highway Patrolman and a Chief of Police ordered us out."

I got back on the bus and one of the persons had used the washroom got back on the bus, too.

As soon as I was seated on the bus, I saw when they began to get the five people in a highway patrolman's car. I stepped off of the bus to see what was happening and somebody screamed from the car that the five workers was in and said, "Get that one there." When I went to get in the car, when the man told me I was under arrest, he kicked me.

I was carried to the county jail and put in the booking room. They left some of the people in the booking room and began to place us in cells. I was placed in a cell with a young woman called Miss Ivesta Simpson. After I was placed in the cell I began to hear sounds of licks and screams. And I could hear somebody say, "Can you say, 'yes, sir,' nigger? Can you say 'yes, sir'?"

And they would say other horrible names.

She would say, "Yes, I can say 'yes, sir.'"

"So, well, say it."

She said, "I don't know you well enough."

They beat her, I don't know how long. And after a while she began to pray, and asked God to have mercy on those people.

And it wasn't too long before three white men came to my cell. One of these men was a State Highway Patrolman and he asked me where I was from. I told him Ruleville and he said, "We are going to check this."

They left my cell and it wasn't too long before they came back. He said, "You are from Ruleville all right," and he used a curse word. And he said, "We are going to make you wish you was dead."

I was carried out of that cell into another cell where they had two Negro prisoners. The State Highway Patrolmen ordered the first Negro to take the blackjack.

The first Negro prisoner ordered me, by orders from the State Highway Patrolman, for me to lay down on a bunk bed on my face.

I laid on my face and the first Negro began to beat. I was beat by the first Negro until he was exhausted. I was holding my hands behind me at that time on my left side, because I suffered from polio when I was six years old.

After the first Negro had beat until he was exhausted, the State Highway Patrolman ordered the second Negro to take the blackjack.

The second Negro began to beat and I began to work my feet, and the State Highway Patrolman ordered the first Negro who had beat me to sit on my feet - to keep me from working my feet. I began to scream and one white man got up and began to beat me in my head and tell me to hush.

One white man - my dress had worked up high - he walked over and pulled my dress - I pulled my dress down and he pulled my dress back up.

I was in jail when Medgar Evers was murdered.

All of this is on account of we want to register, to become first-class citizens. And if the Freedom Democratic Party is not seated now, I question America. Is this America, the land of the free and the home of the brave, where we have to sleep with our telephones off the hooks because our lives be threatened daily, because we want to live as decent human beings, in America?

Thank you.

Source: http://americanradioworks.publicradio.org/features/sayitplain/flhamer.html.

REPRESENTATIONS

7 Esmeralda Santiago, A *Nena Puertorriquena Decente*, 1960s

Popular fiction writer Esmeralda Santiago (1948–) has written about her own coming of age as a Puerto Rican teenager in Brooklyn, New York in the 1960s. In The Turkish Lover, *her third memoir, Santiago reflects on standards of behavior for "decent Puerto Rican girls." The contradictions between ideal and reality raise important questions about the relationship between mothers and daughters during a decade of social change. For Puerto Rican women, generational conflicts intensified under the pressures of migration and the challenges it posed to traditional familial relations.*

"Those *americanas*" were any females my age who were not *nenas puertorriqueñas decentes*. Decent Puerto Rican girls did not wear short skirts, did not wear pants unless they were riding a horse, did not wear makeup, did not tease their hair, did not talk to boys not their brothers, did not go anywhere unchaperoned, did not argue with their mothers, did not challenge adults even when they were wrong, did not look adults in the eyes, especially if they were men, did not disrespect their alcoholic relatives.

A *nena decente* listened to her mother, learned to cook and keep a neat house, left the room when a man visiting her grandmother looked too much in her direction, sat with her legs together even when she was alone minding her own business and reading a book. The person a *nena decente* had to avoid the most was *el hombre que le hizo el daño* – the man who took the virginity of a friend, neighbor, or relative without first marrying her. *El daño* – the damage – spoiled it for the rightful "owner" of her virginity, a legitimate husband in a monogamous relationship.

A *nena puertorriqueña decente* did not give the neighbors cause to gossip. This meant she was conscious at all times of *lo que dirá la gente*, what people would say, and take that into account when weighing her actions, otherwise *¿qué dirán?*

A *nena puertorriqueña decente* was a virgin until she married in a church with her sisters as bridesmaids and her brothers as grooms. Then she became a *mujer puertorriqueña decente*. A decent Puerto Rican woman could wear makeup and dress in a way that pleased her husband but not so sexy as to provoke other men's lust. She could go out accompanied by her husband, children, or female relative *porque si no ¿qué dirán?* She honored her mother and mother-in-law, managed her home efficiently but deferred major decisions to her husband, who was to wear the pants, literally and figuratively, *porque si no ¿qué dirán?* He was served hot, home-cooked Puerto Rican food at every meal. His clothes would be clean and pressed, his shoes shined. He was not to be challenged, corrected, or laughed at, especially in public, for any reason whatsoever, even if he were misinformed, wrong, or a buffoon, *porque si no ¿qué dirán?*

Americanas had too much freedom to do as they pleased, which they abused by being sexually available to any *pendejo* who looked their way. *Americanas* were also disrespectful of their elders, contemptuous of family, lazy housekeepers dependent on prepared foods, and, in spite of their sexual freedom, did not know how to please a man. They also seemed not to care what anyone thought about their behavior, as if *el que dirán* did not exist in English.

I noticed some contradictions.

Mami, a *mujer decente*, had never married Papi and I had never seen her in church. *¿Qué dirán?* Mami dressed to accentuate an hourglass figure crowned by luxurious black hair that, in New York, she cut and learned to dye in shades of brown, blonde, and even red. *¿Qué dirán?* She curled, teased, and sprayed her hair if she had to leave our apartment. She girdled her abdomen to look as if she had not birthed seven children. When she walked down the street in her high heels, her hips swung voluptuously *¿qué dirán?*, which elicited whistles, stares, and promises from men who seemed to stand on corners just to watch women pass by.

Six months after we came to New York, Mami fell in love with Francisco, and by our first summer in Brooklyn, he was living with us in defiance of Tata, who did not think it was appropriate for Mami to "bring a strange man into a house with teenage girls." *¿Qué dirán?* Don Julio, Tata's boyfriend, was exempt from this rule.

Mami did not invent *el que dirán* or the differences between a *nena decente* and an *americana*. Her friends and relatives spouted the same rules to their daughters and we were supposed to listen humbly and without arguments. When our mothers were elsewhere, however, we tried to make sense of what they said as opposed to what they did.

"Maybe," guessed Cousin Alma, "when they say that stuff they're talking about an ideal, not a practical reality."

Source: Esmeralda Santiago, *The Turkish Lover* (Cambridge, MA: DaCapo Press, 2004), pp. 8–9. Reprinted by permission of DACAPO PRESS, a member of Perseus Books Group.

8 *Life Magazine,* How Nice to be a Pretty Girl and Work in Washington, 1962

Life Magazine *published stories such as the essay below from 1962 that glamorized opportunities for young women interested in public service in Washington, DC. The reporting in this popular weekly magazine affirmed a particular set of feminine virtues for women in the 1950s and 1960s. Months earlier, President John F. Kennedy had established the President's Commission on the Status of Women to develop recommendations on a number of serious economic issues.*

A regal and sparkling hostess, Natalie Naugle, 26, formerly of Wichita, Kan., assumes her role in social diplomacy with graceful ease. She works in the State Department's protocol office; at left she sorts place cards for a white-tie dinner given by Secretary of State Dean Rusk for chiefs of foreign missions. On such occasions it is her job to serve as a catalyst, to set the dignitaries at their ease and to encourage them to see eye to eye. She seldom fails, except with the grossly nearsighted.

Well aware of her responsibility, Natalie is a good public servant who feels that she is contributing something of value to her country. She finds her busy official calendar tremendously exciting – at times perhaps too much so. "The only trouble with Washington," she says, "is that there is too much going on. It's impossible to fit it all in." On the next pages she shows that off-duty time in the capital is not total drudgery and, in fact, is as delightful as her work.

On Capitol Hill, as in other official and indeed unofficial sectors, there is always a need for winsome young ladies. Amid all the politicking, lobbying and administering, a pretty girl for some reason seems to improve everyone's mood – and, naturally, "everyone" includes bachelors. "But if you ask me," says one, "it's pretty tough to find an intelligent, attractive girl who isn't all booked up."

A case in point is 25-year-old Layte Bowden, a former Florida State University beauty queen. As secretary-receptionist to Florida's Senator George Smathers, Layte displays a poise and graciousness that puts visiting constituents at ease and has made the senator the envy of some of his less fortunate colleagues. It also results in a full social calendar for Layte. "It is a great 'man' town," she reports and to prove the point a young congressman from Indiana and an Air Force general, among a number of others, vie for her free evenings. At right, the congressman, John Brademas, displays a pretty good vie.

Source: *Life Magazine,* 52(12), March 23, 1962, pp. 30, 36.

DOMESTIC LIVES

9 Del Martin, President's Message to the Daughters of Bilitis, 1956

Eight women in San Francisco including Del Martin founded the Daughters of Bilitis (DOB) in 1955 to support lesbian rights. It began publishing its own newsletter called The Ladder *the following year. Its articles addressed a variety of issues and championed an understanding of the homosexual minority. Lesbians had served the nation in multiple capacities during the war years but suffered discrimination in the post-war emphasis on conformity. The message that follows invites participation in a movement for minority rights.*

Since 1950 there has been a nationwide movement to bring understanding to and about the homosexual minority.

Most of the organizations dedicated to this purpose stem from the Mattachine Foundation which was founded in Los Angeles at that time. Members of these organizations – The Mattachine Society, ONE, and National Association for Sexual Research – are predominantly male, although there are a few hard working women among their ranks.

The Daughters of Bilitis is a women's organization resolved to add the feminine voice and viewpoint to a mutual problem. While women may not have so much difficulty with law enforcement, their problems are none the less real – family, sometimes children, employment, social acceptance.

However, the Lesbian is a very elusive creature. She burrows underground in her fear of identification. She is cautious in her associations. Current modes in hair style and casual attire have enabled her to camouflage her existence. She claims she does not need help. And she will not risk her tight little list of security to aid those who do.

But surely the ground work has been well laid in the past 5½ years. Homosexuality is not the dirty word it used to be. More and more people, professional and lay, are becoming aware of its meaning and implications. There is no longer so much "risk" in becoming associated with it.

And why not "belong?" Many heterosexuals do. Membership is open to anyone who is interested in the minority problems of the sexual variant and does not necessarily indicate one's own sex preference.

Women have taken a beating through the centuries. It has only been in this 20th, through the courageous crusade of the Suffragettes and the influx of women into the business world, that woman has become an independent entity, an individual with the right to vote and the right to a job and economic security. But it took women with foresight and determination to attain this heritage which is now ours.

And what will be the lot of the future lesbian? Fear? Scorn? This need not be – If lethargy is supplanted by an energized constructive program, if cowardice gives way to the solidarity of a cooperative front. If the "let Georgia do it" attitude is replaced by the realization of individual responsibility in thwarting the evils of ignorance, superstition, prejudice and bigotry.

Nothing was ever accomplished by hiding in a dark corner. Why not discard the hermitage for the heritage that awaits any red-blooded American woman who dares to claim it?

Source: *Speaking for Our Lives:, Historic Speeches and Rhetoric for Gay and Lesbian Rights (1892–2000)*, ed. Robert B. Ridinger (New York: Haworth Press, 2004), pp. 52–3.

10 Susan Tracy, We Know What You've Done, 1968

In the 1960s young women faced difficult decisions, often without adequate information, about how to use birth control and protect themselves from pregnancy. Abortions were illegal and often dangerous. This testimonial, recounted almost two decades after an illegal abortion, reveals the complex issues and emotions experienced by a college student at the University of Massachusetts-Amherst, who came of age in the tumult of student activism and changing attitudes towards sexuality. Susan Tracy finished her undergraduate studies and excelled as a student leader, being voted a Distinguished Senior. She subsequently earned a doctorate in history and teaches history and women's studies.

I had an illegal abortion in 1968 when I was an undergraduate at the University of Massachusetts. Those were the years when they told us to "Make Love, Not War." So, taking the phrase seriously, in the true spirit of my generation, I did. As a good Protestant Congregationalist, the first time I made love with anybody, I got pregnant. After I proceeded to throw up for about three weeks and crave oranges and Howard Johnson's hot dogs, I found out that I didn't have an ulcer – that would come ten years later – but that I was pregnant.

Now, you have to understand that in 1968, even though we talk about the women's movement as part of the Sixties, the real women's movement is actually in the 1970s. In 1968 there was a pervasive double standard about sexuality for men and for women – the Sexual Revolution was really a sexual revolution for men. It was okay for men to have sex; it was not okay, really, for women to have sex. In Amherst it was legal for men to go downtown to buy condoms, but it was completely illegal for women who were not married to have any kind of birth control. That was the double standard. That is the world we're going back to if the New Right and the Catholic Church prevail. In addition, since I had grown up in the '50s and '60s, I didn't really know anything about my body – and didn't find out anything about it until *Our Bodies, Ourselves* came out – other than, of course, very carefully studying the directions on the tampon box. But other than that, there was really no information anywhere about my body, because all of the skeletons in the classrooms were males and all the drawings in the textbooks were males. And unfortunately, as I found out later, that was true in medical schools as well.

So, on a day-to-day basis, that's what the double-standard of sexuality meant. It meant that boys went around talking about scoring, and that if you were a young woman and went out and tried to live a sexual life with some measure of sexual freedom, you were still talked about. And if you found yourself pregnant, you were entirely alone.

In my own personal situation, I was especially alone because both my parents had died and a court had placed me with my mother's sister, who was a very conservative Republican on the North Shore of Boston. And since I thought I was fomenting the revolution, you can imagine things were not very comfortable on the home front. In addition to that, I had gotten involved with a 33-year-old man who was Jewish. My mother's sister and her husband wouldn't even allow him into the house. So the idea that I would go home and say that I was pregnant and they would welcome me with open arms was not a reality. What I faced was really a kind of desperate situation. I wasn't in any kind of relationship that was anything [special]. By the time I found out I was pregnant, we had been going out for six weeks. There were no parents I could turn to. So what I faced, when I looked at my options, was that I wouldn't graduate from college, which meant that I wouldn't be able to make a living in any kind of reasonable way as far as I could see. And what I thought I would be doing was consigning myself and this child to poverty. And since I had grown up in poverty, to willingly consign a child to that life I had just left was an anathema to me. Also, as a child who had just had two parents die, the idea of having a child and giving it up felt to me like an abandonment. I just couldn't do it. I knew that I couldn't go through the rest of my life knowing that some place out there, there might be my child, and that I had not taken the responsibility of taking care of that child and that life that I'd brought into the world.

And so, as I thought it out, I thought, well, I've just got to find another way. It turned out that Bill Baird had been in Massachusetts that spring and had been arrested at Boston University for holding up a Dalcon shield. He held it up to the audience and said, "This is a Dalcon shield. This will help you protect yourself from getting pregnant." And he was arrested. Later in that same trip, after he posted bail, he was out at the University of Massachusetts. I and some other people had brought him out, so I knew how to get in touch with him. He had a clinic in Hempstead, Long Island. So the man I was involved with and I went to Hempstead, Long Island, and got a "safe referral."

There is a terrible, terrible loneliness to this whole thing. I think even when abortion is legal, our society is sufficiently screwed up that women are alone in this decision. And to make abortion illegal and not to allow a woman to make what will be the most important decision in her life – *that* is criminal.

The person I was with did not want to tell his parents what was going on. He borrowed some money from them, but pretty much I had to end up by selling almost everything I owned. I sold my winter coats, I sold my books, except for my literature books which I kept. I sold my history books. I sold my stereo. I sold my skis. Because the abortion was $600, which in those days was three times my tuition. It was an enormous amount of money to raise. Today the equivalent might be $3,000 to $5,000.

So we went to this clinic in Long Island. Of course, we were New Englanders and we didn't know how to get to Long Island. We didn't know what bridges to take, and we didn't know how to get off of Long Island once we got there! So we ended up driving and driving and driving for hours looking for the place, while being frantic and scared, because what we were doing was completely illegal. We could be arrested and anybody helping us could be arrested. And so, we went to his clinic and we got the referral. The referral was to Newark, New Jersey. We took out our map and followed it to Newark, New Jersey, getting lost on the way, of course. We ended up in Westchester County and knew it wasn't Newark, New Jersey. Somehow we finally made it over the George Washington Bridge. We got to Newark, New Jersey and got lost again. The place we were sent to was a middle-class black section. It was very clear that we did not belong there. So again we were in danger, and we were putting the black doctor in danger. Our mere presence there put him in danger – put his life in danger, put his patients in danger.

I had what I thought was a safe abortion. It was in a doctor's office. He was very kind. I was knocked out and when I woke up I was in a lot of pain. We started the trip back and decided because I was pretty tired and we were both just exhausted from fright – we didn't really relax until we reached the Massachusetts border and every time we saw a police car we almost died right then and there – to stay in a motel in Holyoke. So we were staying in the motel and I was feeling very bad. I was lying on the bed and I decided I would get up and go into the bathroom. And when I stood up I had the most incredible pain I've ever felt, probably even to this day. It went right up my leg. And then suddenly I had the feeling that all of my insides had just fallen out.

I don't really remember very much after that, other than screaming and fainting and falling on the bed. What had happened was I was hemorrhaging. I was wrapped in a blanket, and my friend and the owner of the motel put me in the car and then drove me at about 80 miles an hour to Cooley Dickinson Hospital where I underwent emergency surgery. All I remember was sort of waking up in the room and seeing bright white lights and feeling very, very cold, and hearing the doctor say, "We know what you've done and we will deal with you in the morning."

I was frightened for my friend, and I was terrified for me. It crossed my mind that I shouldn't let them drug me, because I thought if they drugged me then I'd spill all like they do in the POW (Prisoner of War) camps. I tried to remember that I would just give them my name and my student ID number and nothing else! The next morning the doctor came in and he was very sarcastic. He said, "Well, I suppose you're not going to tell me where you went?" No. "I suppose you're not going to tell me who did this?" No. "And you know I could have you arrested?" Yes. And he said, "But I'm not going to. And you might as well come to see me in my office. You can get birth control pills now that you're ruined. Nobody would want to marry you anyway, so you might as well get birth control pills so you can continue your whorish ways." Something like that. So, I went and got birth control pills from him.

After that I blanked it completely out of my mind. It was one of those things that you could not talk about, because to talk about it was to endanger yourself and just too many people. And so I said nothing to anybody and just put it out of my mind like one does with a very dangerous secret. I didn't talk to anybody about it again until 1973, when *Roe v. Wade* was announced by Walter Cronkite on the CBS Evening News. I was in graduate school at that time and I was with friends. I remember standing in a friend's living room and watching that TV, and when he said that Roe had passed and abortion was legal, I can just remember crying. Tears started falling. Because all of a sudden I realized that I knew what it meant, and that other people wouldn't have to go through what I had gone through – the terror and the loneliness.

Source: *Creating Choice, A Community Responds to the Need for Abortion and Birth Control, 1961–1973*, ed. David P. Cline (New York: Palgrave Macmillan), pp. 55–8.

Questions to Think About

1. What new issues – political, social, economic, domestic – challenged women in the decades following World War II? To what extent did they respond to these challenges differently than in previous generations?
2. How did the civil rights movement and the women's rights movement intersect with each other between 1948 and 1968? Where are the points of convergence and divergence?
3. Do phrases like "the second sex" and "the feminine mystique" capture the variety of ways that women identified themselves between 1948 and 1968?

Chapter 6   Race, Class, Gender, and the Redefinition of America, 1968–88

WORK

1 *Ms. Magazine,* To Love, Honor and … Share: A Marriage Contract for the Seventies, 1973

Ms. Magazine *began publication in 1972 with articles and advertising that supported changes in the economic status of women. When a recently married couple submitted a contract they had drafted in place of wedding vows to* Ms. Magazine, *the editors published it with the caveat that while it might not hold up in court, it reflected an important aspect of an egalitarian marriage. Articles V, VI, and VII address economic issues within the institution of marriage or alternatively marriage as an economic partnership.*

Article V. Careers; Domicile

HARRIETT and HARVEY value the importance and integrity of their respective careers and acknowledge the demands that their jobs place on them as individuals and on their partnership. Commitment to their careers will sometimes place stress on the relationship. It has been the experience of the parties that insofar as their careers contribute to individual self-fulfillment, the careers strengthen the partnership.

THE PARTIES AGREE that, should a career opportunity arise for one of the parties in another city at any future time, the decision to move shall be mutual and based upon the following factors:

(a) *The overall advantage gained by one of the parties in pursuing the new career opportunity shall be weighed against the disadvantages, economic and otherwise, incurred by the other;*

(b) *The amount of income from the new job shall not be controlling;*

(c) *Short-term separations as a result of such moves may be necessary.*

HARVEY HEREBY WAIVES whatever right he may have to solely determine the legal domicile of the parties.

Article VI. Care and Use of Living Space

HARRIETT and HARVEY recognize the need for autonomy and equality within the home in terms of the use of available space and allocation of household tasks. The parties reject the concept that the responsibility for housework rests with the woman in a marriage relationship while the duties of home maintenance and repair rest with the man.

THEREFORE, THE PARTIES AGREE to share equally in the performance of all household tasks, taking into consideration individual schedules and preferences. Periodic allocations of household tasks will be made, in which the time involved in the performance of each party's tasks is equal.

THE PARTIES AGREE that decisions about the use of living space in the home shall be mutually made, regardless of the parties' relative financial interests in the ownership or rental of the home. Each party shall have an individual area within the home in an equal amount, insofar as space is available.

Article VII. Property; Debts; Living Expenses

HARRIETT and HARVEY intend that the individual autonomy sought in the partnership shall be reflected in the ownership of existing and future-acquired property, in the characterization and control of income, and in the responsibility for living expenses.

THEREFORE, THE PARTIES AGREE that this Article of their MARRIAGE CONTRACT, in lieu of the community property laws of the State of Washington, shall govern their interests and obligations in all property acquired during their marriage, as follows:

A. Property

THE PARTIES HAVE MADE full disclosure to each other of all properties and assets presently owned by each of them, and of the income derived therefrom and from all other sources, and AGREE that each party shall have sole management, control, and disposition of the property which each would have owned as a single person, all as specifically described in EXHIBIT A, which is incorporated by reference and made a part of this CONTRACT.

THE PARTIES AGREE that the wages, salary, and other income (including loans) derived by one of the parties will be the separate property of such party and subject to the independent control and or obligation of such party. In order to avoid the commingling of the separate assets, THE PARTIES AGREE to maintain separate bank accounts. At the present time, HARVEY's income consists of his salary as a full-time teacher with Seattle Public Schools; and HARRIETT's income is derived from her savings and government loans, while she is a full-time student at the University of Puget Sound School of Law in Tacoma.

Ownership of all future-acquired property, tangible and intangible, will be determined in accordance with the respective contributions of each party, even in the case of property which is jointly used. Annually, or sooner if required, THE PARTIES AGREE to amend EXHIBIT A of this CONTRACT to include future-acquired property and any changes in the ownership of property presently described in EXHIBIT A. The parties may, by mutual agreement, determine their respective interests in an item of property on a basis other than financial contribution, but such agreement shall not be effective until reduced to writing in EXHIBIT A to this CONTRACT. Gifts, bequests, or devises made to one of the parties will become the separate property of that party, while gifts made to both of the parties will be considered to be jointly owned.

THE PARTIES AGREE to name each other as full beneficiaries of any life insurance policies which they now own or may acquire in the future.

B. Debts

THE PARTIES AGREE that they shall not be obligated to the present or future-incurred debts of the other, including tuition and other educational expenses.

C. Living Expenses

THE PARTIES AGREE to share responsibility for the following expenses, which shall be called LIVING EXPENSES, in proportion to their respective incomes: (1) Mortgage payment or rent, (2) Utilities, (3) Home maintenance,

(4) Food, (5) Shared entertainment, (6) Medical expenses. Other expenses shall be called PERSONAL EXPENSES and will be borne individually by the parties.

THE PARTIES RECOGNIZE that in the absence of income by one of the parties, resulting from unemployment or extended illness, LIVING EXPENSES may become the sole responsibility of the employed party; and in such a situation, the employed party will assume responsibility for the PERSONAL EXPENSES of the other, including, but not limited to the following: (1) Insurance, (2) Transportation, (3) Clothing, (4) Miscellaneous personal items.

THE PARTIES AGREE that extended periods of time in which one or both of the parties will be totally without income will be mutually negotiated.

HARRIETT HEREBY WAIVES whatever right she may have to rely on HARVEY to provide the sole economic support for the family unit.

Source: *Ms. Magazine*, 1(12), June 1973, pp. 62–5. Reprinted by permission of Ms Magazine © 1973.

2 Barbara Kingsolver, Ask Any Miner, 1983

In the mid-1970s Phelps Dodge hired women to work in its copper mines at Ajo and Morenci, Arizona, for the first time since World War II under pressure from a union-backed equal opportunity lawsuit. The work was arduous, both physically and emotionally, but 10 women were hired there in 1973 and 1974. Above all, work in the mines paid more than the pink-collar jobs otherwise available to them. Journalist and novelist Barbara Kingsolver met these women when she reported on a major strike against Phelps Dodge in 1983.

She was one of two women hired at the Morenci pit in 1975, the first since World War II. Doll was twenty-one. "My husband and I had just moved here from Bisbee – he transferred from the mine down there. I didn't know anybody in town, didn't have a job, and was really bored. I cleaned the house three times a day, you know, but there's only so much you can do.... I decided it was either divorce or go to work. I put in my application, and then I would go up to the office every day just to let them know I was still here. I think the secretaries in the office are actually the ones that hired me – they got so used to seeing me.

"I was hired as a lubrication helper. That means you're an assistant to a lubrication mechanic and go around with him in the pit, servicing all the big equipment. I got a lot of harassment. My foreman just didn't want a woman there. He would hassle me, say things like I couldn't talk to my partner. Can you believe that? The two of us would be working under a machine together for eight hours, and we weren't supposed to talk?

"As a helper, I would have to ride around the pit with some guy in the service truck. They would make a pass, and when I pushed them off they'd get mad. Sometimes they wouldn't bring me back to the women's change room when I had to go to the bathroom – they'd tell me just to go out there in the pit, behind a rock or something. The first time a guy made a pass, it made me feel awful; I went home crying. My husband wasn't much help. He said that wasn't a good enough reason to leave work. I could never come home and talk about work. He would talk all about how hard he worked, what happened on his job, but not me – my job wasn't important. And I was actually making more money than he was!

"It was mostly my foreman that made trouble, more than the guys on the job. I got so discouraged at one point I actually quit. I went into the office and tried to explain to Olsen [her supervisor] what was going on. I was crying, but I told him, 'Don't hold crying against me. Sometimes this is what women do – we cry.' Later they told me that after I left he threw my resignation in the trash. They just figured I'd had a bad day." . . .

"There was a twenty-eight-day probation period to see if you could do a new job, and if you wanted the job. One day, right before the end of the twenty-eight days, my foreman told me I was going to have to use the air wrench for eight hours straight. He actually told the other guys not to help me. They told me about this. They knew I pulled my own weight, and they didn't think it was fair. So they showed me how to do certain things easier, and I came through it all right. At the end, the foreman told me if I really wanted the job I could stay. I told him I'd earned that job."

Less than a year after she started work in the locomotive shop, Doll became pregnant. When her foreman found out, he tried once again to make her give up, this time by sending her to the service yard to do work that involved constant squatting and heavy lifting in awkward positions. She pulled an abdominal muscle.

"They sent me to see a company doctor, and I was lucky, I got the good one, Dr. O'Leary. He was really mad when he found out what they had done to me. He wrote a letter telling them I was capable of working but that the squatting was dangerous for me and that I should go back to my old job in repairs. So I got to go back. The company got the idea I wasn't leaving.

"I had to use the men's bathroom, of course. I would kick the door and say, 'Whoever's in there, get out, because I gotta go!' One day one of the head guys was in there, and when he came out, what a look he gave me! Right after that they gave me my own bathroom. The guys built it, fixed it all up for me, and asked me what color I wanted it painted; I said yellow.

They would have painted 'Doll' over the door, but they had to just put 'Women.'"

Her co-workers were not just being solicitous because she was pregnant. She had their honest respect. By this time she was a first-class helper making fifty-six dollars a day and had earned the nickname "Fifty-six dollars worth of a-lotta-help."

Doll's weight went from 94 pounds to 154. By her seventh month, she said, she looked pretty much like a barrel on legs. She had to leave for work a half-hour early each morning, because it took her that long to walk to the pit from the parking lot. "By that time I'd just about had it. One day while I was working, an air hose came loose. They're really heavy and fly all around – it's compressed air – and if they hit you they can really hurt you. The way I stopped it finally was I jumped on it, just stood on it. So there I was, down in this little servicing pit with about two feet of room on each side, pregnant out to here, with that air hose whipping around. I thought to myself, 'I have proven my point,' I stopped working the next day."

At that time there was no maternity leave, and Doll says her union co-workers ridiculed her for even suggesting it. "They would say, 'Why should you get paid leave for being pregnant? You sure had fun getting that way.' I asked them, 'What about a guy that breaks his leg when he's out playing baseball? He had fun doing that, and he gets medical leave!'" Doll's logic, if offbeat, was convincing; she won six weeks' paid leave.

After her son was born she decided to quit, since her family wasn't desperate for the money. But circumstances changed. Within a year she was divorced and in need of a job. She went to work as a secretary for the city. "It was okay for a while, but after working in the mine, $3.10 an hour just didn't make it. I knew I could be making those bucks. So I put in my application. I'd had it in for three weeks when they hired me as a cleanup laborer. They were creating a new department, the leach plant. I started back as a laborer making around $10 an hour. . . .

"He [the superintendant] expected me to do more work than anybody could do in eight hours. I told him that I couldn't do that much in one shift, so he turned my statement around and tried to use it to get me fired – said I'd admitted I couldn't do the job. I was down at Cole's Pizza that night talking about it, and one of the guys there happened to be a grievance man for the Steelworkers. He heard me, and asked me about my situation. The next day I went in and everything was taken care of just like that. I didn't even have to file a grievance. My super wasn't too happy about it. He said, 'I didn't think you would go to the union. We could have worked something out.' Sure! I was impressed when I saw what the union could do for me." . . .

Years ago, when she was a lubricator assistant, Doll occasionally caught sight of a much older woman who'd been working in the mine since World

War II. Her name was Opal. They were in different departments and never really had a chance to talk. Now it's too late. But Doll still wonders about Opal's life: Was it even tougher for women back then? Was the work harder? When the men came home from the war and wanted their jobs back, was the harassment unbearable?

Flossie Navarro says "yes" to all of the above, and she should know. Before getting her medical retirement in 1967, she shoveled rock in the Morenci mine for twenty-three years. She didn't stay there all that time because of any fondness for shoveling, she told me flatly. "I didn't really like the work at all. But we was raising kids, and we needed the money. We raised eleven – Ed had ten already, and then me and him had one. So it wasn't a matter of liking it, it was a matter of having to.

"I don't really have no understanding about the women's movement because I've always drawed the same pay as a man. You got in there and done your part because you was getting paid just as much as he was. I always felt like if he had to do an hour's work I should do it too. The only difference in the paychecks was for the extra day. Back then there was a state law that women could only work six days a week. Then we'd get two days off. After I went to shift work I'd work six days and the seventh you was off. The men, see, could work twenty-eight days straight through and then get their time off.

"I really didn't want to work more than six days, but it would have been better when you was on graveyard shift. You'd work six nights and kind of get your eatin' and sleepin' straightened up, and then you'd be off and have to be up early with the kids. Then you'd have to go back and work six more nights. That was kind of aggravating. You'd rather go ahead and work that one night, not for the money-wise but for the rest you'd get."

Flossie is a union maid, through and through. She began with the CIO, during the war, then joined Mine-Mill, then the United Steelworkers of America. "Twenty-three years I was union. The union made sure everything was fair. The dues I paid every month wasn't that high – it was worth it. Each time the union fought and got us a paid holiday or sick leave or whatever, we just got that right along with the men. When I first went to work we only got two or three holidays a year. In '44 I got sixty-four cents an hour to push that wheelbarrow. It was the unions that got us better pay." Flossie was emphatic on this point. "P.D. wasn't going to give us nothing. They don't say, 'Here it is, come get it.' No, they don't!"

Bringing up the strike proved to be a reliable way to rouse her ire. "I think that's a damn dirty deal, is what I think about that! What's involved in the strike is what we fought for all those years – the unions. And it makes you mad and gets you hot under the collar to see them try to take it away. But what can you do? You'd just like to give someone a rap across the mouth."

Flossie, like so many others, felt that racial equality was especially at stake in the current strike. She had seen the bad old days. "Now, I never wanted a promotion myself. I was just satisfied to go and do my job if they'd leave me alone. But Ed, he tried to go up. Every time he'd come up in line for seniority somebody'd whack him down again to the bottom. Because he was a Mexican."

Ed Navarro, one of Carmina Garcia's two surviving brothers and the man Flossie married, had grown up among the peach and quince orchards at Eagle Creek. His family had been driven from their farm, and he was working as a laborer in the mine when Flossie came in. Because of poor health, he wasn't drafted, and he remained in Morenci through the war. Not surprisingly, this was when he was finally promoted to repairman – when the only alternative would have been to promote a woman.

Ed still had vivid forty-year-old memories of working with women in the mine – including the one who became his bride. "Oh, I saw them push those wheelbarrows. They would get a good load on them and haul it about fifty yards over there and dump it. It kind of hurt you to see women doing that."

I asked Ed if he respected Flossie for doing such hard work. His eyes sparkled, and he answered without hesitation, "Yes. That's how come she married me."

Marriages between Anglos and Hispanics were extremely uncommon in those days, but Flossie insists this wasn't a problem for her. "Oh, people didn't think much of it; they would say things. Now, my family always treated him good – they couldn't believe he was a Mexican. They didn't see too many back in Arkansas. When we went back there people would stare at us. But I'll tell you one thing. If you are in a restaurant, they would take your money. If you stayed in a motel, they'd take your money. They didn't ask if it was 'mixed' money.

"There was another thing I could never understand. If a Mexican woman married a white man, people around here didn't think that was so bad. The woman would change her name, you know, and all. But if a white woman married a Mexican man, that was different; they didn't like that. To me, I never could see the difference. The kids are going to come out mixed, ever which way they manage it!"

Regardless of popular opinion, she and Ed consider their union successful. "We'll soon be married thirty-four years, and we never fought over money. Right, Ed? I brought home that paycheck, too, so I felt like I could always do what I wanted with the money, and we agreed on things. I always figured what was his was mine, and if what I had wasn't his, that was his fault!"

Flossie sometimes thinks she might have liked to stay home with the children, but with eleven, that simply was never an option. There wasn't enough money. She sighed, remembering the year they had two graduating from high school and two from eighth grade, all at once. "Kids have to have an awful lot," she said.

"We never told our kids what to do. We just raised them to go to school and behave theirselves and not get in trouble, and thank God we never did have one get locked up, I don't think. Well, really that's something to be thankful for, isn't it?" She leaned back, clapped her hands down on the arms of her overstuffed chair, and looked across the room at Ed. And laughed. "We raised eleven kids, and now here we are looking at each other." . . .

Source: Barbara Kingsolver, *Holding the Line: Women in the Great Arizona Mine Strike of 1983* (Ithaca, NY: ILR Press, 1989), excerpts from pp. 73–80.

3 Seth Mydans, Children of Chinatown Get a Day-Care Center, 1984

New York City's Chinatown was the site of a historic strike in 1982 that resulted in favorable contract negotiations between the International Ladies Garment Workers Union (ILGWU) and the manufacturers. Wage increases over three years and a benefit package that included holiday pay for piece workers, greater employer contributions to health and welfare funds, and a cost of living adjustment improved the conditions of labor for piece workers, many of whom spoke only Chinese. After the strike, activists continued to work towards a Chinatown day-care center for garment workers.

It took a Chinese-language petition signed by 3,000 immigrant seamstresses to get it started, and today it will be opened formally: the Garment Industry Day Care Center of Chinatown.

The dedication of the little red-brick schoolhouse in the heart of Chinatown culminates a cooperative effort by government and private business that the city would like to see duplicated, officials said.

The cost of the center is being borne, in small part, by the parents of the children themselves. The idea for the center, however, came totally from the people involved, immigrant women who labor long hours as they struggle to make their way in their new country.

Day Care Common in China

"In China, any unit that you belong to has a day-care center as a matter of course," said Katie Kwan, a union activist who helped lead a campaign to open the center.

She said the immigrant mothers "can't believe it when they get here and there's nobody to take care of their kids."

Because most of the husbands work in restaurants while their wives sew piecework, she said, the children were often taken along to work or left in groups with untrained babysitters for lack of an alternative.

Mrs. Kwan and other members of Local 23–25 of the International Ladies Garment Workers Union drew up a petition and spent their lunch hours carrying it up and down the narrow stairs of many of Chinatown's 500 small garment factories to gather the signatures. There were delays, she said, but in the end the union championed their cause.

Costs are Subsidized

The center, at 115 Chrystie Street, opened its first classes last Nov. 28. It now cares for 70 pre-kindergarten children of union members.

The Agency for Child Development of the city's Human Services Administration will be paying about half the operating costs....

Private assistance comes from the Greater Blouse, Skirt and Undergarment Association Inc., which is made up of owners of the small factories for whom the immigrant seamstresses work. The association will pay $32 of the weekly cost of $82 per child.

To cover the rest of the cost, parents will be assessed by the city on a sliding scale pegged to income. The cost will range from $2 to $8 a week for each child.

CITIZENSHIP

4 Angela Davis, Free Angela Davis, 1972

Angela Y. Davis, (1944–), an intellectual and political activist, worked on behalf of the Student Nonviolent Coordinating Committee (SNCC) and the Black Panther Party. She had studied Marxism and joined the Communist Party in 1968. In 1970 the Federal Bureau of Investigation (FBI) put her on its Ten Most Wanted List on charges stemming from her efforts on behalf of the Soledad Brothers on trial in Marin County, California, for murder of a federal judge. She was arrested in New York City and held at the Women's House of Detention. She became the subject of an international campaign to "Free

*Angela Davis," and was acquitted following her trial in 1972. Davis stood
at the center of the Black Power movement; her writings focus on class, race,
and gender and themes of oppression and self-determination.*

The inside of this jail stood in stark contrast to the building I had just left. The FBI headquarters was modern, antiseptically clean, its plastic texture illuminated by fluorescent lights. The Women's House of Detention was old, musty, dreary and dim. The floor of the receiving room was unpainted cement, dirt from the shoes of thousands of prisoners, policemen and matrons etched into its surface. There was a single desk where all the paperwork seemed to be done, and rows of long benches which looked as though they had once been pews in a storefront church.

I was told to sit on the front bench in the right-hand row. A few other women were scattered unsystematically throughout the benches. Some, I learned, had just been booked; others had come in from a day in court. Food was brought in to us, but I had no appetite for the wrinkled hot dogs and cold potatoes.

Suddenly there was a loud rumble outside the gate. Scores of women were walking up to the entrance, waiting for the iron gate to be opened. I wondered what could have led to such a massive bust, but one of the sisters inside told me that these were the women returning from court on the last bus.

All the women I could see were either Black or Puerto Rican. There were no white prisoners in the group. One of the Puerto Rican sisters called out, "Are you Spanish?" At first I didn't think she could mean me, but then I remembered how I must have looked with my hair straight and flat after the agents had snatched the wig away. I said "no" with as warm a tone as I could manage, trying to convey that it did not really matter: the same jailers would be holding the same hammer over our heads. While the women who had returned from court were still standing outside the iron gates, I was led out of the room. I thought that I was on my way to the cells, but instead I found myself in a large windowless room, a dim light bulb barely illuminating the center of the ceiling. There were the same filthy cement floors, drab yellow tile walls and two very old office desks.

A robust white matron was in charge. When I discovered, amid the papers taped to the wall, my picture and description on an FBI Wanted poster, she snatched it down. My eyes shifted to the next poster. To my surprise it bore the photograph and description of a woman whom I had known in high school. Kathy Boudin had been in my eleventh- and twelfth-grade classes at Elisabeth Irwin High School. Now she was on the FBI's Wanted list.

When the work shift changed, I was still waiting in that dingy room. A new officer was sent to guard me. She was black, she was young – younger than I – she wore a natural, and as she approached, she showed none of the belligerence and arrogance I had learned to associate with jail matrons.

It was a disarming experience. Yet it was not the fact that she was black that threw me. I had encountered black matrons before – in jails in San Diego and Los Angeles – but it was her manner: unaggressive and apparently sympathetic.

At first she was taciturn. But after a few minutes, in a quiet voice, she told me, "A lot of officers here – the black officers – have been pulling for you. We've been hoping all along that you would get to someplace that was safe."

I wanted to talk to her, but I felt it was best to be wary of any involved conversation. For all I knew, she might have been instructed to assume this sympathetic posture. If I appeared to be deluded by her sympathy, if I appeared to become familiar with her, it would lend credibility should she decide to lie about the content of our conversations. I would be safer if I maintained the distance, the formality.

Thinking that I might be able to pry some information out of her about my predicament, I asked her why the delay was so long. She didn't know all the details, she said, but she thought that they were trying to decide how they could keep me away from the main jail population. The problem was the lack of facilities for isolation. It was her feeling that they would put me in 4b, the area of the jail reserved for women with psychological problems.

I looked at her in disbelief. If they locked me up in a tank for mental patients, their next step might be to declare me insane. Perhaps they would try to say that communism is a psychological illness – something akin to masochism, exhibitionism or sadism.

Surprised at my reaction, she tried to console me by saying that I'd probably be happier there – sometimes the women would ask to be moved to the "mental" cellblock because they couldn't tolerate the noise in the main population. But to me, jail was jail – there were no degrees of better or worse. And nothing could detract from the thought that they wanted to isolate me because they feared the impact the mere presence of a political prisoner would have on the other women.

I reminded the officer that I had not yet made the two telephone calls due me. I needed a lawyer, and I knew I had the right to contact one.

"A lawyer by the name of John Abt has been trying to get in to see you," she said. "But visiting hours for attorneys are over at five o'clock. I'm sorry I can't do anything."

"If I can't see him, at least I ought to be able to call him."

"These people," she said, "haven't decided how to deal with you. They say you're a federal prisoner, under the jurisdiction of the federal marshals.

We have federal prisoners all the time. The marshals are the ones who should have let you make the two phone calls. At least, that's what the captain said."

"For five hours," I insisted, "I have been trying to make a phone call, and everybody I ask gives me the run-around."

"You know, no prisoners here are actually allowed to use the phone. You have to write out your number and your message on a form and a special officer does the calling."

I started to protest, but soon realized that nothing I said would make them give me access to a telephone that evening. The only thing they relinquished was a card John Abt had left at the front gate.

The crowd of women just back from court had apparently been "processed," and I could now return to the receiving room to await my turn for this mysterious "process." As I entered the room, I saw a figure lying on a hospital cart, almost completely covered with a sheet. I didn't know whether it was living or dead. It was simply there, unattended, in the least conspicuous corner of the receiving room. When I tried to inspect it as carefully as I could from a distance, I noticed an elevation in the middle that seemed to be moving. It was a pregnant prisoner about to deliver – and soon. Wasn't anybody going to *do* anything? Were they going to let her have the baby right here in this dump? Even if they did take her to a halfway decent hospital, what would happen to the infant once it was born? Would it be placed in an orphanage while she did her time? I felt angry but helpless as I watched the sister go further and further into labor. Soon the iron gates opened, and the attendants of a police ambulance came to take her away. I watched them carry the stretcher into the night.

At last it was my turn. The print of my forefinger was stamped on an orange card, which, they informed me, was the jail identification that every prisoner had to keep with her at all times. Then came another body search. I vigorously protested this second search – the FBI had already done it once. The officer assigned to search me was ambivalent about the procedure. While I undressed in the shower room, she discreetly pretended to be looking for something. She gave me a hospital dressing gown and directed me to sit on a bench outside a closed door. From the women already waiting there, I learned that we were about to be searched internally. Each time prisoners left the jail for a court appearance, and upon their return, they had to submit to a vaginal and rectal examination.

It was one A.M. before they actually booked me into the jail. There were only three women left in the receiving room. One of them stared at me for a long time and finally asked whether I was Angela Davis. When I smiled and nodded, she said that coming in from court she had seen crowds outside demonstrating for me. All kinds of people – young, old, black, white.

"What? Where?" I was tremendously excited by the possibility that people in the movement were near.

The sister told us to be quiet for a moment. If we listened especially hard, we might be able to hear some of the chants. Sure enough, muffled rhythms were penetrating these massive walls. Just outside the building, the sister said, they were chanting, "Free Angela Davis." The sister describing the scene was in jail for possession of heroin. (The first thing she was going to do when she got out, she said, was to look up her connection.) With an expression of triumph on her face, she assured me that I was going to win. She said this knowing that according to jail standards, I was facing very heavy charges.

The entire jail was shrouded in darkness when I finally reached the cell in 4b. It was no more than four and a half feet wide. The only furnishings were an iron cot bolted to the floor and a seatless toilet at the foot of the bed. Some minutes after they had locked me in, the officer in charge of that unit – another young black woman – came to the iron door. She whispered through the grating that she was shoving a piece of candy under the door. She sounded sincere enough, but I couldn't take any chances. I didn't want to be paranoid, but it was better to be too distrustful than not cautious enough. I was familiar with jailhouse "suicides" in California. For all I knew, there might be poison in the candy.

The first night in jail, I had no desire to sleep. I thought about George and his brothers in San Quentin. I thought about Jonathan. I thought about my mother and father and hoped that they would make it through this ordeal. And then I thought about the demonstration outside, about all the people who had dropped everything to fight for my freedom.

I had just been captured; a trial awaited me in California on the charges of murder, kidnapping and conspiracy. A conviction on any one of these charges could mean death in the gas chamber. One would have thought that this was an enormous defeat. Yet, at that moment, I was feeling better than I had felt in a long time. The struggle would be difficult, but there was already a hint of victory. In the heavy silence of the jail, I discovered that if I concentrated hard enough, I could hear echoes of slogans being chanted on the other side of the walls. "Free Angela Davis." "Free All Political Prisoners."

Source: Angela Davis, *An Autobiography* (New York: Random House, 1974), pp. 18–23.

5 Letter from Esther Peterson to Martha Griffiths, 1971

The Equal Rights Amendment (ERA) first introduced in 1923, was reintroduced in Congress in 1972 by Martha Griffiths and quickly ratified by 30 states. Esther Peterson was appointed by President Kennedy in 1961 to head the Women's Bureau in the Department of Labor and as vice chairman of the President's Commission on the Status of Women. She initially opposed the ERA fearing that it would undo decades of work to protect working women. However, she decided to support the ERA in 1971 agreeing with many working women who wanted equal pay for equal work and equal opportunity in the industrial workplace. The AFL-CIO formally endorsed the ERA in 1973.

7714 13th Street, N.W.
Washington, D.C. 20012
October 12, 1971

Dear Martha:

As you know, I have in the past been reluctant to support the equal rights amendment because of a long-standing concern for the low-income women workers who are so frequently exploited. Then, too, I was deeply involved in the work of the President's Commission on the Status of Women and concurred with its conclusions that the Constitution embodies equality of rights for women in the fifth and fourteenth amendments. We did not feel that a constitutional amendment was needed at that time. We urged that definitive court pronouncement, particularly by the United States Supreme Court be sought so as to establish the principle of equality firmly in constitutional doctrine.

The action we had hoped for in the courts has not materialized and the increasingly conservative nature of the Supreme Court leads one to conclude that women's chances for assistance through judicial action are slight.

After much soul searching I have come to the conclusion that the time for waiting for court action is past and enactment of the equal rights amendment would be a constructive step. It is difficult for me to make this statement. I realize that it will come as a disappointment to many individuals and organizations with whom I shared the opposite view for many years. However, such has happened in the past decade to improve the prospects for women – the Equal Pay Act, extension of coverage of the Fair Labor Standards Act, Title 7 of the Civil Rights Act, prohibiting sex discrimination in employment policies, and the amended Executive Order 11246. Also heartening are efforts to strengthen this recent legislation.

In the process, such state protective legislation for women has been, in effect, nullified. I note that all but twelve states have either repealed or relaxed their hours laws. Now I believe we should direct our efforts toward replacing discriminatory state laws with good labor standards that will protect both men and women.

History is moving in this direction and I believe women must move with it. But it entails a shared responsibility for all citizens. That is why I would urge women who have found changes in the laws to be to their advantage to make every effort to assist those who still may be exploited.

My congratulations to you, Martha, for taking a courageous and fore-sighted position. I am happy that I can now share it with you.

Sincerely,

EP/pam

Source: Esther Peterson to Martha Griffiths, October 12, 1971, Esther Peterson Papers, 1884–1998, Box 54, Folder 1061, Schlesinger Library, Radcliffe Institute for Advanced Study, Harvard University. Available from Alexander Street Press at http://aspbnew.alexanderstreet.com/was2/was2.browse.documents.aspx by Letter=L&sortorder=title&pagePos=10.

6 Phyllis Schlafly, Women Should Not Serve in Combat, 1979

The ERA served as a lightning rod along with reproductive rights to galvanize an anti-feminist movement in the early 1970s largely among married white women, mostly Christian, and devout in religious practice. Phyllis Schlafly had worked as a researcher for Senator Joseph McCarthy at the peak of anti-communist hysteria in 1953. In 1972 she effectively used her skills as a lawyer, public speaker, and writer to organize a campaign to STOP-ERA.

The push to repeal the laws that exempt women from military combat duty must be the strangest of all aberrations indulged in by what has become known as the women's liberation or feminist movement. The very idea of women serving in military combat is so unnatural that it almost sounds like a death wish for our species.

Last Sunday's newspapers carried a front-page picture of a man express-ing the disgust of the average American with the humiliation of our nation by the radicals in Iran. The man held up a large sign that said, "Kick me, I'm an American." Yet, here we are at a House committee hearing at which representatives of the women's liberation movement are, in essence, saying, "Kick me, I'm a woman. I want to be sent into war where I can be shot at and captured just like a man." Some men seem willing to let that happen.

Has our nation sunk so low that we are willing to send our daughters into battle? Is chivalry completely dead? Breathes there a man with soul so dead that he will not rise up and defend his wife, his sweetheart, his mother, or his daughter, against those who want to wound or capture them, whoever they may be?

There is no evidence in all history for the proposition that the assignment of women to military combat jobs is the way to promote national security, improve combat readiness, or win wars. Indeed, the entire experience of recorded history teaches us that battles are *not* won by coed armies or coed navies. Even Hitler and the Japanese, when they ran short of manpower, found it more efficient to use underage and overage men in combat than to use female troops. Of the thousands of books written about World War II, no one ever wrote that Hitler or the Japanese should have solved their manpower shortage problem by using women in combat.

Every country that has experimented with women in combat has abandoned the idea. Israel used women in combat for a few weeks in the war of 1948 but never did so in later military operations. Women are now treated very differently from men in the Israeli armed forces. They serve only about half as long; they are housed in separate barracks, they have an automatic exemption if they marry or have a baby. Israel has a smaller percentage of women in its armed forces than the United States.

The Soviet Union used some female troops in World War II but has since abandoned this altogether. Women make up less than one per cent of Soviet troops today. There must be a reason for the unanimous verdict of history that the armed forces demand different roles for men and women.

The first reason is that women, on the average, have only 60 percent of the physical strength of men. This truism, so self-evident to those with eyes to see, has been confirmed by many studies. However, under pressure from the feminist movement, much of this evidence is not allowed to see the light of day or, if it does, is couched in apologetic terms. For example, a report by the Comptroller General of the United States called *Job Opportunities for Women in the Military: Progress and Problems* surveyed the actual experience of enlisted women placed on military jobs formerly reserved for men. The Comptroller General said, "If as the Air-Force Surgeon General has concluded, females are only 60 percent as strong as males, it seems there are some jobs that males, on the average can do better than females."

As I travel around the country, I do many radio call-in programs. Everywhere I go, I hear the same complaint from men in the U.S. Armed Services: the women are getting the same pay and have the same rank as the men, but they are not doing the equal work, and the male soldiers must do part of the women's jobs for them. This situation is not just and is destructive of morale and good personnel relations.

Sex-neutral treatment of men and women in the military is just as unfair to women as it is to men. If you interview the women who are army privates or navy sailors, you get a different story from that of the officers who must toe the administration line.

The second reason for the unanimous verdict of history that the armed forces demand different roles for men and women is that women get pregnant and men do not. That particular sex-role stereotype has become a tremendous problem in the military today. Why should anyone be surprised? When young men and women in the age group of eighteen to twenty-five are required to live in close proximity, often doing unpleasant tasks and suffering from loneliness away from home, the inevitable happens. News stories report that the pregnancy rate is about 15 percent among servicewomen. Another 5 percent have had their babies and brought them back to the post. The rape rate is also said to be about twice what it is in civilian life.

Yet we are told that the armed services cannot discharge a woman who becomes pregnant because that would be "sex discrimination" unless the services also discharge the father of the baby! And it would be obviously impossible for the armed services to discharge every man who fathers a baby. The services are required to ignore the obvious fact that pregnancy keeps a woman from doing her job in a way that fatherhood does not interfere with a man's performance on the job.

How did we get into our present situation, in which our military officers are issuing maternity uniforms, opening nurseries on army posts, and pretending that women can do anything that men can do? For the answer to that, we must look at two of the false dogmas of the women's liberation movement.

The first false dogma is that there really is no difference between the sexes (except those obvious ones we need not discuss) and that all those other differences you think you see are not inherent but are due merely to sex-role stereotyping which can and must be erased by sex-neutral education, laws, and changed attitudes. The sex-neutral dogma is variously called gender free, unisex, or the elimination of sexism from our society and attitudes.

Neither Congress nor the military will ever be able to cope with the problems and demands raised by the feminists until we realize that the feminists look upon the military as a vehicle to achieve the gender-free goals of the women's liberation movement – not as an instrument to defend the United States of America. Since the armed services are an institution where people must obey orders, it is the perfect vehicle to enforce the sex-neutral goals of the feminist movement. Feminists look upon the armed services as a giant social welfare program, designed to provide upward social mobility for minorities which, according to their peculiar definitions, include women.

The national security of the United States, justice to the majority of young men and women, respect for the wishes of the great majority of the

American people, and rational behavior all demand that we continue to structure the armed services of our nation on the commonsense premise that there must be different roles for men and women in the military. We cannot allow those values to be upset and disoriented by the strident demands of a few over-draft-age feminists who have high-level affirmative-action jobs in the Pentagon, or by the handful of high-ranking women officers who seek greater recognition at the expense of their sisters who will have to march in the combat infantry.

It is interesting that the desire of women for sex-neutral treatment in the military is usually in inverse proportion to their rank. A few of them have delusions of grandeur that women must be accepted as army-chair generals and admirals, but the price that our own daughters will have to pay in the ranks, in case of another war or a reinstated draft is far too high, as is the price of reduced combat readiness.

The second false dogma of the women's liberation movement is that we must be neutral between morality and immorality, and between the institution of the family and alternative lifestyles. As the national conference on International Women's Year at Houston in 1977 proved, the feminists demand that government policy accord the same dignity to lesbians and prostitutes as to wives, to illegitimate births as to legitimate, to abortions as to live births, and that we support immoral and anti-family practices with public funds. In deference to feminists, the armed services are now supporting and maintaining servicewomen who engage in immoral practices and bring their babies back to the posts. We must stop this public funding of immorality.

The purpose of the armed services is to defend the United States of America – not to create a tax-funded haven for sexually active young men and women, nor is it to serve as a giant social welfare institution. The need for combat-ready troops and a stronger national defense has never been greater in our country's history. The very idea of ordering women into combat jobs would send a message to the world that we have reduced the strength of our troops to the physical strength of the average female. It would be a sign of weakness because it would tell the world we do not have enough men willing to defend America.

I urge Congress to reject all demands to repeal the laws that exempt servicewomen from combat jobs. I urge Congress to maintain and reinforce the time-tested rule that there must be different roles for men and women in the United States armed services. Anything less than that will waste the valuable energies of our military officers on the exhausting task of coping with the escalating demands of a few feminist spokesmen who do not speak for anyone but their own narrow group. The first priority of the armed services should be to rebuild the military strength and the combat effectiveness of the United States.

Source: Phyllis Schlafly, Testimony to the House Armed Services Committee, Military Personnel Subcommittee, November 16, 1979, in *Feminist Fantasies* (Dallas, TX: Spence Publishing, 2003), pp.161–5.

7 Sister Theresa Kane, Welcome to Pope John Paul II, October 7, 1979

Sister Theresa Kane, a religious with the Sisters of Mercy and head of the Leadership Conference of Women Religious, welcomed Pope John Paul II on his first visit to the United States in 1979. Although the Pope opposed the ordination of women Sister Kane nevertheless used this most public occasion to ask the Pope to open all the Church's ministries to women. During the 1970s the ordination of women created new possibilities for female clerics in Judaism and Protestantism.

October 7, 1979

In the name of the women religious gathered in this Shrine dedicated to Mary, I greet you, Your Holiness Pope John Paul II. It is an honor, a privilege and an awesome responsibility to express in a few moments the sentiments of women present at this shrine dedicated to Mary the Patronness of the United States and the Mother of all humankind. It is appropriate that a woman's voice be heard in this shrine and I call upon Mary to direct what is in my heart and on my lips during these moments of greeting.

I welcome you sincerely; I extend greetings of profound respect, esteem and affection from women religious throughout this country. With the sentiments experienced by Elizabeth when visited by Mary, our hearts too leap with joy as we welcome you – you who have been called the Pope of the people. As I welcome you today, I am mindful of the countless number of women religious who have dedicated their lives to the church in this country in the past. The lives of many valiant women who were the catalysts of growth for the United States Church continue to serve as heroines of inspiration to us as we too struggle to be women of courage and hope during these times.

Women religious in the United States entered into the renewal efforts in an obedient response to the call of Vatican II. We have experienced both joy and suffering in our efforts. As a result of such renewal women religious approach the next decade with a renewed identity and a deep sense of our responsibilities to, with and in the church.

Your Holiness, the women of this country have been inspired by your spirit of courage. We thank you for exemplifying such courage in speaking to us so directly about our responsibilities to the poor and oppressed

throughout the world. We who live in the United States, one of the wealthi-
est nations of the earth, need to become ever more conscious of the suffering
that is present among so many of our brothers and sisters, recognizing that
systemic injustices are serious moral and social issues that need to be
confronted courageously. We pledge ourselves in solidarity with you in
your efforts to respond to the cry of the poor.

As I share this privileged moment with you, Your Holiness, I urge you to
be mindful of the intense suffering and pain which is part of the life of many
women in these United States. I call upon you to listen with compassion and
to hear the call of women who comprise half of humankind. As women we
have heard the powerful messages of our Church addressing the dignity and
reverence for all persons. As women we have pondered upon these words.
Our contemplation leads us to state that the Church in its struggle to be
faithful to its call for reverence and dignity for all persons must respond by
providing the possibility of women as persons being included in all ministries of our Church. I urge you, Your Holiness, to be open to and respond to
the voices coming from the women of this country who are desirous of
serving in and through the Church as fully participating members.

Finally, I assure you, Pope John Paul, of the prayers, support and fidelity of
the women religious in this country as you continue to challenge us to be women
of holiness for the sake of the Kingdom. With these few words from the joyous,
hope-filled prayer, the Magnificat, we call upon Mary to be your continued
source of inspiration, courage and hope: "May your whole being proclaim and
magnify the Lord; may your spirit always rejoice in God your Saviour; the Lord
who is mighty has done great things for you; Holy is God's Name."

Source: Sister Theresa Kane, RSM, "Welcome to Pope John Paul II," October 7,
1979, Donna Quinn Collection 5/Pope's US Visit – 1979, 1 of 3, Women and
Leadership Archives, Loyola University, Chicago, IL. Available from Alexander
Street Press at http://aspbnew.alexanderstreet.com/was2/was2.object.details.aspx?
dorpid=1000689866.

REPRESENTATIONS

8 Bil Keane, When I Grow Up, 1973

This cartoon by Bil Keane inspired a reader to write to Ms. *Magazine that it
had converted her to a feminist. Raising awareness through reading and small-
group discussions played a significant role in second-wave feminism. It is
difficult to figure out what Bil Keane intended by "just."*

THE FAMILY CIRCUS   By Bil Keane

"When I grow up I don't want to be ANYTHING! I'm just going to be a mommy and a grandma."

Figure 6.1   Bill Keane When I Grow Up 1973
Source: Family Circus Cartoon submitted as part of a letter to the editor of *Ms. Magazine*, 1(12), June 1973, p. 6. © Bill Keane Inc.

9 Gloria Anzaldúa, To Live in the Borderlands means you, 1999

Gloria Anzaldúa (1942–2004) challenged women of color to write from their own epicenter and to share with others both what defined them and what set them apart. Her reflection on women of color in the last quarter of the twentieth century used powerful imagery to raise serious questions about women's lives. When Anzaldúa died in 2004, she left behind a body of work which makes impossible to ignore what she referred to as women at the borderlands.

To live in the Borderlands means you
    are neither *hispana india negra española*
    ni gabacha, eres mestiza, mulata, half-breed
    caught in the crossfire between camps
    while carrying all five races on your back
    not knowing which side to turn to, run from;

To live in the Borderlands means knowing
    that the *india* in you, betrayed for 500 years,
    is no longer speaking to you,
    that *mexicanas* call you *rajetas,*
    that denying the Anglo inside you
    is as bad as having denied the Indian or Black;

Cuando vives en la frontera
    people walk through you, the wind steals your voice,
    you're a *burra, buey,* scapegoat,
    forerunner of a new race,

half and half – both woman and man, neither –
a new gender;

To live in the Borderlands means to
   put *chile* in the borscht,
   eat whole wheat *tortillas,*
   speak Tex-Mex with a Brooklyn accent;
   be stopped by *la migra* at the border checkpoints;

Living in the Borderlands means you fight hard to
   resist the gold elixir beckoning from the bottle,
   the pull of the gun barrel,
   the rope crushing the hollow of your throat;

In the Borderlands
   you are the battleground
   where enemies are kin to each other;
   you are at home, a stranger,
   the border disputes have been settled
   the volley of shots have shattered the truce
   you are wounded, lost in action
   dead, fighting back;

To live in the Borderlands means
   the mill with the razor white teeth wants to shred off
   your olive-red skin, crush out the kernel, your heart
   pound you pinch you roll you out
   smelling like white bread but dead;

To survive the Borderlands
   you must live *sin fronteras*
   be a crossroads.

gabacha – a Chicano term for a white woman
rajetas – literally, "split," that is, having betrayed your word
burra – donkey
buey – oxen
sin fronteras – without borders

Source: "To Live in the Borderlands Means You" from Borderlands/La Frontera: The New Mestiza. Copyright © 1987, 1999, 2007 by Gloria Anzaldúa. Reprinted by permission of Aunt Lute Books, www.auntlute.com.

DOMESTIC LIVES

10 Barbara Susan Kaminsky, An Abortion Testimonial, n.d.

Reproductive freedom was a battleground for women already engaged in debates over feminism, the ERA, and female sexuality. Activists fought to decriminalize abortion by challenging laws most significantly in New York in 1971 but they struggled elsewhere until the Supreme Court ruled it unconstitutional for states to make abortion a crime and set a critical precedent in interpreting the "right of privacy... to encompass a woman's decision whether or not to terminate her pregnancy" (Roe v. Wade, 1973).

I became pregnant. I had incomplete knowledge of contraception. I was sane and healthy, therefore ineligible for a legal abortion. Not being criminal or sophisticated I had no access to illegal means of abortion. I asked my mother for money to cover the cost of a trip to Japan where abortion was legal. She was not wealthy. She refused. She became hysterical. I became hysterical. Twenty-four hours later I was married. Eight months later I was delivered of an infant. Shortly afterwards the child was adopted and my marriage dissolved.

At the time of conception, I was capable of a love relationship but not a parent-child relationship. The state forced me into becoming a parent by denying me the right to a legal abortion. I would like to sue the state for damages resulting from that maternity.

I was forced into a marriage relationship through pressure from my family. Pressure, which since I was in a vulnerable position, I was unable to resist. My husband had no money. I left college and took a full-time job. By taking a leave of absence from college I forfeited a regents scholarship (which was the only reason I was able to attend school). Also, the school had a rule which did not allow pregnant women to register. In effect, I had no freedom to pursue the goals which I had set up for myself. The state was punishing me for my sexual behavior. I no longer had control of my life. At seventeen years of age it had been interrupted by forced maternity.

I decided to give the child up for adoption. I had to defend that decision against family and friends who had been so influenced by the legal sanctions given to motherhood that they found it impossible to accept my decision. They tried to convince me to stay married and become a mother. I was unprepared for motherhood financially, emotionally, and morally.

I decided to dissolve the marriage. After the birth of the child I returned to school. I was also working at that time to pay off legal bills, medical bills, and to support myself. (I had been fired from my previous job when they discovered I was pregnant.) After one term I left school and got a full-time job. My present occupation as an art teacher and a painter is not a very lucrative one, and can barely support me, let alone enable me to return to school.

When I tried to take control of my life (have an abortion), I faced opposition. The state was on the side of the opposition. I feel it is unconstitutional for the state to have taken any position in relation to the moral and emotional way in which I chose to conduct my life. The state should compensate me for the emotional ordeal it put me through. Moreover, the state should be made to support me while I finish my education.

Source: Barbara Susan Kaminsky, Testimony before the New York State Assembly in *"Takin' it to the Streets": A Sixties Reader,* ed. Alexander Bloom and Wini Breines (New York: Oxford University Press, 2003), pp. 428–9.

11 Senator George McGovern, The Pill and Informed Consent, 1970

In May 1960 the United States Food and Drug Administration approved the marketing of a synthetic birth control pill, Enovid, by drug manufacturer G.D. Searle. First approved in 1957 for the treatment of menstrual disorders, the pill offered healthy women new ways to assume greater control over family planning. The marketing of the pill fed new attitudes towards sexuality, reproductive freedom, and women's rights. Although clinical trials had shown dangerous side effects that included blood clots and heart attacks, drug companies downplayed the risks. Then, in 1969, Barbara Seaman, a medical journalist published the results of her investigation in The Doctors' Case Against the Pill. *Shortly thereafter, Senator Gaylord Nelson conducted hearings regarding its safety and the importance of informed consent for women who opted to use the pill for contraception. This statement from Senator George McGovern followed the Nelson hearings.*

Mr. McGOVERN. Mr. President, there was no small measure of public vexation produced by Senator GAYLORD NELSON's recent investigation of whether users of oral contraceptives are being adequately warned of possible risks as well as benefits.

It is my view that we have been well served by the Wisconsin Senator's insistence that those who choose this method of contraception should be able to base their decision on "informed consent."

His hearings demonstrated that some two-thirds of the users of the pill were not advised of the known risks, even though medical witnesses were nearly unanimous in the view that the user should have such information as a matter of right.

When Senator NELSON announced the hearings last November he argued that information sheet on the pill should be included with each package, and he called for substantial additional research on oral contraceptives. Every witness testifying at the hearings agreed that the need for more research is crucial.

Where the question of warning is concerned, it is interesting to note that, on the last day of the hearings, Dr. Charles C. Edwards, Commissioner of the Food and Drug Administration, confirmed Senator NELSON's view on informed consent. He said:

I have come to the conclusion that the information being supplied to the patient in the case of the oral contraceptive is insufficient and that a re-evaluation of our present policies is in order. . . . The action we must take now, immediately in my opinion, is to help inform the 8½ million American women now taking oral contraceptives of the risks involved.

And Dr. Edwards then announced that an informational sheet would henceforth be included with each pill package.

The Washington Evening Star's distinguished medical writer, Judith Randal, recognized the importance of the issue involved in the pill hearings in a Washington Close-up column on March 13 entitled "Pill Raises Issue of Right To Know." It is significant that she saw a connection on this score between the pill and the pesticide DDT, particularly since it was also Senator NELSON who 5 years ago began introducing legislation to ban the use of the slow degrading pesticide because of its effects on the environment.

Mr. President, I ask unanimous consent that the column to which I have referred be printed in the RECORD.

There being no objection the article was ordered to be printed in the RECORD, as follows:

"PILL." RAISES ISSUE OF RIGHT TO KNOW (By Judith Randal)

Two weeks ago today, Sen. Gaylord Nelson, D-Wis., then conducting hearings on oral contraceptives, raised one of the most crucial issue confronting society in the 1970s.

By that time, Nelson had been charged with inciting the press to sensationalism, fostering scare headlines, and – by bringing to public attention what the scientific community already knew about possible risks from "the pill" – threatening efforts to contain the population explosion. But what no one else had said in so many words was that the real issue raised was the public's right to know.

Nelson saw the opportunity to bring this issue to the fore when Dr. Alan F. Guttmacher, president of Planned Parenthood-World Population, came to the witness table. After pointing out that other contraceptive measures, as well as pregnancy, also carry risks, Guttmacher indicated that the dangers of the pill would better have been aired behind closed doors.

"I have little faith in detailing the hazards of a drug...to a patient," he said, explaining that scientific data is too complicated for laymen to understand.

Nelson saw this as a "right-to-know" issue and decided to attack it head-on. Said he:

"We debated on the floor of the Senate at great length the anti-ballistic missile, which is an incredibly complicated mechanical device which probably nobody in the Congress could explain from a technical standpoint. Should that be discussed because it is complicated and the public really cannot understand it, or should it not?

"...Do we have a right...to withhold knowledge developed by the Federal government itself through research and studies and conferences like (those held by) the National Institutes of Health, or should these matters be made a matter of public knowledge, counting, as it seems we always have to do, upon the ultimate good judgment of the public to come to a reasonable conclusion?"

Nelson, who is on record in favor of family planning and who is an advocate of zero population growth in this country and abroad, has touched a sensitive nerve. We are increasingly finding in our society that too little public advance consideration of possible results from scientific or technological progress may cause a dangerous, even catastrophic, overaction. The process goes about like this:

A scientific advance is made, and its manifest promise causes it to be oversold to the public. At the same time, research on what now seems a solved problem slows or grinds to a halt. The public adopts the new advance and uses it enthusiastically without really understanding its pluses and minuses.

In time, drawbacks begin to come to public attention. General revulsion sets in and, lacking possible benefits of continuing research, the public tunes out. At this point, the very real possibility exists that efforts to solve the problem will be abandoned for good.

What is even more serious, perhaps, is that changing attitudes in advanced countries like ours bring themselves to bear in other parts of the world that rely on us for technological inputs. The pill is one example, and DDT is another.

There is no question that DDT has been overused in the United States, where it is threatening the environment. Developed countries may well get along nicely without it, but if they decide to abandon it for more expensive forms of pest control, underdeveloped countries that cannot afford such options are likely to follow suit.

If this happens, countless deaths from malaria may occur in Southeast Asia and tropical Africa because of decisions made in the United States and Sweden.

This, of course, is written with 20–20 hind-sight. Nevertheless, where both the pill and DDT are concerned, something very like what has happened could easily have been predicted – in the case of the pill because its hormonal components exert an influence on many body systems, in the case of DDT because its poisonous properties persist in the environment long after their initial purpose is served.

Which brings us back to the public's right to know. Had society at large been informed of the hazards of DDT that were known or suspected 10 years ago, perhaps laws regarding its use would be different from those on the books.

Similarly, if women had been told about the hazards in the pill of which the medical profession long has had inklings, two things might have happened. First, many woman might have opted for other measures of birth control, which would have been further developed than they now are: and, second, research into safer and equally effective "pills" might have had top-priority attention, which to date it has not.

Source: *The Congressional Record*, April, 1970.

12 New Jersey Lesbian Caucus, How Do You Define "Lesbianism?" 1976

The women's liberation movement and increased public presence of lesbianism occurred simultaneously in the 1970s. While the two movements remained distinct, both promoted discussion about sexual identity, sexual attraction, and sexual relations. Lesbianism originated as love for and between women not as hatred of men. As an act of self-determination, lesbianism defined itself openly, positively, and increasingly without fear that society could discriminate against women sexually oriented towards women.

In our sexist and sex-oriented society lesbians have generally been defined as women who have sexual relations with other women. We reject this identification on purely sexual terms, just as non-lesbian women hopefully reject their identification only and solely by their sexual activities.

Martin and Lyon in their book *Lesbian/Woman* define a lesbian as "a woman whose primary erotic, psychological and social interest is in a member of her own sex..." Rita Mae Brown in an article in the now defunct FURIES defined a lesbian as a woman who loves lesbians.

We feel that both of these definitions are only partly valid, and that lesbianism and lesbians are far more difficult to define.

Last year National NOW convened a task force on "Lesbianism and Sexuality." We of the Lesbian Caucus disagree with the combination of sexuality and lesbianism as if they were part of the same issue. They are not. Lesbianism is a way of being, while sexuality is basically an act.

When women – sometimes women-oriented women – try to tell us that the only difference between us and other women is what we do in bed, we need to ask these women several questions. For one, what about women who for shorter or longer periods decide to be celibate? Are these women "nothing"? Also, if lesbianism is only a sexual act, then, when a lesbian leaves her bedroom, does she cease being a lesbian? The absurdity of these statements is obvious: a celibate woman is either a lesbian or straight, and when I leave my bedroom I am still a lesbian. I do not suddenly become straight because I leave my bed and my bed-partner behind.

Another reason for a need to define who and what we are is the spread of the feminist movement causing women to learn to relate to each other as working partners, friends, and possibly more than that. When we work with people and form close relationships, we tend to develop feelings beyond "accepted" limits, including at times – sexual feelings. Some women become frightened when this happens, and leave the movement. Others less inhibited decide to explore their feelings and get emotionally and sometimes sexually involved with other women. While many of these women explore with other women in similar circumstances, some feel that only a "true" lesbian will do, putting many lesbian sisters in sticky situations where they are damned if they accede, and even more damned if they refuse the advances of the straight woman.

The question naturally arises whether these previously straight women are now "becoming lesbians," and the attending question is whether lesbianism is something one decides to "become," like joining a party or a club. Also, most if not all of these women undoubtedly will eventually return to their previous lifestyle, and men, and the question arises whether lesbianism is a "stage" in a woman's life.

These questions have become especially urgent in the past months, as we see movement "lesbians" return to a male-oriented lifestyle, such as Jill Johnston who has been exhibited as "Lesbian #1" to the American public by the media, and who has written books about her life as a "lesbian."

Those of us who have always been lesbians, have lived the lesbian lifestyle for many years, and who identify as radical lesbian/feminists, are understandably disturbed by these events, because they seriously threaten the credibility of our lifestyle. After all, if Jill Johnston after writing books and being so very public...is returning into the male-female fold, doesn't it prove that lesbianism is just a passing fancy...a man-hating phase which will go away as soon as the woman meets the "right" man? Doesn't it prove that "dykes" are sickies at worst, and poor women who cannot get a man at best? That lesbianism is not a valid and permanent lifestyle? Of course, we reject all such conclusions.

Then, who or what IS a lesbian, and what IS lesbianism? We are here trying to formulate some kind of a position, as best we can, because there is, of course, no pat answer to a way of living, relating and loving.

We feel that lesbianism is a "given": that a woman either IS, or IS NOT a lesbian, and that she has basically no choice in the matter. She DOES have a choice as to whether she will ACT upon her lesbianism. Or not. But she has NO choice in whether she is, or is not, emotionally basically oriented towards women in contrast to non-lesbians who are basically oriented towards men. This is where the difficulty arises: because in our society the emphasis is on the male-female relationship, and many lesbians marry men, have children, and try to live a conventional lifestyle. This does not, in our opinion, make these women "straight" – it simply means that these women have opted for a lifestyle not "natural" FOR THEM, but easier (in their opinion) in our society as it is. On the other hand, we see women who have been poorly treated by men ADOPT a same-sex lifestyle which is also not natural FOR THEM...adopt a preference for females out of an aversion to males. It is these women who eventually return to the male/female lifestyle, because it is natural for them to do so, and "playing" lesbian is not.

It must be emphasized that lesbianism is never hating men (negative) but rather that it is only and solely a positive attitude of loving women.

Lesbianism is then, basically, a head trip, and one that is developed early in a woman's life. We don't know how early, but we know some women who were aware of their total involvement with women early in life, at age 3 or 4. Others do not come to this realization until their "teens," and for others the assurance of where their heads and hearts are comes even later, often after some years of marriage and several children.

Many of these women have felt a vague uneasiness about themselves all of their lives. They never felt "right," but could not determine what was wrong. Sometimes when such women finally become aware of their lesbianism, the feeling of "wrong" disappears immediately. With others the realization is more gradual and the adjustment not so sudden.

We have so far mentioned sexuality only at the very beginning. What about sex and sexual orientation? Sexual orientation is, of course, mostly a matter of choice or *preference*. Most people are sexual, and can function at least to some degree with either or both sexes. Most people make a deliberate choice when they choose a sex partner. The lesbian, however, will never feel fulfilled with a male, as the non-lesbian woman will never be fully fulfilled with a female sex partner, meaning both emotionally and physically. Most of us can go through the motions, but true fulfillment is another matter.

We reject the sexual definition of "lesbian" mainly because we feel that lesbians relate sexually to other women *because* they are totally women-centered in their entire outlook. We do not feel that women are lesbians by virtue of relating sexually to other women. In other words, we feel that same-sex expression is a *consequence of*, rather than a *criterion for* being a lesbian.

Source: *Gaylife*, reprinted in *Speaking for Our Lives, Historic Speeches and Rhetoric for Gay and Lesbian Rights 1892–2000*, ed. Robert Ridinger (Haworth Press, 2004) pp. 271–3.

Questions to Think About

1. How did the intersections of race, class, ethnicity, sexual orientation, and life cycle affect the public and private experiences of American women between 1968 and 1988?
2. What issues divided women activists between 1968 and 1988? Where did they find common ground in addressing questions that affected women's collective experiences?
3. How did women respond in different ways to the backlash against women's liberation?

Chapter 7   Globalization, Glass Ceilings, and the Good Life? 1988–2008

WORK

1 Felice N. Schwartz, Management Women and the New Facts of Life, 1989

Educated women entered the ranks of middle and upper management in greater numbers in the 1980s. Still they encountered challenges in balancing work and family, ambition and sacrifice, expenses and salaries. Under pressure to develop their human resources, companies responded in various ways to the presence of women in corporate America. The article by Felice Schwartz generated huge debate over what came to be called "the Mommy Track."

The cost of employing women in management is greater than the cost of employing men. This is a jarring statement, partly because it is true, but mostly because it is something people are reluctant to talk about. A new study by one multinational corporation shows that the rate of turnover in management positions is 2½ times higher among top-performing women than it is among men. A large producer of consumer goods reports that one half of the women who take maternity leave return to their jobs late or not at all. And we know that women also have a greater tendency to plateau or to interrupt their careers in ways that limit their growth and development. But we have become so sensitive to charges of sexism and so afraid of confrontation, even litigation, that we rarely say what we know to be true. Unfortunately, our bottled-up awareness leaks out in misleading metaphors ("glass ceiling" is one notable example), veiled hostility, lowered expectations, distrust, and reluctant adherence to Equal Employment Opportunity requirements.

Career interruptions, plateauing, and turnover are expensive. The money corporations invest in recruitment, training, and development is less likely to produce top executives among women than among men, and the invaluable company experience that developing executives acquire at every level as they move up through management ranks is more often lost.

The studies just mentioned are only the first of many, I'm quite sure. Demographic realities are going to force corporations all across the country to analyze the cost of employing women in managerial positions, and what they will discover is that women cost more.

But here is another startling truth: The greater cost of employing women is not a function of inescapable gender differences. Women *are* different from men, but what increases their cost to the corporation is principally the clash of their perceptions, attitudes, and behavior with those of men, which is to say, with the policies and practices of male-led corporations.

It is terribly important that employers draw the right conclusions from the studies now being done. The studies will be useless – or worse, harmful – if all they teach us is that women are expensive to employ. What we need to learn is how to reduce that expense, how to stop throwing away the investments we make in talented women, how to become more responsive to the needs of the women that corporations *must* employ if they are to have the best and the brightest of all those now entering the work force.

The gender differences relevant to business fall into two categories: those related to maternity and those related to the differing traditions and expectations of the sexes. Maternity is biological rather than cultural. We can't alter it, but we can dramatically reduce its impact on the workplace and in many cases eliminate its negative effect on employee development. We can accomplish this by addressing the second set of differences, those between male and female socialization. Today, these differences exaggerate the real costs of maternity and can turn a relatively slight disruption in work schedule into a serious business problem and a career derailment for individual women. If we are to overcome the cost differential between male and female employees, we need to address the issues that arise when female socialization meets the male corporate culture and masculine rules of career development – issues of behavior and style, of expectation, of stereotypes and preconceptions, of sexual tension and harassment, of female mentoring, lateral mobility, relocation, compensation, and early identification of top performers.

The one immutable, enduring difference between men and women is maternity. Maternity is not simply childbirth but a continuum that begins with an awareness of the ticking of the biological clock, proceeds to the

anticipation of motherhood, includes pregnancy, childbirth, physical recu-
peration, psychological adjustment, and continues on to nursing, bonding,
and child rearing. Not all women choose to become mothers, of course, and
among those who do, the process varies from case to case depending on the
health of the mother and baby, the values of the parents, and the availability,
cost, and quality of child care.

In past centuries, the biological fact of maternity shaped the traditional
roles of the sexes. Women performed the home-centered functions that
related to the bearing and nurturing of children. Men did the work that
required great physical strength. Over time, however, family size contracted,
the community assumed greater responsibility for the care and education of
children, packaged foods and household technology reduced the work load
in the home, and technology eliminated much of the need for muscle power
at the workplace. Today, in the developed world, the only role still uniquely
gender related is childbearing. Yet men and women are still socialized to
perform their traditional roles.

Men and women may or may not have some innate psychological disposition toward these traditional roles – men to be aggressive, competitive,
self-reliant, risk taking, women to be supportive, nurturing, intuitive, sensitive, communicative – but certainly both men and women are capable of
the full range of behavior. Indeed, the male and female roles have already
begun to expand and merge. In the decades ahead, as the socialization of
boys and girls and the experience and expectations of young men and
women grow steadily more androgynous, the differences in workplace
behavior will continue to fade. At the moment, however, we are still plagued
by dispartes in perception and behavior that make the integration of men
and women in the workplace unnecessarily difficult and expensive.

Let me illustrate with a few broadbrush generalizations. Of course, these
are only stereotypes, but I think they help to exemplify the kinds of preconceptions that can muddy the corporate waters.

Men continue to perceive women as the rearers of their children, so they
find it understandable, indeed appropriate, that women should renounce
their careers to raise families. Edmund Pratt, CEO of Pfizer, once asked me
in all sincerity, "Why would any woman choose to be a chief financial
officer rather than a full-time mother?" By condoning and taking pleasure
in women's traditional behavior, men reinforce it. Not only do they see
parenting as fundamentally female, they see a career as fundamentally
male – either an unbroken series of promotions and advancements toward
CEOdom or stagnation and disappointment. This attitude serves to legit-
imize a woman's choice to extend maternity leave and even, for those who
can afford it, to leave employment altogether for several years. By the same
token, men who might want to take a leave after the birth of a child know

that management will see such behavior as a lack of career commitment, even when company policy permits parental leave for men.

Women also bring counterproductive expectations and perceptions to the workplace. Ironically, although the feminist movement was an expression of women's quest for freedom from their home-based lives, most women were remarkably free already. They had many responsibilities, but they were autonomous and could be entrepreneurial in how and when they carried them out. And once their children grew up and left home, they were essentially free to do what they wanted with their lives. Women's traditional role also included freedom from responsibility for the financial support of their families. Many of us were socialized from girlhood to expect our husbands to take care of us, while our brothers were socialized from an equally early age to complete their educations, pursue careers, climb the ladder of success, and provide dependable financial support for their families. To the extent that this tradition of freedom lingers subliminally, women tend to bring to their employment a sense that they can choose to change jobs or careers at will, take time off, or reduce their hours.

Finally, women's traditional role encouraged particular attention to the quality and substance of what they did, specifically to the physical, psychological, and intellectual development of their children...

Even so, incredibly, I don't know of more than one or two companies that have looked into their own records to study the absolutely critical issue of maternity leave – how many women took it, when and whether they returned, and how this behavior correlated with their rank, tenure, age, and performance. The unique drawback to the employment of women is the physical reality of maternity and the particular socializing influence maternity has had. Yet to make women equal to men in the workplace we have chosen on the whole not to discuss this single most significant difference between them. Unless we do, we cannot evaluate the cost of recruiting, developing, and moving women up.

Now that interest is replacing indifference, there are four steps every company can take to examine its own experience with women:

1. Gather quantitative data on the company's experience with management – level women regarding turnover rates, occurrence of and return from maternity leave, and organizational level attained in relation to tenure and performance.
2. Correlate this data with factors such as age, marital status, and presence and age of children, and attempt to identify and analyze why women respond the way they do.
3. Gather qualitative data on the experience of women in your company and on how women are perceived by both sexes.

4. Conduct a cost-benefit analysis of the return on your investment in high-performing women. Factor in the cost to the company of women's negative reactions to negative experience, as well as the probable cost of corrective measures and policies. If women's value to your company is greater than the cost to recruit, train, and develop them – and of course I believe it will be – then you will want to do everything you can to retain them.

Source: *Harvard Business Review*, 67(1) (January February 1989), pp. 65–7, 75.

2 *New York Times*, More and More, Women Risk All to Enter U.S., 2006

Women from Asia, Africa, and Latin America are a significant presence in the paid labor force in American cities. Many work for low wages in factories and in service jobs including health, food, and childcare. The often heartbreaking story of Mexican women coming north both legally and illegally frequently makes headlines. The following front-page news article, DATELINE: Tuscon, is representative of reporting on the complex problems of women, immigration, and the challenges of reform.

It took years for Normaeli Gallardo, a single mother from Acapulco, to drum up the courage to join the growing stream of Mexican women illegally crossing the border on the promise of a job, in her case working in a Kansas meat-packing plant for $5.15 an hour.

First, she had to grapple with the idea of landing in an unfamiliar country, all alone, with no grasp of English and no place to live.

Then she had to imagine crossing the Arizona desert, where immigrants face heat exhaustion by day, frostbite by night and the cunning of the "coyotes" – smugglers who charge as much as $1,500 to guide people into the United States and who make a habit of robbing and sexually assaulting them.

And finally, Ms. Gallardo, 38, who earned $50 a week at an Acapulco hotel, had to contemplate life without her two vivacious daughters, Isabel, 7, and Fernanda, 5. That once unimaginable trade-off – leaving her children behind so they could one day leave poverty behind – had suddenly become her only option.

She simply did not earn enough money, she said. If she paid the electric bill, she fell behind on rent; if she paid the water bill, she could forget about new clothes for the children.

"My heart broke, my heart broke," said Ms. Gallardo, who crumbled as she recounted her decision to leave her girls with her sister and make the uncertain journey across the border. "But I had to give them a better life. I told them I would go and work, and we could buy a small plot of land and build a little house and have a dog."

Undaunted by a backlash against illegal immigrants here, Ms. Gallardo is part of what some experts say is a largely unnoticed phenomenon: the increasing number of women, many without male companions, enduring danger and the risk of capture to come to the United States to work and to settle.

As many as 11 million illegal immigrants are thought to be living and working in the United States, though estimates vary.

No one knows how many people illegally cross the Mexico-United States border, trekking through the desert, hiding in cars and trucks, or walking through points of entry with false papers. But academics, immigration advocates and Border Patrol agents all agree that the number of women making the trip is on the rise.

Katharine Donato, an associate professor of sociology at Rice University in Houston who studies Mexican migration to the United States, estimates that as many as 35 percent to 45 percent of those crossing the border illegally today are women. Twenty years ago, fewer than 20 percent of the people crossing illegally were women, she said.

The increase, which has occurred gradually, comes at a time when anger over illegal immigration is on the upswing, especially in states near the border. Some of that anger is directed at women who have babies in American hospitals and send their children to public schools.

The House recently passed a hard-hitting bill that seeks to beef up border enforcement and make it a federal crime to live in the United States illegally.

But to most of the women who cross the border, the debate over illegal immigration and the ire of taxpayers has little bearing, if any, on the difficult decision they make to undertake the journey. "Vale la pena," said Kat Rodriguez, an organizer for the Human Rights Coalition in Tucson, echoing a refrain among the women. "It's worth it"

Some women cross simply to keep their families together and join their husbands after long separations, a situation that has grown more pronounced since the Border Patrol agency began stepping up enforcement 10 years ago. With the border more secure in California and Texas, many people are now being funneled into the rugged territory of Arizona – an effort that virtually requires the help of an expensive coyote to cross successfully.

Yet a growing number of single women, like Ms. Gallardo, are coming not to join husbands, but to find jobs, send money home and escape a bleak future in Mexico. They come to find work in the booming underground economy, through a vast network of friends and relatives already employed here as maids, cooks, kitchen helpers, factory workers and baby sitters. In these jobs, they can earn double or triple their Mexican salaries.

"It remains a story about family reunification, but the proportion of women coming to the U.S. who are not married and working full time has gone up substantially," Professor Donato said. "So we see the single migrant woman motivated by economic reasons coming to the United States that we saw very little of 30 years ago."

Still, the promise of a sweeter future often goes unfulfilled.

Ms. Gallardo never made it to Kansas. She never made it beyond the desert. After walking eight hours at night and committing $500 to a coyote, she stumbled down a rocky hill near Tucson and broke her ankle. The coyote left her sitting on a nearby highway in the desert, where the Border Patrol eventually found her, took her to a local emergency room and deported her to Nogales, Mexico, the next day.

A Mexican immigrant group, Grupo Beta, took her to a Mexican hospital where she was told she needed surgery on her ankle at a cost of 3,000 pesos, or seven weeks' salary. She also owes the friends who gave the coyote $500.

A month and a half earlier, Margarita Ximil Lopez, 20, had her hopes dashed, too. She sat in a dismal holding cell at the United States Border Patrol station in Nogales in October and tried to hide her tears from her son, Edel, who is about to turn 6.

It was for his sake, she said, that she illegally crossed the border, only to be abandoned by the coyote and picked up at a motel by American immigration officers. Ms. Ximil, from Puebla, a large city southeast of Mexico City, had hoped to join her sister, who had lined up a job for her as a waitress in Los Angeles.

Here in Arizona, a tide of anti-immigrant sentiment has swelled along with the number of border crossers, some of it directed particularly at women. Many taxpayers say they resent that their tax dollars are being spent to educate these women's children and pay for their delivery costs at local hospitals.

Reacting to the surge in illegal border crossings, voters in Arizona passed Proposition 200 in November 2004, which, among other things, requires people applying for some public benefits to show proof of citizenship.

The economic reality of illegal immigration is complex. Whether these workers cost taxpayers more than they contribute has been debated for years, factoring in the taxes collected, the unclaimed Social Security funds and the undesirable jobs filled at low wages.

Pregnant women who are already in the United States illegally invariably use hospitals to give birth, though statistics are unreliable because emergency room patients are not asked their legal status. Children born in

America are automatically granted citizenship, and some critics accuse the mothers of exploiting that guarantee.

But advocates for illegal immigrants maintain that the women's reasons for coming here reach far beyond citizenship for their children; few women come to the United States expressly to have babies, collect benefits and visit the emergency room, the advocates say. Jim Hawkins, a Tucson sector Border Patrol agent, said such instances were rare but not unheard of.

"I had a woman sit on the south side of the fence until she went into labor, then jumped the fence," Mr. Hawkins said. "She was coached well: she immediately asked for an ambulance."

After she gave birth, the woman was ordered to return to Mexico. Rather than have her baby put up for adoption, Mr. Hawkins said, she took the baby back to Mexico with her.

The nation's roiling immigration debate weighs little on the minds of the women who cross here. Nor do the dangers of the crossing itself, which they know routinely include sexual harassment or assault. As the borders have become tighter, the coyotes have become more violent and desperate, law enforcement officials and immigration advocates say.

"These poor aliens are nothing but product to these animals," said Mr. Hawkins, adding that many women are raped, robbed and abandoned at the first sign of trouble and are given amphetamines to keep them moving faster at night.

Since most women do not come forward to report the crimes – because they do not speak the language and are illegal, ashamed and scared of deportation – few hard numbers exist. But there is ample anecdotal information to bolster the claim.

Maria Jimenez, 29, who is from Oaxaca and came here to work and join her husband, has experienced most of what can go wrong. The first time she crossed into Arizona three years ago, she was told by a coyote to expect a three-hour evening walk across the desert. She packed no water. The journey took two nights and three days, and Ms. Jimenez grew desperately dizzy and disoriented.

Then the coyote, an American, tried to sexually assault her and her sister-in-law, she said. "I told him no," Ms. Jimenez said. "I started to cry." He left her alone, but robbed her of the $300 in her pocket. Then just as they neared a highway, the Border Patrol arrested the group.

She tried again a month later carrying drinks with electrolytes but no money in her pocket. She made it, joining her husband in Tucson, where she got a job at a restaurant and had a baby, Stephanie. A family emergency in Oaxaca forced her to return home last year. But in November, she came back into the country, this time with a group of eight people – four of them women she met in Nogales.

During the trip, Ms. Jimenez slipped and fell, spraining her ankle. She wrapped it in discarded clothes strewn across the desert by other immigrants, and she hobbled on.

After a night of walking, they reached the railroad tracks and hopped a freight train to Tucson. Her husband paid the coyote $1,000.

Ms. Jimenez, her husband and baby now share a house with another family. She found work quickly in a restaurant kitchen for $5.25 an hour, no breaks, no sick days.

"We are all scared when we cross," she said. "But the thought that we can help people back home makes it worth it."

CITIZENSHIP

3 Anita Hill, Statement to the U.S. Senate Judiciary Committee for the Hearings on Clarence Thomas, 1991

Sexual harassment in the workplace became the focus of public attention during confirmation hearings of Clarence Thomas, the second African American appointed to the Supreme Court. Anita Hill testified Thomas had sexually harassed her when they worked together at the Equal Employment Opportunity Commission. Hill's testimony before an all-male Senate committee was broadcast nationwide and prompted Thomas to complain about a "high tech lynching for uppity blacks." Hill's commitment to speak out as an African American woman held special significance in a culture where race and gender have a complicated relationship reflected in sexual stereotypes and violence against both women and men. For many women, the hearings underscored the underrepresentation of women in electoral politics and indeed, since 1992, the gender gap has become an analytic tool for political scientists, pollsters, and news commentators.

MR. CHAIRMAN, SENATOR THURMOND, members of the committee:

My name is Anita F. Hill, and I am a professor of law at the University of Oklahoma. I was born on a farm in Okmulgee County, Oklahoma, in 1956. I am the youngest of thirteen children.

I had my early education in Okmulgee County. My father, Albert Hill, is a farmer in that area. My mother's name is Erma Hill. She is also a farmer and a housewife.

My childhood was one of a lot of hard work and not much money, but it was one of solid family affection as represented by my parents. I was reared in a religious atmosphere in the Baptist faith, and I have been a member of the Antioch Baptist Church in Tulsa, Oklahoma, since 1983. It is a very warm part of my life at the present time.

For my undergraduate work, I went to Oklahoma State University and graduated from there in 1977. I am attaching to this statement a copy of my resume for further details of my education....

I graduated from the university with academic honors, and proceeded to the Yale Law School, where I received my J.D. degree in 1980.

Upon graduation from law school, I became a practicing lawyer with the Washington, DC, firm of Wald, Harkrader & Ross. In 1981 I was introduced to now Judge Thomas by a mutual friend.

Judge Thomas told me that he was anticipating a political appointment, and asked if I would be interested in working with him.

He was in fact appointed as assistant secretary of education for civil rights. After he had taken that post, he asked if I would become his assistant, and I accepted that position.

In my early period there, I had two major projects. First was an article I wrote for Judge Thomas's signature on the education of minority students. The second was the organization of a seminar on high-risk students, which was abandoned because Judge Thomas transferred to the EEOC, where he became the chairman of that office.

During this period at the Department of Education my working relationship with Judge Thomas was positive. I had a good deal of responsibility and independence. I thought he respected my work, and that he trusted my judgment.

After approximately three months of working there, he asked me to go out socially with him. What happened next, and telling the world about it, are the two most difficult things – experiences of my life.

It is only after a great deal of agonizing consideration, and a number of sleepless nights, that I am able to talk of these unpleasant matters to anyone but my close friends.

I declined the invitation to go out socially with him, and explained to him that I thought it would jeopardize what at the time I considered to be a very good working relationship. I had a normal social life with other men outside the office. I believed then, as now, that having a social relationship with a person who was supervising my work would be ill advised. I was very uncomfortable with the idea and told him so.

I thought that by saying no and explaining my reasons, my employer would abandon his social suggestions. However, to my regret, in the following few weeks, he continued to ask me out on several occasions.

He pressed me to justify my reasons for saying no to him. These incidents took place in his office, or mine. They were in the form of private conversations, which would not have been overheard by anyone else.

My working relationship became even more strained when Judge Thomas began to use work situations to discuss sex. On these occasions he would call me into his office for a course on education issues and projects, or he might suggest that because of the time pressures of his schedule we go to lunch to a government cafeteria.

After a brief discussion of work, he would turn the conversation to a discussion of sexual matters. His conversations were very vivid. He spoke about acts that he had seen in pornographic films involving such matters as women having sex with animals, and films showing group sex or rape scenes.

He talked about pornographic materials depicting individuals with large penises or large breasts, involving various sex acts.

On several occasions, Thomas told me graphically of his own sexual prowess.

Because I was extremely uncomfortable talking about sex with him at all, and particularly in such a graphic way, I told him that I did not want to talk about these subjects. I would also try to change the subject to education matters or to nonsexual personal matters, such as his background or his beliefs.

My efforts to change the subject were rarely successful.

Throughout the period of these conversations, he also from time to time asked me for social engagements. My reaction to these conversations was to avoid them by limiting opportunities for us to engage in extended conversations.

This was difficult because, at the time, I was his only assistant at the office of education – or office for civil rights. During the latter part of my time at the Department of Education, the social pressures, and any conversation of his offensive behavior, ended. I began both to believe and hope that our working relationship could be a proper, cordial, and professional one.

When Judge Thomas was made chair of the EEOC, I needed to face the question of whether to go with him. I was asked to do so, and I did.

The work itself was interesting, and at that time it appeared that the sexual overtures which had so troubled me had ended.

I also faced the realistic fact that I had no alternative job. While I might have gone back to private practice, perhaps in my old firm or at another, I was dedicated to civil rights work and my first choice was to be in that field. Moreover, at that time, the Department of Education itself was a dubious venture. President Reagan was seeking to abolish the entire department.

For my first months at the EEOC, where I continued to be an assistant to Judge Thomas, there were no sexual conversations or overtures. However, during the fall and winter of 1982 these began again. The comments were random and ranged from pressing me about why I didn't go out with him to remarks about my personal appearance. I remember his saying that some day I would have to tell him the real reason that I wouldn't go out with him.

He began to show displeasure in his tone and voice and his demeanor and his continued pressure for an explanation. He commented on what I was wearing in terms of whether it made me more or less sexually attractive. The incidents occurred in his inner office at the EEOC.

One of the oddest episodes I remember was an occasion in which Thomas was drinking a Coke in his office. He got up from the table at which we were working, went over to his desk to get the Coke, looked at the can, and asked, "Who has put pubic hair on my Coke?"

On other occasions, he referred to the size of his own penis as being larger than normal and he also spoke on some occasions of the pleasures he had given to women with oral sex. At this point, late 1982, I began to be concerned that Clarence Thomas might take out his anger with me by degrading me or not giving me important assignments. I also thought that he might find an excuse for dismissing me.

In January of 1983, I began looking for another job. I was handicapped because I feared that if he found out, he might make it difficult for me to find other employment and I might be dismissed from the job I had. Another factor that made my search more difficult was that this was during a period of a hiring freeze in the government.

In February 1983 I was hospitalized for five days on an emergency basis for acute stomach pain, which I attributed to stress on the job. Once out of the hospital I became more committed to find other employment and sought further to minimize my contact with Thomas. This became easier when Allyson Duncan became office director because most of my work was then funneled through her and I had contact with Clarence Thomas mostly in staff meetings.

In the spring of 1983, an opportunity to teach at Oral Roberts University opened up. I participated in a seminar, taught an afternoon session in a seminar at Oral Roberts University. The dean of the university saw me teaching and inquired as to whether I would be interested in further pursuing a career in teaching beginning at Oral Roberts University.

I agreed to take the job, in large part because of my desire to escape the pressures I felt at the EEOC due to Judge Thomas.

When I informed him that I was leaving in July, I recall that his response was that now I would no longer have an excuse for not going out with him. I told him that I still preferred not to do so. At some time after that meeting, he asked if he could take me to dinner at the end of the term. When I declined, he assured me that the dinner was a professional courtesy only and not a social invitation. I reluctantly agreed to accept that invitation but only if it was at the very end of a working day.

On, as I recall, the last day of my employment at the EEOC in the summer of 1983, I did have dinner with Clarence Thomas. We went directly from work to a restaurant near the office. We talked about the work I had done, both at Education and at the EEOC. He told me that he was pleased with all of it except for an article and speech that I had done for him while we were at the Office for Civil Rights. Finally he made a comment that I will vividly remember. He said that if I ever told anyone of his behavior that it would ruin his career. This was not an apology; nor was it an explanation. That was his last remark about the possibility of our going out or reference to his behavior.

In July of 1983 I left the Washington, DC, area and I've had miminal contacts with Judge Clarence Thomas since....

It is only after a great deal of agonizing consideration that I am able to talk of these unpleasant matters to anyone except my closest friends, as I've said before. These last few days have been very trying and very hard for me and it hasn't just been the last few days this week.

It has actually been over a month now that I have been under the strain of this issue.

Telling the world is the most difficult experience of my life, but it is very close to having to live through the experience that occasioned this meeting.

I may have used poor judgment early on in my relationship with this issue. I was aware, however, that telling at any point in my career could adversely affect my future career, and I did not want, early on, to burn all the bridges to the EEOC.

As I said, I may have used poor judgment. Perhaps I should have taken angry or even militant steps, both when I was in the agency or after I had left it. But I must confess to the world that the course that I took seemed the better as well as the easier approach.

I declined any comment to newspapers, but later, when Senate staff asked me about these matters, I felt that I had a duty to report.

I have no personal vendetta against Clarence Thomas. I seek only to provide the committee with information which it may regard as relevant.

It would have been more comfortable to remain silent. I took no initiative to inform anyone. But when I was asked by a representative of this committee to report my experience, I felt that I had to tell the truth. I could not keep silent.

Source: *Feminism in Our Time: The Essential Writings, World War II to the Present*, ed. Miriam Schneir (New York: Random House, 1994), pp. 469–77.

4 Rebecca Walker, Becoming the Third Wave, 1992

*The decision to reclaim feminism as a meaningful term took shape in the
1990s as a new generation of women identified with and apart from the
historical memory of a century of struggle. As a movement, Third Wave
feminism strives to represent women across a broad and multidimensional
spectrum of color and sexuality and gives voice to contemporary and often
global concerns of justice in public and private lives. Rebecca Walker wrote
"Becoming the Third Wave" in 1992 at a critical moment in her own
coming of age as she separated her feminism from that of her mother,
Alice Walker. Alice Walker and others who represented "Second Wave
Feminism" served as icons of both the women's movement of the 1960s and
the civil rights movement. Rebecca Walker's words tap a well-spring of
emotion that shed light on the potential of feminism in the twenty-first
century.*

I am not one of the people who sat transfixed before the television watching
the Senate hearings. I had classes to go to, papers to write, and frankly, the
whole thing was too painful. A black man grilled by a panel of white men
about his sexual deviance. A black woman claiming harassment and being
discredited by other women.... I could not bring myself to watch that
sensationalized assault of the human spirit.

To me, the hearings were not about determining whether or not Clarence
Thomas did in fact harass Anita Hill. They were about checking and
redefining the extent of women's credibility and power.

Can a woman's experience undermine a man's career? Can a woman's
voice, a woman's sense of self-worth and injustice, challenge a structure
predicated upon the subjugation of our gender? Anita Hill's testimony
threatened to do that and more. If Thomas had not been confirmed, every
man in the United States would be at risk. For how many senators never told
a sexist joke? How many men have not used their protected male privilege
to thwart in some way the influence or ideas of a woman colleague, friend,
or relative?

For those whose sense of power is so obviously connected to the health
and vigor of the penis, it would have been a metaphoric castration. Of
course this is too great a threat.

While some may laud the whole spectacle for the consciousness it raised
around sexual harassment, its very real outcome is more informative. He
was promoted. She was repudiated. Men were assured of the inviolability of
their penis/power. Women were admonished to keep their experiences to
themselves.

The backlash against U.S. women is real. As the misconception of equality between the sexes becomes more ubiquitous, so does the attempt to restrict the boundaries of women's personal and political power. Thomas' confirmation, the ultimate rally of support for the male paradigm of harassment, sends a clear message to women: "Shut up! Even if you speak, we will not listen."

I will not be silenced.

I acknowledge the fact that we live under siege. I intend to fight back. I have uncovered and unleashed more repressed anger than I thought possible. For the umpteenth time in my 22 years, I have been radicalized, politicized, shaken awake. I have come to voice again, and this time my voice is not conciliatory.

The night after Thomas' confirmation I ask the man I am intimate with what he thinks of the whole mess. His concern is primarily with Thomas' propensity to demolish civil rights and opportunities for people of color. I launch into a tirade. "When will progressive black men prioritize my rights and well-being? When will they stop talking so damn much about 'the race' as if it revolved exclusively around them?" He tells me I wear my emotions on my sleeve. I scream "I need to know, are you with me or are you going to help them try to destroy me?"

A week later I am on a train to New York. A beautiful mother and daughter, both wearing green outfits, sit across the aisle from me. The little girl has tightly plaited braids. Her brown skin is glowing and smooth, her eyes bright as she chatters happily while looking out the window. Two men get on the train and sit directly behind me, shaking my seat as they thud into place. I bury myself in *The Sound and the Fury*. Loudly they begin to talk about women. "Man, I fucked that bitch all night and then I never called her again." "Man, there's lots of girlies over there, you know that ho, live over there by Tyrone? Well, I snatched that shit up."

The mother moves closer to her now quiet daughter. Looking at her small back I can see that she is listening to the men. I am thinking of how I can transform the situation, of all the people in the car whose silence makes us complicit.

Another large man gets on the train. After exchanging loud greetings with the two men, he sits next to me. He tells them he is going to Philadelphia to visit his wife and child. I am suckered into thinking that he is different. Then, "Man, there's a ton of females in Philly, just waitin' for you to give 'em some." I turn my head and allow the fire in my eyes to burn into him. He takes up two seats and has hands with huge swollen knuckles. I imagine the gold rings on his fingers slamming into my face. He senses something, "What's your name, sweetheart?" The other men lean forward over the seat.

A torrent explodes: "I ain't your sweetheart, I ain't your bitch, I ain't your baby. How dare you have the nerve to sit up here and talk about women that way, and then try to speak to me." The woman/mother chimes in to the beat with claps of sisterhood. The men are momentarily stunned. Then the comeback: "Aw, bitch, don't play that woman shit over here 'cause that's bullshit." He slaps the back of one hand against the palm of the other. I refuse to back down Words fly.

My instinct kicks in, telling me to get out. "Since I see you all are not going to move, I will." I move to the first car. I am so angry that thoughts of murder, of physically retaliating against them, of separatism, engulf me. I am almost out of body, just shy of being pure force. I am sick of the way women are negated, violated, devalued, ignored. I am livid, unrelenting in my anger at those who invade my space, who wish to take away my rights, who refuse to hear my voice. As the days pass, I push myself to figure out what it means to be a part of the Third Wave of feminism. I begin to realize that I owe it to my self, to my little sister on the train, to all of the daughters yet to be born, to push beyond my rage and articulate an agenda. After battling with ideas of separatism and militancy, I connect with my own feelings of powerlessness. I realize that I must undergo a transformation if I am truly committed to women's empowerment. My involvement must reach beyond my own voice in discussion, beyond voting, beyond reading feminist theory. My anger and awareness must translate into tangible action.

I am ready to decide, as my mother decided before me, to devote much of my energy to the history, health, and healing of women. Each of my choices will have to hold to my feminist standard of justice.

To be a feminist is to integrate an ideology of equality and female empowerment into the very fiber of my life. It is to search for personal clarity in the midst of systemic destruction, to join in sisterhood with women when often we are divided, to understand power structures with the intention of challenging them.

While this may sound simple, it is exactly the kind of stand that many of my peers are unwilling to take. So I write this as a plea to all women, especially the women of my generation: Let Thomas' confirmation serve to remind you, as it did me, that the fight is far from over. Let this dismissal of a woman's experience move you to anger. Turn that outrage into political power. Do not vote for them unless they work for us. Do not have sex with them, do not break bread with them, do not nurture them if they don't prioritize our freedom to control our bodies and our lives.

I am not a postfeminism feminist. I am the Third Wave.

Source: *The Essential Feminist Reader*, ed. Estelle B. Freedman (New York: Modern Library, 2007), pp. 397–401.

5 Carolyn Maloney, The Spirit of Stonewall, 1999

A routine police raid of the Stonewall Inn, a gay bar in Greenwich Village on June 28, 1969, sparked an unexpected response when bar patrons refused to leave peacefully. For five days riots and public protest called attention to the violation of the civil rights of gays and lesbians. In its aftermath, the modern gay rights movement became a more visible and powerful political force. The historic memory of Stonewall is emblematic of efforts within the women's movement to support the civil and human rights of all Americans. To that end, Carolyn Maloney, a member of the House of Representatives from New York State who had worked for women's rights, commemorated the event on the floor of the House. Her text reflected a change in attitude on the part of many elected officials to champion the rights of all their constituents.

Mr. Speaker, I rise to commemorate the thirtieth anniversary of the modern gay rights movement. On Friday, June 27, 1969, the New York City Police Department raided and attempted to close the Stonewall Inn for the perceived crime of operating a dance bar that catered to homosexuals. Recall, that in 1969 it was illegal for men to dance with men, although, oddly, it was legal for women to dance with women.

In New York City and almost everywhere, police raids on gay bars were routine. Usually, the patrons scurried, fearful of the repercussions of being caught in a gay bar. On this night, brave young men and women stood up to the police. They were no longer willing to accept daily harassment and the abridgment of their civil rights.

The Police operated in their customary fashion, hurling a string of homophobic comments, as they evicted the bar patrons one by one. As patrons and onlookers gathered outside, the crowd grew. A parking meter was uprooted and used to barricade the door. Thirteen gay people were arrested that first night.

This was the beginning of a number of nights of demonstrations that drew national attention. Moreover, it demonstrated to the gay community that there was an alternative to continued oppression. It also showed the community at large that gays were no longer willing to be silent in the face of injustice. After that night the movement to protect the rights of gays, lesbians, bisexuals and the transgendered gained strength and respectability.

In the last thirty years much has changed. Gay bars can be found in almost every town – from Anchorage, Alaska to Wheeling, West Virginia. More important, bookstores, hotlines and support groups have appeared in smaller communities to ease the isolation previously felt by many gays. The legacy of Stonewall can be seen in the lives of hundreds of thousands of men and women who are able to live their lives honestly and out of the closet. The Stonewall Revolution inspired men and women to "come out" and showed young gays and lesbians that they are not alone. Today, an openly gay person is no longer automatically disqualified from holding public office or other positions of trust. Now, numerous communities have embraced the post-Stonewall reality by passing laws specifically protecting against discrimination based on real or perceived sexual preference.

I am proud to represent thousands of gays and lesbians, in Manhattan and Queens, and I am proud of my close relationship with and support of the Stonewall Veterans Association, a group of those actually present on that fateful night.

As we celebrate the anniversary of the modern gay rights movement, we recognize the expansion of freedom has not been uniform and much remains to be done. So we celebrate the important, but incomplete, steps toward equality for those previously banished to the closet. Much more remains to be done to eliminate irrational prejudice against those who are different. And we must recommit ourselves to the fight against all types of bigotry, whether based on race, religion, national origin, sex or perceived sexual preference.

Source: *Congressional Record*, June 7, 1999, E1144, reprinted in *Speaking for Our Lives: Historic Speeches and Rhetoric for Gay and Lesbian Rights (1892–2000)* (New York: Harrington Park Press, 2004), pp. 756–7.

REPRESENTATIONS

6 Guerilla Girls, Do Women Have to Be Naked to Get into the Met. Museum? 1989

The Guerrilla Girls explain who they are:

"*We're a bunch of anonymous females who take the names of dead women artists as pseudonyms and appear in public wearing gorilla masks. We have produced posters, stickers, books, printed projects, and actions that expose sexism and racism in politics, the art world, film, and the culture at large. We use humor to convey information, provoke discussion, and show that feminists can be funny. We wear gorilla masks to focus on the issues rather than our personalities. Dubbing ourselves the conscience of culture, we declare ourselves feminist counterparts to the mostly male tradition of anonymous do-gooders like Robin Hood, Batman, and the Lone Ranger.*"

The poster below is a visual display of their provocative art.

Figure 7.1 *Guerrilla Girls, Do Women Have to be Naked to Get into the Met. Museum?*

7 Susan Power, Museum Indians, 2002

Artifacts preserved behind glass cases tell the stories of people from long ago and often forgotten. Susan Power's short story "Museum Indians" evokes two worlds and the bridges between them. An enrolled member of Standing Rock Sioux tribe, Power explores the social construction of memory from the intersecting perspectives of the Native American and female identities.

A snake coils in my mother's dresser drawer, it is thick and black, glossy as sequins. My mother cut her hair several years ago, before I was born, but she kept one heavy braid. It is the three-foot snake I lift from it's nest and handle as if it were alive.

"Mom, why did you cut your hair?" I ask. I am a little girl lifting a sleek black river into the light that streams through the kitchen window. Mom turns to me.

"It gave me headaches. Now put that away and wash your hands for lunch."

"You won't cut *my* hair, will you?" I'm sure this is a whine.

"No, just a little trim now and then to even the ends"

I return the dark snake to its nest among my mother's slips, arranging it so that its thin tail hides beneath the wide mouth sheared by scissors. My mother keeps her promise and lets my hair grow long, but I am only half of her; my thin brown braids will reach the middle of my back, and in maturity will look like tiny garden snakes.

My mother tells me stories every day while she cleans, while she cooks, on our way to the library, standing in the checkout line at the supermarket. I like to share her stories with other people, and chatter like a monkey when I am able to command adult attention.

She left the reservation when she was sixteen years old," I tell my audience. Sixteen sounds very old to me, but I always state the number because it seems integral to my recitation. "She had never been on a train before, or used a telephone. She left Standing Rock to take a job in Chicago so she could help out the family during the war. She was petrified of all the strange people and new surroundings; she stayed in her seat all the way from McLaughlin, South Dakota, to Chicago, Illinois, and didn't move once."

I usually laugh after saying this, because I cannot imagine my mother being afraid of anything. She is so tall, a true Dakota woman; she rises against the sun like a skyscraper, and when I draw her picture in my notebook she takes up the entire page. She talks politics and attends sit-ins, wrestles with the Chicago police and says what's on her mind.

I am her small shadow and witness. I am the timid daughter who can rage only on paper.

We don't have much money, but Mom takes me from one end of the city to the other on foot, on buses. I will grow up believing that Chicago belongs to me, because it was given to me by my mother. Nearly every week we tour the Historical Society, and Mom makes a point of complaining about the statue that depicts an Indian man about to kill a white woman and her children: "This is the only monument to the history of Indians in this area that you have on exhibit. It's a shame because it is completely one-sided. Children who see this will think this is what Indians are all about."

My mother lectures the guides and their bosses, until eventually that statue disappears.

Some days we haunt the Art Institute, and my mother pauses before a Picasso.

"He did this during his blue period," she tells me.

I squint at the blue man holding a blue guitar. "Was he very sad?" I ask.

"Yes, I think he was." My mother takes my hand and looks away from the painting. I can see a story developing behind her eyes, and I tug on her arm to release the words. She will tell me why Picasso was blue, what his thoughts were as he painted this canvas. She relates anecdotes I will never find in books, never see footnoted in a biography of the master artist. I don't even bother to check these references because I like my mother's version best.

When Mom is down, we go to see the mummies at the Field Museum of Natural History. The Egyptian dead sleep in the basement, most of them still shrouded in their wrappings.

"These were people like us," my mother whispers. She pulls me into her waist. "They had dreams and intrigues and problems with their teeth. They thought their one particular life was of the utmost significance. And now, just *look* at them." My mother never fails to brighten. "So what's the use of worrying too hard or too long? Might as well be cheerful."

Before we leave this place, we always visit my great-grandmother's buck-skin dress. We mount the stairs and walk through the museum's main hall – past the dinosaur bones all strung together, and the stuffed elephants lifting their trunks in a mute trumpet.

The clothed figures are disconcerting because they have no heads. I think of them as dead Indians. We reach the traditional outfits of the Sioux in the Plains Indian section, and there is the dress, as magnificent as I remembered. The yoke is completely beaded – I know the garment must be heavy to wear. My great-grandmother used blue beads as a background for the geometrical design, and I point to the azure expanse.

"Was this her blue period?" I ask my mother. She hushes me unexpectedly, she will not play the game. I come to understand that this is a solemn call, and we stand before the glass case as we would before a grave.

"I don't know how this got out of the family," Mom murmurs. I feel helpless beside her, wishing I could reach through the glass to disrobe the headless mannequin. My mother belongs in a grand buckskin dress such as this, even though her hair is now too short to braid and has been trained to curl at the edges in a saucy flip.

We leave our fingerprints on the glass, two sets of hands at different heights pressing against the barrier. Mom is sad to leave.

"I hope she knows we visit her dress," my mother says.

There is a little buffalo across the hall, stuffed and staring. Mom doesn't always have the heart to greet him. Some days we slip out of the museum without finding his stall.

"You don't belong here," Mom tells him on those rare occasions when she feels she must pay her respects. "We honor you," she continues, "because you are a creature of great endurance and great generosity. You provided us with so many things that helped us to survive. It makes me angry to see you like this."

Few things can make my mother cry; the buffalo is one of them.

"I am just like you," she whispers. "I don't belong here either. We should be in the Dakotas, somewhere a little bit east of the Missouri River. This crazy city is not a fit home for buffalo or Dakotas."

I take my mother's hand to hold her in place. I am a city child, nervous around livestock and lonely on the plains. I am afraid of a sky without light pollution – I never knew there could be so many stars. I lead my mother from the museum so she will forget the sense of loss. From the marble steps we can see Lake Shore Drive spill ahead of us, and I sweep my arm to the side as if I were responsible for this view. I introduce my mother to the city she gave me. I call her home.

Source: "Roofwalker" from *Roofwalker* by Susan Power (Minneapolis: Milkweed Editions, 2002). Copyright © 2002 by Susan Power. Reprinted with permission from Milkweed Editions (www.milkweed.org).

DOMESTIC LIVES

8 National Center for Health Statistics, Death Rates for Selected Causes of Death for White and Black Women, 1970 and 1993

> *The National Center for Health Statistics (NCHS) publishes data to support policies that aim to improve the health of American people. In 1995 Secretary of Health and Human Services Donna Shalala released a special report on the Health of American Women at the same time that NCHS published its twentieth annual report concluding that, "we need to pay more attention to women's health issues." Heart disease, breast and lung cancers, AIDs, and violence affected female life expectancy differently depending on race and class. The NCHS identifies women's health problems; politics informs the allocation of resources.*

Death rates for selected causes of death for white and black women, 1970 and 1993[1]

	White Women		Black Women	
	1970	1993	1970	1993
	Death Rate	Death Rate	Death Rate	Death Rate
Heart disease	167.8	99.2	251.7	165.3
Malignant neoplasms (cancers)	107.6	110.1	123.5	135.3
Cerebrovascular diseases (e.g., stroke)	56.2	22.7	107.9	39.9
Unintentional injuries (accidents)	27.2	16.6	35.3	20.1
Pneumonia and influenza	15.0	10.4	29.2	13.5
Diabetes mellitus	12.8	10.0	30.9	26.9
Chronic liver disease and cirrhosis	8.7	4.6	17.8	6.6
Suicide	7.2	4.6	2.9	2.1

Chronic obstructive pulmonary disease	5.3	17.8	—	12.2
Homicide and legal intervention	2.2	3.0	15.0	13.4
Nephritis, nephrotic syndrome, and nephritis (diseases of the kidneys)	—	3.2	—	9.2
HIV/AIDS	—	1.9	—	17.3

[1]Deaths per 100,000 resident population; rates are age-adjusted.

Source: National Center for Health Statistics, Health, United States, 1995, 1996, Table 30 in *The American Woman, 1999–2000*, ed. Cynthia Costello *et al.* (New York: Norton, 1998), p. 253.

9 Barbara Seaman, The Doctors' Case Against the Pill 1969, 1995

Twenty-five years after Barbara Seaman published The Doctors' Case Against the Pill, *she updated this landmark book with information on Norplant. The testimonies of dozens of women, typical of those who suffered devastating consequences from both the pill and Norplant, served to inform others at a time when advocacy replaced silence in what for decades had been a personal and private issue.*

FROM 1969

According to the best available estimates, somewhere between twelve and fifteen million women around the world are taking oral contraceptives with their own consent, if not with eagerness. Some eight million of these women are Americans. During premarital physical examinations at first-rate U.S. medical institutions, eight out of ten young women ask for the pill. "They give the physician a look ordinarily reserved for a museum piece if he explains that other means of contraception do exist," according to Dr. C. D. Christian of Duke University.

Unhappily, very few women anywhere are ever exposed to detailed explanations of alternatives. And so, for the vast majority of pill-using women, even in the United States, where we pride ourselves on ready access to the most intimate information, the deceptively easy act of swallowing the innocent-looking little pill is, in fact, an act of *uninformed* consent. Very few pill-users have the slightest notion of the potency of the drugs they are ingesting, or how the little pills may affect their own health or their still unborn children.

It seems incredible, but it is tragically true.

How many pill-users would still be taking these drugs if wives and husbands were fully informed about the drugs' risks and about the disenchantment and dismay that are increasingly disturbing the inner councils of the medical profession? There is no way of knowing until the full facts are laid before the public. Up to now, pill-users have heard almost exclusively about the pill's effectiveness and convenience. Most of them have yet to hear the full story of its dreadful drawbacks. And that is what this book will present.

How could it happen, in an era when electronics can alert everybody, everywhere, about anything at an instant's notice, that crucial knowledge about oral contraceptives – the most powerful, most widely used unnecessary drug ever developed in the history of mankind – has not been made generally available?

One answer is that bad news in medicine, unlike bad news of wars, tends to travel slowly, especially when it is fed, as is true in the case of the pill, by many sources in many countries and many medical specialties, all operating with surprising autonomy from each other. Much of the evidence has been buried, in bits and pieces, in technical journals that are not accessible to the public, or even to the typical, well-intentioned pill-prescribing gynecologist and general practitioner. For example, a most important warning appeared in an article entitled "Oral Contraceptives and Cerebrovascular Complications" in the February, 1969, issue of *Radiology*. There are some 300,000 physicians in the United States; *Radiology* has a circulation of only 9,699 and most radiologists rarely, if ever, prescribe birth control.

The second answer is that the precise extent of the seriousness of the case against the pill, much like the precise status of the case against smoking cigarettes, is not yet final and conclusive. It is merely so strongly suggestive that women who have a free choice in their use of contraceptives (and most readers of this book have this choice) would be unwise to use the pill without their *informed* consent.

The final and most significant answer is that all the logical sources of new information about the pill – the Government, the pill manufacturers and the practicing physicians – have until now preferred to keep these unhappy developments largely to themselves. Each had its own honorable reason.

The Government is traditionally reluctant to restrict the freedom of citizens, especially such productive and vocal ones as doctors and highly profitable tax-paying manufacturers.

The Pill Bandwagon

The profit motive and the wish to help curb the worldwide population explosion could explain the general reluctance of the drug manufacturers. Dependence on revenue from pharmaceutical advertising may explain the apparent reluctance of the editors on some medical journals to publish anti-pill research. Furthermore, most people are not aware that many prominent doctors, including medical school professors, derive much of their research money from drug companies or organizations specifically devoted to "population control."

The wish not to trigger undue alarm among patients inhibits many doctors. This is particularly true of those practitioners who, pressured by their patients and supplied with inadequate information about the effects of oral contraceptives, jumped on the pill bandwagon early and perhaps now regret it.

One prominent clinical researcher compared the pill to the war in Vietnam: "We got into it with the best of intentions, and now we don't know how the hell to get out."

Dr. David Clark, a world-famous neurologist from the University of Kentucky School of Medicine, summed up the situation with these stark words: "The pill allows experiments on the general population that would never be allowed as a planned experiment."

Many women feel well and look well on the pill, but this is no guarantee that it is good for them. It is now recognized that a large number of subtle changes occur in the body chemistry of virtually all pill-users, and may create no serious symptoms until many years have passed.

In a cautiously worded speech, which he says "is suddenly getting very popular" in medical circles, Dr. John J. Schrogie, who directs the research on oral contraceptives for the U.S. Food and Drug Administration, warned: "The estrogenic and progestational components of oral contraceptive drugs, as we know them today, are extremely active hormonal agents which have effects on many biological systems within the body... in fact, the contraceptive effects of these drugs may be merely incidental to many other pharmacological effects.... Although these various effects are now coming under closer attention, precise quantification of risk and identification of patients at increased risk still largely remains to be determined."

To put it in plain English, medicine's knowledge about the pill is still so vague that no doctor can answer the following crucial question with any degree of precision: for which women is the pill merely risky, and for which women is it very dangerous? ...

One doctor said: "We've been using a cannon to shoot down a sparrow." ...

In Atlanta, Dr. John R. McCain, clinical professor of gynecology and obstetrics at Emory University School of Medicine, knows how to make up for this lack of explanatory material in the pill packages. He told us: "For the ordinary patient contraceptives are available that work extremely well, if her doctor gives her careful directions, and she follows them. I have great confidence in the time-proven mechanical methods and I convey this to my patients." Even Dr. McCain's newlywed patients do not regard him as a "museum piece" when he cautions them against the pill:

"I take down my *Physician's Desk Reference* [a book containing the same information as the "package inserts"] and show them the long, long list of complications and dangers. I translate the medical terms for them. I answer their questions. Yes, even brides accept the diaphragm!"

Some doctors are shocked to hear that colleagues show *Physician's Desk Reference* to their patients. Dr. William Barfield, an Augusta gynecologist and associate clinical professor at the Medical College of Georgia, says: "I don't think it is necessary to talk about depression, loss of energy or loss of libido....I would not suggest to any patient that the pill might cause headaches."

"I Don't Suggest Symptoms"

Dr. Elizabeth Connell of New York City's Metropolitan Hospital, a mother of six ("all planned"), admits that she is "not 100 per cent secure about the safety of the pill. Anyone who is, doesn't know what he's talking about." But then we asked her: "If a woman who is happy using a diaphragm came to you and had been using it successfully, but wanted to try the pill just because her neighbors were using it or her husband thought sex might be a little more fun, would you tend to discourage her – as long as she was using the diaphragm successfully?"

Dr. Connell replied: "No, it's up to her. I would not encourage her either way. I think this is the patient's decision. If she wanted to switch, I would switch her. If she had an inclination to remain on the diaphragm I would leave her on."

While Dr. Connell maintained that the choice of a birth-control method is up to the patient, she did not seem to feel that *informed* choice is necessary.

We asked her: "Which risks do you mention to the patient?"

She replied: "Oh, usually the thrombophlebitis [blood clotting disorders] and not too much else. They don't understand anything else. You scare the heck out of them. We tell her that in case of anything abnormal she is to call. You don't have to outline it for them and make trouble. You don't have to plant seeds about what they're going to call about. If you tell them the symptoms they'll have them by the next day."

Dr. Connell points out that she works in impoverished Harlem, but would apply the same standard in a middle-class practice.

Dr. Hans Lehfeldt, director of Bellevue Hospital's Contraceptive Clinic, maintains a Park Avenue private practice at the same time. Like Dr. Connell he insists that it is a doctor's duty to use the "same rules" for his private and clinic patients. Dr. Lehfeldt says: "I don't suggest symptoms to any of my patients because it might produce them, but I do tell them to call me if *anything* unusual occurs."

On the other side of the argument, Dr. Harold Speert, a noted Columbia University gynecologist, told us flatly: "Doctors assume unwarranted responsibility if they prescribe the pill without discussing it." Dr. Speert prescribes the pill for perhaps one contraceptive patient in ten, or twenty, and only after a detailed dialogue about alternatives. Whenever he does prescribe the pill it's "a compromise of some sort. What may be good for humanity as a whole – the population explosion and so on – may be very bad for a New York woman with easy access to other techniques."

And Dr. Hugh Davis of Johns Hopkins University maintained: "Everyone has the right to select his own form of suicide. We now know that the pill carries a definite risk and if you're going to use it you must inform your patients of the risks – fully. It's true that if you mention headaches you may get 99 annoying phone calls from 99 suggestible women with imagined discomforts. But your hundredth phone call might be from a lady whose life is at stake, whose headache is a warning symptom that she must discontinue the pill."

In certain cases, medication should be discontinued at once. Mrs. Cynthia Y. of Salt Lake City is a graduate of Vassar. A week after she went on the pill she started developing headaches. A few more weeks passed and they worsened, but did not yet seem severe enough to require medical attention. Mrs. Y. thought that perhaps her "sinus was acting up."

"One Tuesday on vacation in Los Angeles I had these tremendous headaches all day long and I just thought I really couldn't see. It just went on and on. I finally threw up and then I felt better. At least I was able to sleep. I decided to give up the pill because it was the only thing I could think of that I had changed, that might be causing it. I couldn't reach my gynecologist at home – he was on vacation, too – and I didn't know a doctor in Los Angeles. I was afraid to give up the pill right on the spot. I thought something awful might happen if you suddenly stopped in mid-cycle. When I got home my doctor apologized for having been unreachable; in fact, he got very angry at the doctor who was supposed to be covering for him, and said that he would never use him again. He told me I was most fortunate to be alive and well, and that I should have stopped the pills immediately when the headaches became so intense."

The case of Mrs. Y., who may have been about to suffer a stroke illustrates the necessity for informed communication between doctor and pill-user. An exceptionally bright woman, Mrs. Y. made the connection between her headaches and her pills; many less intelligent pill-takers would have failed to do so. Moreover, Mrs. Y's doctor had only given her a two-month prescription, unlike many doctors who hand out prescriptions for six months or longer, even when a patient is first beginning the pill. Yet, when Mrs. Y. developed a potentially life-threatening symptom, she still did not have sufficient information to know how to proceed in his absence.

So there are highly esteemed gynecologists who do not think it wise to discuss the pill's dangers and warning signs too specifically with their patients. Other equally respected specialists insist that it is mandatory to give detailed facts, particularly since other good alternative birth-control devices are available and the pill is not usually being used to cure a disease. And the fact is that users selected the pill for convenience, not need.

Among the good and careful doctors, the difference of views dates back to Plato, who made a sharp distinction between physicians treating slaves and free men. Plato urged that in treating a slave a doctor should prescribe like an authority figure, as if he were absolutely sure of himself and his potions. In treating a free man, the physician was expected to "enter into discourse with the patient *and* his family" and was not entitled to proceed with any medication or surgery until the patient was "convinced."

This standard is not always applicable today. When a doctor must perform an emergency operation he may not have time to discuss the merits of one anesthetic or surgical procedure vis-à-vis another. But, in choosing a contraceptive Plato's distinction applies. The reader whose physician troubles himself to discuss the pros and cons of various methods with her is being treated like a free adult. The reader whose physician merely pushes a pill prescription across the desk is being treated like something a good deal less.

Most doctors used to go along with a loose-reined approach to prescribing oral contraception. But in 1968, as more and more adverse reports surfaced, especially the authoritative British inquiry into blood clotting, the tide started to turn. Even a marketing "strategy report" by a leading pill manufacturer acknowledged that the typical doctor has been "confronted with a rising tide of [medical] journal articles focused on morbidity and mortality associated with oral contraceptives. It therefore should be assumed that his attitudes toward presently available products are undergoing rapid change."

Often, a conscientious doctor may have trouble making his warnings stick. When Mrs. Sandra T. arrived for her semi-annual checkup in her Vermont physician's office in the spring of 1969 and asked for a refill of her pill prescription, the doctor urged her to give the pill up. He told her that her varicose veins were looking worse, and explained that this might mean she was in danger of developing a clotting disorder. He explained that the incidence of clotting disorders in pill-users was proving to be much higher than originally suspected. He showed Mrs. T. several popular articles which he considered well documented and, as he explained, were in line with reports he'd been reading in "practically every issue" of the medical journals he received. One was a clipping from *Newsweek* of May, 1969, quoting Dr. Roy Hertz of the National Institutes of Health as suggesting that by 1971 breast cancer may start to occur increasingly among the women who take oral contraceptives....

FROM 1995

In 1960, when Enovid opened the era of modern contraception (and some would say, a sexual revolution), American women were deeply passive toward our doctors and our health care. We allowed ourselves to be drugged, shaved, painted, humiliated, patronized, and stuck up in stirrups to have our babies delivered. We handed over our hard-earned cash to infant-formula companies for a product billed as "nutritionally superior to mother's milk." We fretted if our orgasms were merely clitoral and not vaginal, as Sigmund Freud had ordained they ought to be to prove we were "mature." We believed that the early high-dose killer pills were, as we had been told, "natural, physiologic, and therefore safe." It wasn't until about the end of the decade that we learned to question authority.

Today, we check the claims for new products. With Norplant, women's health advocates are performing and publishing their own studies, and pooling information at international conferences. In the United States, through such organizations as the National Women's Health Network, the Boston Women's Health Book Collective, the Black Women's Health Project, the Native American Women's Health Education Resource Center, and the Committee on Women, Population and the Environment, we are spreading awareness.

And finally – perhaps most hopefully – the Population Council has come to recognize that contraception is for couples, and is developing an implant system for men, a male vaccine, and a plastic condom providing long shelf life and greater strength than latex.

Source: Barbara Seaman, *The Doctors' Case Against the Pill* (Alameda, CA: Hunter House Publishers, 1995), pp. 12–19, 252.

10 Antonia I. Castañeda, History and the Politics of Violence Against Women, 1995

Castañeda used astounding statistics to describe the violence against women in the 1990s. At a time when murder and burglaries declined, rape became the fastest-growing violent crime. Most rapes are intra-racial and committed by men against women. In response, activists established battered women's shelters, rape crisis centers, and increased efforts to promote women's self-defense. The following analysis locates rape and violence against women in the context of sexual politics, a powerful expression of male power and dominance.

I dedicate this talk to the soul of the Mayan woman who was thrown alive to the dogs because she refused to have sex with her captor.

Statistics: Local and National

Rape is the fastest growing violent crime in the nation. In San Antonio, reports of sexual assault rose by more than 16 percent in 1995 – from 565 cases to 658 – while the number of other major crimes, including murders and burglaries, plummeted.

One in three women will raped in her lifetime.

Ninety percent of all rapes are intraracial; the assailant and the victim are of the same "race."

Only one in ten rapes are reported to law enforcement.

Two hundred women per hour are physically abused by spouses or live-in partners.

Of all women killed in Texas, 38 percent were murdered by their intimate male partners. The national average is 30 percent.

Battering is the number one crime and cause of injury to women in the United States.

Seventy percent of men who batter their wives also batter their children.

In 95 percent of all domestic violence assaults, the assaults are committed by men against women.

Two hundred million dollars, or five hours of military spending, could pay for the annual support of 1,600 rape crisis centers and battered women's shelters.

We are here in the name of twenty-year-old Ada Powell – shot and killed on her way to work by two men in a car who first honked and waved at her and her sister, then followed them onto the San Diego Freeway, and shot to kill on an early spring day in 1992.

We are here in the name of fifty-one-year-old Shirley Lowery, who was stabbed nineteen times by her live-in partner in a Milwaukee courthouse, where she had gone to get a two-year injunction against him because he repeatedly raped her and threatened to kill her if she left him. He succeeded.

We are here in the name of Joanne Little and Inés Garcia, who in the 1970s killed the jailers who raped them in their cells after they had been arrested and were in police custody.

We are here in the name of Anna Mae Ashquash, the Cree woman who was murdered for her political activities in the Indian Rights Movement.

We are here in the name of Anita Hill, who broke the silence about sexual harassment at the highest levels of government and made it impossible for the nation to ignore the reality of sexual harassment, sexual threat, and sexual assault that women face daily in the workplace.

We are here in the name of all women, so that every woman – whatever her race, sexual orientation, culture, class, age, or physical condition can be in the streets, at school, at work, at play, or any other place by herself, can be with anybody of her own choosing, in a manner of her own desire, wearing whatever she pleases, and can do so freely – without the abiding threat and actuality of rape and all of the other forms of sexual and other violence that constantly assault our bodies, our psyches, our spirits, our emotions, our souls. We see ourselves daily displayed, violated, dismembered, abused, objectified, and discarded – on TV, in music, books, rape jokes, sexual harassment at work, in the classroom, on the street, grocery store porn magazines, billboards, record jackets, soap operas, films.

Let us be clear at the very outset that rape and other violence against women are acts of domination – acts of power – the direct expression of sexual politics, and thus are violent political acts of sexual and other aggression against women. Rape and other forms of sexual violence are primary instruments of terrorism used against women to maintain hetero-sexual male supremacy, to sustain the patriarchy and all its structures, and to preserve the gender status quo. Violence against women is a logical extension of sexism and the politics of male domination.

Let us be equally clear about the relationship of sexism/violence to other forms of domination, and the importance of rape in maintaining those other forms of domination. I am speaking here specifically about the relationship between sexism and racism, classism, and homophobism. While sexism affects women most directly, the latter three affect both women and men and thus cut across gender. Yet all these forms of domin-ation originate in a sexism/male domination which is itself rooted in a normative heterosexuality that conceptualizes and defines male sexuality as aggressive and female sexuality as submissive.

Thus, it is imperative that we understand that in the United States, in the Americas, rape and sexual violence are inextricably tied to a pervasive racism with its attendant, vicious violence against people of color – against African Americans, Asian Americans, Chicanos/Latinos, and Native Americans; it is tied to a pervasive homophobism with its attendant violence against lesbians and gays; and to pervasive classism with its attendant violence against the economically poor, "lower classes," now called "the urban underclass."

All of these forms of power, of domination, of oppression are interrelated. They derive from, feed upon, and sustain one another; they are rooted in the invasion of the Americas, in a colonialist domination that began over 500 years ago with Columbus, and which today is the common legacy we live with daily – albeit from different positions of power and privilege depending on our gender, our race, our sexual orientation, our class, and our physical condition.

That legacy is rooted in sexual and other violence against women. The first political acts of domination were acts of rape and sexual aggression against women – first against Native American women, then against their mestiza daughters, and then against black women torn from their African homelands, enslaved and raped to labor themselves and to produce laborers to feed the colonial economies of Spain, England, and subsequently, the United States.

Michele de Cuneo, a nobleman from Savona who came with Columbus on the second journey in 1493–1496, left us an account of the first documented rape in the Americas. He was the perpetrator and, in 1493, he wrote boastfully to a friend:

> While I was in the boat, I captured a very beautiful Carib woman, whom the aforesaid Lord Admiral (Columbus) gave to me, and with whom, having brought her into my cabin, and she being naked as is their custom, I conceived the desire to take my pleasure. I wanted to put my desire to execution, but she was unwilling for me to do so, and treated me with her nails in such wise that I would have preferred never to have begun. But seeing this (in order to tell you the whole event to the end), I took a rope-end and thrashed her well, following which she produced such screaming and wailing as would cause you not to believe your ears. Finally we reached an agreement such that, I can tell you, she seemed to have been raised in a veritable school of harlots.

This narrative written by the rapist himself 503 years ago, establishes the interpretation of rape upon which this country's rape laws were based until less than twenty years ago. This interpretation, upheld and sanctioned by the courts, by the judicial system, by society and culture, is one in which a woman may first resist, but then succumbs to what "she wanted all along." The mentality and underlying assumptions this interpretation conveys is:

1. That Women ask for it because of the way they are dressed.
2. That "no" really means "yes."
3. That women enjoy being raped.
4. That historically women of color could be raped, beaten, worked to death or killed with impunity precisely because they are of color.

Racism intersects with sexism to pit women of color and white women against each other. Women of color are sexualized and racialized. White women are reified as the incarnation of both sexual and racial purity. That reification is bought at the price of the devaluation of women of color.

It is important that we reflect upon the origins and on the contemporary effects of these interrelated multiple oppressions.

When California entered the nation as a free state in 1850, meaning slavery was outlawed, it simultaneously passed a law to allow apprenticeship or indenture of Indian males under eighteen, and females under fifteen years old – a euphemism for enslavement. Under the cover of the apprenticeship provisions of the laws of 1850 and 1860, the abduction and sale of Indians – especially young women and children – were carried on as a regular business enterprise in California. The price depended on age, sex, and usefulness, and ranged from $30 to $200. A common feature of the trade was the seizure of Indian girls and women who were held by their captors as sexual partners or sold to other whites for sexual purposes. Dealers in Indian women in the early 1850s classified their "merchandise," as "fair, middling, inferior, refuse," and set their prices accordingly.

Mexican women, whose country lost the war, were now among the conquered. Rosalia Vallejo de Leese, who was pregnant during the Bear Flag Revolt in June 1846, described how John C. Fremont and his band of outlaws held her captive and threatened to torch her home, with her female relatives in it, unless she complied with their demands.

The commonly held notion that women, due to their scarcity during the California gold rush, were afforded moral, emotional, and physical protection and respect by Anglo miners, does not hold for either Indian or Mexican women. Mexicanas, as part of the nation that lost the war and part of the group of more knowledgeable, experienced, and initially successful miners competing with Anglos in the gold fields, became one object of the violence and lawlessness directed against Mexicanos/Latinos. It is significant that Juanita of Downieville and Cheptia of San Patricio, the only women hanged in California and in Texas, were Mexican. Both had killed white men who tried to assault them.

Similarly, Asian American historian Sucheng Chan finds the intersection of gender, race, sexuality, and labor to be key to the legislation on Chinese exclusion and immigration from the 1870s to 1943. Contrary to the common belief that Chinese laborers were the target of the first exclusion act, the effort to bar another group of Chinese – prostitutes – preceded the prohibition against male workers who had been brought in to work as unskilled laborers in the racially segmented labor force that kept them mobile, transient, exploitable, and expendable.

Chinese women, like men, were brought to the United States as contract workers – as another source of mobile, exploitable, expendable, and cheap labor. Unlike men, however, Chinese women were brought for the purposes of sexual labor – to "provide sexual services to the Chinese male workers," at the moment that the miscegenation laws prohibiting interracial marriage were extended to include Asians. Most often, Chinese women were brought under false pretenses, including abduction and enslavement. Once in California, their sexuality was impugned. Chinese women's sexuality was a pivotal issue in legislative hearings, committee meetings, and statutes, in municipal ordinances, and in the Chinese-exclusion laws. The laws barred all Chinese women who sought admission into the United States. The government's targeted exclusion of Chinese women effectively prevented Chinese families, and thus a full-fledged Chinese society (societies), from establishing themselves in the United States during the 19th century. And no Chinese woman in California, regardless of her social standing, was safe from harassment.

For women of color, the inseparable, interlocking oppressions have produced a conceptualization of our sexuality as promiscuous women who offered their favors to white men. Thus these stereotypes, which abound in the historical and popular literature as well as in all aspects of nineteenth- and twentieth-century popular culture in the United States, include the placed Indian "squaw" who readily gives her sexual favors, the passionate black or mulatto women who is always ready and sexually insatiable, the volatile Mexican woman who is fiery eyed and hot blooded, and the languid, opium-drowsed Asian woman whose only occupation is sex.

Let me underscore the relationship between the past and the present. The legacy of the Americas is violence and exploitation based on sex, gender, race, sexuality, class, culture, and physical condition – based on the power and privilege to exploit and oppress others that each of those elements confer on us. We all share the historical legacy – it is our common heritage. Today, it is evident in Propositions 187 and 209 in California; in the recent violent beating of undocumented workers Alicia Sotero and Enrique Flores in El Monte, California; in the anti-gay ordinance in Colorado; in the dismantling of affirmative action, such as the Hopwood decision in Texas; in the attacks against welfare mothers; and in environmental racism, Nafta, and multiple forms of attacks against working peoples.

Where do each of us stand on each of these interlocking elements? And what will each of us do with this historical legacy? I would ask each of us to interrogate ourselves, our organizations, our workplaces, our families – to examine our individual gender, sexual, racial, and class politics, and our power and privilege in each realm.

We cannot change the last 500 years, but we can change the next 500. We must take personal responsibility to act against rape, sexual violence, racism, sexism, homophobism, classism. Every time we remain silent and do not take a stand against these interlocking evils wherever we encounter them, we become complicitous with them and we reproduce them. In brief, we become perpetrators of the sexual and other violence that is being committed.

I challenge each of us individually and all of us collectively to recognize the privilege and power that we have – to examine our gender, racial, sexual, and class politics. We must challenge ourselves and each other to define a politic where we use every ounce of our power and privilege to stop rape, to stop sexual and all other forms of violence against women specifically, and to stop all of the multiple violences of sexism, racism, homophobism, and classism in our lives and society, beginning right here today in San Antonio.

What can you do? You can resist. Whoever you are, you can say *No – it stops here – it stops with me.* And we can find ways to take individual and collective political action.

Women

1. Break the silence if you have been raped, molested, sexually assaulted, sexually harassed. Register and file complaints and grievances, bring charges against the perpetrator or perpetrators.
2. Work with organizations such as rape crisis centers to help other women and victims of sexual crimes.
3. March, rally, protest, and take back the night.
4. Work with and vote for politicians who support women's sexual, reproductive, and civil rights.
5. Take a personal stand – no matter how unpopular. Challenge and speak out clearly and directly to friends, family, teachers, co-workers, and so on against any form of sexism, racism, homophobism, ableism, or any other kind of violence that is occurring in your presence.
6. Take self-defense classes and teach what you have learned to other women.

Men

1. Learn about your unearned male privilege and power and about how you use that male power and privilege to perpetuate sexism and other violences against women.
2. Recognize and do not participate, do not perpetuate any form of sexism and its attendant violences against women under any circumstances.
3. Break the silence and the protection that men have historically afforded each other: Do not protect other perpetrators. Stand up to your peers – take the heat of their disapproval.
4. Work to politicize and educate other men about their sexism and its attendant violences.
5. Work with and vote for politicians who support women's sexual, reproductive, and civil rights.
6. Determine the multiple ways in which you perpetuate the structures of power and domination and work against those structures, to tear them down – to change them.

Source: *Living Chicana Theory*, ed. Carla Trujillo (Berkeley, CA: Third Woman Press, 1998), pp. 310–19.

Questions to Think About

1. Discuss the different meanings conveyed in the phrase "sexual politics."
2. How have the representations of women changed over the course of the twentieth century?
3. Describe how contemporary women use the power of memory as a tool for shaping their lives.

Bibliography

This bibliography is suggestive rather than exhaustive.

General Histories and Collections of Documents

Anderson, Karen (1996) *Changing Woman: A History of Racial, Ethnic Women in Modern America*. New York: Oxford University Press.

Baxandall, Rosalyn and Linda Gordon, eds. (2000) *Dear Sisters: Dispatches from the Women's Liberation Movement*. New York: Basic Books.

Blackwelder, Julia Kirk (1997) *Now Hiring: The Feminization of Work in the United States, 1900–1995*. College Station: Texas A&M University Press.

Cott, Nancy, ed. (2000) *No Small Courage: A History of Women in the United States*. New York: Oxford University Press.

D'Emilio, John and Estelle B. Freedman (1988) *Intimate Matters: A History of Sexuality in America*. New York: Harper & Row.

DuBois, Ellen Carol and Lynn Dumenil (2009) *Through Women's Eyes, an American History with Documents*. Boston: Bedford/St. Martin's Press.

Kleinberg, S. Jay *et al.*, ed. (2007) *The Practice of U.S. Women's History: Narratives, Intersections, and Dialogues*. New Brunswick: Rutgers University Press.

Ruiz, Vicki and Ellen Carol DuBois, eds. (1994) *Unequal Sisters: A Multicultural Reader in U.S. Women's History, 2nd edition*. New York: Routledge.

White, Deborah Gray (1999) *Too Heavy a Load: Black Women in Defense of Themselves, 1894–1994*. New York: W.W. Norton.

Chapter 1

Blewett, Mary (1991) *We Will Rise in Our Might: Workingwomen's Voices from Nineteenth-Century New England*. Ithaca: Cornell University Press.

Bordin, Ruth (1986) *Frances Willard, a Biography*. Chapel Hill: University of North Carolina Press.

Hunter, Tera W. (1997) *To 'joy my freedom: Southern Black Women's Lives and Labors after the Civil War*. Cambridge: Harvard University Press.

Jones, Jacqueline (1985) *Labor of Love, Labor of Sorrow: Black Women, Work and the Family from Slavery to the Present*. New York: Basic Books.

Pascoe Peggy (1990) *Relations of Rescue: The Search for Female Moral Authority in the American West, 1874–1939*. New York: Oxford University Press.

Riley, Glenda (1996) *Building and Breaking Families in the American West*. Albuquerque: University of New Mexico.

Sklar, Kathryn Kish (1995) *Florence Kelley and the Nation's Work*. New Haven: Yale University Press.

Sneider, Allison (2008) *Suffragists in an Imperial Age: U.S. Expansion and the Woman Question, 1870–1929*. New York: Oxford University Press.

Yung, Judy (1995) *Unbound Feet: A Social History of Chinese Women in San Francisco*. Berkeley: University of California Press.

Chapter 2

Blair, Karen (1980) *The Clubwoman as Feminist: True Womanhood Redefined, 1868–1914*. New York: Holmes & Meier.

Cott, Nancy F. (1987) *The Grounding of Modern Feminism*. New Haven: Yale University Press.

DuBois, Ellen Carol (1997) *Harriot Stanton Blatch and the Winning of Woman Suffrage*. New Haven: Yale University Press.

Enstad, Nan (1999) *Ladies of Labor, Girls of Adventure: Working Women, Popular Culture, and Labor Politics at the turn of Twentieth Century*. New York: Columbia University Press.

Ford, Linda (1991) *Iron-Jawed Angels: The Suffrage Militancy of the National Woman's Party, 1912–1920*. Lanham: University Press of America.

Frankel, Noralee and Nancy S. Dye (1991) *Gender, Class, Race, and Reform in the Progressive Era*. Lexington: University Press of Kentucky.

Higginbotham, Evelyn Brooks (1993) *Righteous Discontent: The Women's Movement in the Black Baptist Church, 1880–1920*. Cambridge: Harvard University Press.

Muncy, Robyn (1991) *Creating a Female Dominion in American Reform, 1890–1935*. New York: Oxford University Press.

Orleck, Annelise (1995) *Common Sense and a Little Fire: Women and Working-Class Politics in the United States, 1900–1965*. Chapel Hill: University of North Carolina Press.

Parker, Alison M. (1997) *Purifying America: Women, Cultural Reform, and Pro-Censorship Activism, 1873–1933*. Urbana: University of Illinois Press.

Peiss, Kathy (1986) *Cheap Amusements: Working Women and Leisure in Turn of the Century New York*. Philadelphia: Temple University Press.

Chapter 3

Andersen, Kristi (1996) *After Suffrage: Women in Partisan and Electoral Politics Before the New Deal*. Chicago: University of Chicago Press.

Benson, Susan Porter (2007) *Household Accounts: Working-Class Family Economies in the Interwar United States*. Ithaca: Cornell University Press.

Cohen, Miriam (1993) *Workshop to Office: Two Generations of Italian Women in New York City, 1900–1950*. Ithaca: Cornell University Press.

Cook, Blanche Wiesen (1992) *Eleanor Roosevelt vol. 1 and 2*. New York: Viking.

Goodwin, Joanne (1997) *Gender and the Politics of Welfare Reform: Mothers' Pensions in Chicago, 1911–1929*. Chicago: University of Chicago Press.

Hall, Jacqueline Dowd et al. (1987) *Like a Family: The Making of a Southern Cotton Mill World*. Chapel Hill: University of North Carolina Press.

Strom, Sharon Hartman (1992) *Beyond the Typewriter: Gender, Class, and the Origins of Modern American Office Work, 1900–1930*. Urbana: University of Illinois Press.

Ware, Susan (1987) *Partner and I: Molly Dewson, Feminism, and New Deal Politics*. New Haven: Yale University Press.

Chapter 4

Glenn, Evelyn Nakano (1986) *Issei, Nisei, War Bride: Three Generations of Japanese American Women in Domestic Service*. Philadelphia, Temple University Press.

Clark-Lewis, Elizabeth (1994) *Living In, Living Out: African American Domestics in Washington D.C., 1910–1940*. Washington: Smithsonian Institution Press.

Gluck, Sherna Berger (1988) *Rosie the Riveter Revisited: Women, the War, and Social Change*. New York: New American Library.

Honey, Maureen, ed. (1999) *Bitter Fruit: African American Women in World War II*. Columbia: University of Missouri Press.

Kessler-Harris, Alice (2001) *In Pursuit of Equity: Women, Men, and the Quest for Economic Citizenship in Twentieth Century America*. New York: Oxford University Press.

Milkman, Ruth (1987) *Gender at Work: The Dynamics of Job Segregation by Sex during World War II*. Urbana: University of Illinois Press.

Ruiz, Vicki (1987) *Cannery Women, Cannery Lives: Mexican Women, Unionization, and the California Food Processing Industry, 1930–1950*. Albuquerque: University of New Mexico Press.

Ruiz, Vicki (1998) *From Out of the Shadows: Mexican Women in Twentieth-Century America*. New York: Oxford University Press.

Chapter 5

Baker, Ellen (2007) *On Strike and on Film, Mexican American Families and Black-listed Filmmakers in Cold War America*. Chapel Hill: University of North Carolina Press.

Curry, Constance (1996) *Silver Rights*. San Diego: Harcourt Brace.

Harrison, Cynthia (1988) *On Account of Sex: The Politics of Women's Issues, 1945–1968*. Berkeley, University of California Press.

Hartmann, Susan (1989) *From Margin to Mainstream: American Women and Politics Since 1960*. New York: Knopf.

Meyerowitz Joanne, ed. (1994) *Not June Cleaver: Women and Gender in Postwar America, 1945–1960*. Philadelphia: Temple University Press.

Ransby, Barbara (2003) *Ella Baker and the Black Freedom Movement: A Radical Democratic Vision*. Chapel Hill: University of North Carolina Press.

Peiss, Kathy (1998) *Hope in a Jar: The Making of America's Beauty Culture*. New York: Metropolitan Books.

Chapter 6

Breines, Winifred (2006) *The Trouble Between Us: An Uneasy History of White and Black Women in the Feminist Movement*. New York: Oxford University Press.

Cobble, Dorothy Sue (2004) *The Other Women's Movement: Workplace Justice and Social Rights in Modern America*. Princeton: Princeton University Press.

Critchlow, Donald (2005) *Phyllis Schlafly and Grassroots Conservatism: A Woman's Crusade*. Princeton: Princeton University Press.

Faderman, Lillian (1991) *Odd Girls and Twilight Lovers: A History of Lesbian Life in Twentieth-Century America*: New York: Columbia University Press.

Farrell, Amy Erdman (1998) *Yours in Sisterhood: Ms. Magazine and the Promise of Popular Feminism*. Chapel Hill: University of North Carolina Press.

Luker, Kristin (1984) *Abortion and the Politics of Motherhood*. Berkeley: University of California Press.

MacLean, Nancy (2006) *Freedom is Not Enough: The Opening of the American Workplace*. New York: Russell Sage Foundation; Cambridge, Harvard University Press.

McGirr, Lisa (2001) *Suburban Warriors: The Origins of the New American Right*. Princeton: Princeton University Press.

Moraga, Cherrie and Gloria Anzaldua, eds. (2002) *This Bridge Called My Back: Writings by Radical Women of Color, 3rd Edition*. Berkeley: Third Woman Press.

Nadasen, Premilla (2005) *Welfare Warriors: The Welfare Rights Movement in the United States*. New York: Routledge.

Nelson, Jennifer (2003) *Women of Color and the Reproductive Rights Movement*. New York: New York University Press.

Chapter 7

Baumgardner, Jennifer and Amy Richards (2000) *Manifesta: Young Women, Feminism and the Future*. New York: Farrar, Straus and Giroux.

Evans, Sarah M. (2003) *Tidal Wave: How Women Changed America at Century's End*. New York: Free Press.

Louie, Miriam Ching Yoon (2001) *Sweatshop Warriors: Immigrant Women Workers Take on the Global Factory*. Cambridge: South End Press.

Rosen, Ruth (2007) *The World Split Open: How the Modern Women's Movement Changed Amercia, 2nd edition*. New York: Viking.

Solinger, Rickie (1998) *Abortion Wars: A Half Century of Struggle, 1950–2000*. Berkeley: University of California Press.

Stiehm, Judith Hicks ed. (1996) *It's Our Military Too!: Women and the U.S. Military*. Philadelphia, Temple University Press.

Index

abortion, 7–8, 120, 183–6, 206, 211–12
abuse, physical, 14–15, 47 *see also*
    violence against women
    sexual, 55, 74–5, 99, 172, 223–6 *see
    also* rape
activism, 127, 135, 183, 197, 253–4
adolescence, female, 179–80
advertising, 162, 162–9, 174
affirmative action, 206, 253
African American women, 10, 12–15,
    23, 52–8, 74–5, 115, 130–3, 142,
    149, 176–8, 198–201, 227–31,
    232–3, 240–1
amendment, fifteenth, 176–8
    fifth, 202
    fourteenth, 169–70, 176–8, 202–3
    nineteenth, 3, 8, 31, 96, 161 *see also*
    suffrage
American Birth Control League, 116
American Civil Liberties Union, 169–73
American Federation of Labor, 125
American Federation of Labor –
    Congress of Industrial
    Organizations (AFL–CIO), 194,
    202–3
American Woman Suffrage
    Association, 17
Anthony, Susan B., 20
Anzaldúa, Gloria, 209–10

arrests, of women, 128, 178 *see also*
    prison conditions
art, museum, 236–7, 238

Baker, Ella, 173–6
Betty Boop, 114
biological clock, 220
birth control, 7–8, 118–20, 183–6 *see
    also* contraception, family planning
    pill, 186, 212–15, 241–7 *see also*
    reproductive rights
Blanket Equality Bill, 96–101
Bolshevism, 76, 102 *see also* Russian
    Revolution
Brandeis, Brief, 63–74
Breckinridge, S.P., 71
Bryn Mawr Summer School for Women
    Workers, 93–5
Burroughs, Nannie Helen, 64–5

career women, 75, 175, 189, 219–23
cartoons, 114, 209
Catholicism, 87, 114, 120, 127–9, 137,
    184, 207–8
Catt, Carrie Chapman, 101, 108
charity organizations, 16, 35, 76, 117
child labor, 101
childcare, non-maternal, 28–31, 53–8,
    90, 196–7, 205–6

Chinatown, 40–6, 122–4, 196–7
citizenship, Indian, 31, 86–8
Civil Rights Act, 202
common law, 173
Communism, Communist Party,
    123, 197
Congress of Industrial Organizations
    (CIO), 125, 194
Congressional Union for Woman
    Suffrage, 80–1
Consumer Movement, 60
consumerism, 163–9
contraception, 36–9, 116–18, 211–12,
    241–8 *see also* birth control,
    reproductive rights
Crawford, Joan, 143

dating, 87, 181, 235
Daughters of Bilitis (DOB), 182–3
Davis, Angel, 197–201
Democratic National Convention,
    176–8
Democratic National Committee,
    Bureau of Women's Activities, 107
Department of Labor, Women's Bureau,
    10, 202–3
Dewson, Molly, 107
discrimination, racial (racism), 126,
    132, 176–8, 195, 249
disorderly conduct, 13, 92
divorce, 97, 115–16, 143, 173, 191, 193

Eastman, Crystal, 79
education, 22–3, 76, 85, 88, 118–19,
    128, 130, 133, 134, 135–7, 146
    see also school, public
    in business school, 47, 141
    in college, 113, 133–4, 140–1
    industrial, 19
    professional, 23
Ellis, Havelock, 64
emancipation, 20, 21–2, 59, 172
Enovid *see* birth control pill
Equal Employment Opportunity
    Commission (EEOC), 220, 227–31

Equal Pay Act, 202
equal rights, 21–2, 96–101, 110–11,
    171–3, 173–6, 202, 235–6
Equal Rights Amendment (ERA), 96,
    108, 202–3, 203–7
equal wages, 19, 194
equality, legal, 96–7, 108, 191–6, 202–3
eugenics, 116–18

family life, 147–8
    African American, 57–8, 149
    children, 146, 149, 209
    family planning, 118, 241–7 *see also*
        birth control
    immigrant, 76
    marital sex, 36–9, 59, 192, 195
    Mexican American, 157–61
    mother/daughter relationship, 31–4,
        119, 167, 179–80, 233–4, 237–40
    play, 33, 149
    see also marriage
fashion, 20, 88, 130, 168
Federal Bureau of Investigation (FBI),
    197
Federal Emergency Relief Association,
    146
The Feminine Mystique, 162–9
Feminism, Second Wave, 162–9, 208–9
Feminism, Third Wave, 232–4
Feminist Movement, 204–7, 222,
    236–7
film, 89, 93, 104
    Hollywood movies, 75, 114, 143, 156
Flynn, Elizabeth Gurley, 58–62
Fox-Genovese, Elizabeth, 7
free speech, 79, 102
Freedom of Contract, 97
Friedan, Betty, 162
friendship, among women, 50–1,
    83, 129

Gay Rights Movement, 235–6
gender, social construction, 175–6
General Federation of Women's Clubs,
    31, 105, 114

glass ceiling, 219
Goldmark, Josephine, 63

Hamer, Fannie Lou, 176–8
Hamilton, Alice, 118–20
harassment, sexual, 5, 55–6, 58, 152,
    158, 178, 191–6, 227–31, 232–4,
    235–6, 249–54
Hayden, Casey, 173–6
health, complaints, female hygiene,
    65–8, 192, 240, 241–7, 244–7
health, occupational, 63–74, 118, 192
Heterodoxy Club, 75
Hill, Anita, 227–31, 232, 249
homemaking, scientific principles, 55,
    163, 166–7 see also work,
    household
homosexuality, 182–3
hospitalization, 48–51, 90, 230
House Un-American Activities
    Committee (HUAC), 156
housewives, 163–9, 170–3
Hoyt, Gwendolyn, 169–73
Hull House, 118–20

immigration, illegal, 223–7, 252
immigration, Japanese, 135
immigration legislation, 116
    Chinese, 39–46, 122–6, 136,
        196–7, 252
    Eastern European, 75–8, 89–92, 118
Indian Rights Movement, 249
Indian women, 31–4, 86–8, 237–40
    see also Native American
    women
Informed Consent, 212–15, 241–7
    see also birth control, birth control
    pill, reproductive rights
inter-faith relations, 20
International Ladies Garment Workers
    Union (ILGWU), 122, 196–7
International Pecan Shellers Union,
    127–9
International Women's Year at
    Houston, 206

International Workers of the World
    (IWW), 58, 129
internment, Japanese, 135–41
inter-racial relations, 14, 26–7, 83, 87

jail, chain gang, 13
Jews, 75–8, 89, 118, 120
jobs, pink-collar, 191–6
jury service, 169–73

Kelley, Florence, 63, 96
Kenyon, Dorothy, 169–73
King, Mary, 173–6
Knights of Labor, 15
Ku Klux Klan, 3, 116, 127, 176–8

labor contract, 57
labor strikes, 12, 60–2, 72, 92–5, 124–6,
    127–9, 191, 194–5, 196 see also
    wives, labor strikes
    picket lines, 62, 92–4, 124–5,
        156–61
labor, unions, 15, 54, 59–61, 93–5,
    127–9, 152, 193–6
The Ladder, 182–3
lawyers, female, 63, 75, 227–31
Leadership Conference of Women
    Religious, 207–8
League of Women Voters, 172
legislation, protective labor, 19, 63–74,
    96–100, 202–3
leisure, 54, 69, 84–5, 88, 93, 235
Lerner, Gerda, 6–7
lesbian, 182–3, 206, 215–18, 235–6
Levien, Sonya, 75–8
Love, Nancy Harkness, 133–4
lynching, 23–8, 227

Ma Ferguson, 127
Maloney, Carolyn, 235
Manzanar, 135–41
marriage, 50, 98, 119, 130, 135, 146,
    152, 181–91, 192, 211–12 see also
    family relationships
    interracial, 195–6, 252

legal status, 98, 188–91, 252
Marxism, 76, 197
mass meetings, 14
maternity leave, 219–22
McGovern, George, 212
memory 1, 34, 40–5, 52, 75–7, 93–5,
    186, 238–9, 250–3
menstruation, 67
mental illness, 198–201
mentoring, 220
Mestiza, 127–9, 195–6, 209, 250
Metropolitan Museum of Art, 237
Mexican, 127–9, 195, 209–10, 223–4,
    250–1
Mexican American, 127–9, 136,
    156–61, 209–10, 248–54
Mildred Pierce, 143
military service, women, 203–6
minimum wages, 99, 101, 124–6
mining, 156–61, 191–6 *see also* Western
    Federation of Miners
Mommy Track, 219–23
mortality, infant and child, 70–4, 85, 92,
    99, 120, 129
mortality rates, 99, 240–1
motherhood, 19, 119, 170–2, 174–5,
    221
Ms. Magazine, 188–91, 208–9
Muller v. Oregon, 63–74

National American Woman Suffrage
    Association (NAWSA), 17–18,
    74, 80
National Center for Health Statistics,
    240–1
National Consumers' League (NCL),
    63, 96, 105
National Organization for Women
    (NOW), 161, 216
National Woman Suffrage
    Association, 17
National Woman's Party, 96, 101
Native American, 31–4, 86–8, 127
    see also Women, Indian
natural rights, 20–3

Norplant, 247
nuns, 129, 137, 207–8
nurse, nanny, 53–8, 130
nursing, medical, 85, 86–8, 130, 141

oral history, 93–5, 122–6, 135–41
oral interviews, 36–9, 40–6, 93–5,
    122–6, 130–3, 135–41, 191–6
ordination, women, 19, 207–8
Our Bodies, Ourselves, 184

Park, Maud Wood, 101–7
Paul, Alice, 80
peace movements, 101, 110
Planned Parenthood, 214
pluralism, cultural, 136
political parties
    Democratic, 176–8
    Mississippi Freedom Democratic
        Party (MFDP), 178
    Republican, 184
pregnancy, 68, 146, 183, 192–3, 200,
    205, 225–6
President's Commission on the Status of
    Women, 181, 202–3
prison conditions, 178 *see also* arrests,
    of women
prisoners, political, 82, 198–201
prostitution, 34, 47, 49, 50–2, 59,
    206, 252

rape, 99, 205, 229, 248–5 *see also*
    abuse, sexual
    old threadbare lie, 24–7
    rape crisis centers, 248
Reagan, Ronald, 229
reproductive rights, 4, 8, 203, 253
    see also birth control,
    contraception, abortion
riots, 138–9
Roe v. Wade, 8, 186
Roosevelt, Eleanor, 107–13
Roosevelt, Theodore, 76
Rosie the Riveter, 142
Russian Revolution, 79–80

Salt of the Earth, 156–61
Sanger, Margaret, 116–18
Schlafly, Phyllis, 203
school, public, 76, 85, 133 *see also*
    education
Seaman, Barbara, 241–7
The Second Sex, 4
segregation, 56–7, 130–3, 161, 176–8
Settlement Movement, 75–8, 118
sex discrimination (sexism), 107–13,
    130, 202–7, 219, 236–7, 249–53
sexual revolution, 183–6
sexuality, 115–16, 164–5, 168, 179–80,
    182–3
Shampanier, Phyllis, 169–73
sharecropping, 130, 147, 177
single women, head of household,
    28–31, 224
Smith-Rosenberg, Carol, 7
Social Purity, 19, 22, 35, 49, 69, 75
Socialist Party, 59–62
Socialists, 59, 76, 103
Stanton, Elizabeth Cady, 17–18, 20–3
stereotypes, women, 143, 181, 205–7,
    209, 220–2, 249, 252
    African American, 24–7, 56
    Chinese, 39–46, 252
    elderly, 92
    Mexican American, 156–61
    Puerto Rican, 179–80
    Yankee, 16–7
Stonewall, 235–6
Student Nonviolent Coordinating
    Committee (SNCC), 173–6, 197
suffrage, 17, 20–3, 31, 60–2, 74–5, 78,
    96, 111, 117, 176–8
suffragists, African American, 74–5

teachers, 23
Tennessee Valley Authority, 144–9
Texas, 127, 130–3
textile workers, 93
Thomas, Clarence, 227–31, 232–4
trafficking in women (white slavery), 34
Triangle Factory Fire, 58

underground economy, 224–5
United Cannery, Agricultural, Packing,
    and Allied Workers of America
    (UCAPAWA), 127
United Nations, 172–3
United States Congress, 20
United States Industrial Commission,
    64, 73

violence, against women, 15 *see also*
    abuse, physical

wage-earning, women, 62, 63–74, 76–7
wages, 3, 17, 47–8, 52, 54–9, 61–2, 69,
    72, 76–7, 89–92, 93, 96, 99–101,
    119, 124, 127, 130, 137, 150, 190,
    192–3, 196, 223
    see also equal wages, minimum wages
Walker, Rebecca, 232–3
War Department, United States, 105–7,
    133–4
Webb, Mrs. Sidney (Beatrice), 69–70, 73
Wells, Ida B., 23–8
Welty, Eudora, 10, 149
Western Federation of Miners, 61
    see also mining
widowhood, 53, 83, 98, 135, 141
Willard, Frances, 17–20, 25–7
Wilson, Woodrow, 79–80, 80–2
wives, strikes, 61–2, 196–7
Woman's Christian Temperance Union
    (WCTU), 17, 23, 25–7, 34–5
Woman's Convention, National Baptist
    Convention, 74
Woman's International Council, 18–19
Woman's National Council, 17, 19
Woman's Peace Party, 79–80
Woman's Suffrage Party of New York, 78
women, letter writing, 47–52, 83–6,
    86–8, 150–5
Women Airforce Service Pilots (WASP),
    133–4
women and politics, 103–8, 108–13,
    235
women and public service, 112

women of color, 20, 115, 209–10,
    232–4, 250–3
Women's Council for World
    Disarmament, 104–5
Women's International League for Peace
    and Freedom, 104–5
Women's Joint Congressional
    Committee, 101–7
women's rights, 20
work
    agricultural, 84–6, 128, 144–8
    contract, 252
    department stores, 68, 131
    domestic service, 13, 22–3, 53–8,
        130–3, 142, 225
    factory operatives, 15–17,
        63–74, 91

    household, 59, 84–5, 91–2, 130, 146,
        163–9, 189 *see also* homemaking
    industrial, 83, 91, 142
    night work (graveyard shift), 48, 53,
        150–3, 194
    office, 47–8, 67, 130, 137–41, 150–4,
        162, 181, 193
    piecework, 90–1
    sewing, 91, 146, 196–7
    textiles, 92
    washerwomen, 13, 70
Works Progress Administration (WPA),
    10, 149
World War I, 76–8, 79–80, 81–2,
    86–8, 113
World War II, 4, 130, 133–4, 135–44,
    150–5, 164, 191, 193–5, 204